Puritans, Indians, and Manifest Destiny

Charles M. Segal
and David C. Stineback

Foreword by
SACVAN BERCOVITCH

G. P. PUTNAM'S SONS   NEW YORK

SBN: 399-11928-0 (Hardcover)
SBN: 399-50378-1 (Softcover)

Library of Congress Cataloging in Publication Data

Main entry under title:

Puritans, Indians, and manifest destiny.

   Bibliography
   Includes index.
   1. Indians, Treatment of—New England—Sources.
2. Puritans—New England—History—Sources. 3. New
England—History—Colonial period, ca. 1600-1775—Sources.
I. Segal, Charles M. II. Stineback, David C.
E78.N5P87   1977   974'.02   77-3858

PRINTED IN THE UNITED STATES OF AMERICA

PURITANS, INDIANS, AND MANIFEST DESTINY

Acknowledgments

Roger Williams, "A Key into the Language of America," from Vol. 1 of *The Complete Writings of Roger Williams,* reproduced from the Narragansett Edition (1866) with the addition of a seventh volume, edited by Perry Miller (New York: Russell & Russell, 1963). Reprinted by permission.

Roger Williams, "Christenings Make Not Christians," from Vol. 7 of *The Complete Writings of Roger Williams,* reproduced from the Narragansett Edition (1866) with the addition of a seventh volume, edited by Perry Miller (New York: Russell & Russell, 1963). Reprinted by permission.

William Bradford, *Of Plymouth Plantation, 1620–1647,* the complete text, with notes and an introduction by Samuel Eliot Morison, pp. 26, 62, 296, 396–98. Copyright © 1952 by Samuel Eliot Morison. Reprinted by permission of the publisher, Alfred A. Knopf, Inc.

Wilcomb E. Washburn, "Governor Berkeley and King Philip's War," *The New England Quarterly,* 30 (1957), 371. Reprinted by permission of the author.

Benjamin Thompson, "New England's Crisis," edited by Howard Judson Hall and reprinted in *American Thought and Writing,* Vol. I, edited by Russel B. Nye and Norman S. Grabo (Boston: Houghton Mifflin, 1965). Excerpts from this poem are reprinted by permission of the Board of Trustees of the Leland Stanford Junior University.

John Cotton, *The Way of Congregational Churches Cleared,* in Larzer Ziff, ed., *John Cotton on the Churches of New England* (Cambridge: The Belknap Press, 1968), pp. 268, 272–74, 278–79. Reprinted by permission.

Letter, John Winthrop to His Wife, May 15, 1629, in Allyn B. Forbes, ed., *Winthrop Papers, 1623–1630,* Vol. II (Boston: Massachusetts Historical Society, 1931), 91. Courtesy Massachusetts Historical Society.

"General Observations: Higginson Copy," in Allyn B. Forbes, ed., *Winthrop Papers, 1623–1630,* Vol. II (Boston: Massachusetts Historical Society, 1931), 120. Courtesy Massachusetts Historical Society.

"Reasons to Be Considered, and Objections with Answers," in Allyn B. Forbes, ed., *Winthrop Papers, 1623–1630,* Vol. II (Boston: Massachusetts Historical Society, 1931), 141. Courtesy Massachusetts Historical Society.

"Sir John Eliot's Copy of the New England Tracts," in Allyn B. Forbes, ed., *Winthrop Papers, 1623–1630,* Vol. II (Boston: Massachusetts Historical Society, 1931), 145. Courtesy Massachusetts Historical Society.

ACKNOWLEDGMENTS

Letter, John Winthrop to His Wife, July 23, 1630, in Allyn B. Forbes, ed., *Winthrop Papers, 1623-1630,* Vol. II (Boston: Massachusetts Historical Society, 1931), 303. Courtesy Massachusetts Historical Society.

Letter, —— Pond to William Pond, n.d., in Allyn B. Forbes, ed., *Winthrop Papers, 1631-1637,* Vol. III (Boston: Massachusetts Historical Society, 1943), 17. Courtesy Massachusetts Historical Society.

Letter, Jonathan Brewster to John Winthrop, Jr., June 18, 1636, in Allyn B. Forbes, ed., *Winthrop Papers, 1631-1637,* Vol. III (Boston: Massachusetts Historical Society, 1943), 270-71. Courtesy Massachusetts Historical Society.

Letter, John Higginson to John Winthrop, *ca.* May, 1637, in Allyn B. Forbes, ed., *Winthrop Papers, 1631-1637,* Vol. III (Boston: Massachusetts Historical Society, 1943), 404-7. Courtesy Massachusetts Historical Society.

Letter, Roger Williams to John Winthrop, May, 1637, in Allyn B. Forbes, ed., *Winthrop Papers, 1631-1637,* Vol. III (Boston: Massachusetts Historical Society, 1943), 412-14. Courtesy Massachusetts Historical Society.

Letter, Richard Davenport to Hugh Peter, *ca.* July 17, 1637, in Allyn B. Forbes, ed., *Winthrop Papers, 1631-1637,* Vol. III (Boston: Massachusetts Historical Society, 1943), 452-54. Courtesy Massachusetts Historical Society.

Letter, Roger Williams to John Winthrop, Providence, Dec. 28, 1637/1638, in Allyn B. Forbes, ed., *Winthrop Papers, 1638-1644,* Vol. IV (Boston: Massachusetts Historical Society, 1944), 17. Courtesy Massachusetts Historical Society.

Letter, William Piggott to John Winthrop, May 4, 1647, in Allyn B. Forbes, ed., *Winthrop Papers, 1645-1649,* Vol. V (Boston: Massachusetts Historical Society, 1947), 155. Courtesy Massachusetts Historical Society.

Daniel Gookin, "History of the Christian Indians," *Transactions* (Cambridge, Massachusetts, 1836), 2:450-51, 528-29. Reprinted by permission of the American Antiquarian Society.

The William Harris Papers, *Collections* (Providence, 1902). 10:177-78. Reprinted by permission of the Rhode Island Historical Society.

"Cartwright's Answer to the Massachusetts Narrative of Transactions with the Royal Commissioners," in The Clarendon Papers, *Collections* (1869), pp. 90-93, 102-4. Reprinted by permission of the New-York Historical Society.

For the Stinebacks:
George and Ruth

And the Segals:
Nessa, Shari, Lisa,
Deborah, and Julie

Contents

Preface

This book has a double purpose: (1) to introduce readers to the basic issues and attitudes of Puritan-Indian contact in seventeenth-century New England, and (2) to contribute a new point of view to the stimulating scholarly debate on the nature of Puritan and Indian relations. Both purposes are served by our making available, for the first time in this century, an extensive collection of primary documents dealing with the various aspects of Puritan-Indian contact: land and trade, government relations, the Pequot War, the conversion of Indians to Christianity, and King Philip's War. Thus the chapter "Land and Trade" includes an introduction to the issues raised by seventeenth-century events and by surviving documents from the period, and a selection of nine key documents on the economics of Puritan and Indian relations. Each of the other four chapters of the book follows the same pattern. In all, fifty-five primary documents from the seventeenth century (under forty-five subheadings) are presented in part or in full for the reader's own evaluation.

The order of the five chapters of the book needs a further word of explanation. Within each topic—"Land and Trade," "Government Relations," etc.—the introductory narrative and the documents themselves move in a more or less chronological fashion. The five topics are then chronologically arranged according to their inception as important concerns in Puritan-Indian relations: economic dealings ("Land and Trade") between Puritans and Indians preceded the first political arrangements ("Government Relations"), which came before the onset of the Pequot War. Similarly, the missionary effort to the Indians ("Christianizing the Indians") was initiated after the Pequot War and before King Philip's War. Our reason for resorting to this unusual organizational principle was simple: it provides the reader with a general historical perspective while allowing him to concentrate on an individual topic in a single chapter of the book.

The new point of view that we presume to argue in this combined narrative and anthology is our conviction—supported, we feel, by an objective choice of documents—that the history of Puritan and Indian relations is best seen as a cultural conflict with a philosophical (or theological) basis. The two most significant studies of the same subject—Alden Vaughan's *New England Frontier: Puritans and Indians, 1620-1675* (1965), and Francis Jennings's *The Invasion of America: Indians, Colonialism, and the Cant of Conquest* (1975)—take opposite positions on the nature of Puritan-Indian contact, but neither is a fair assessment of the extent and sincerity of the religious outlooks that characterized the two cultures in New England. By emphasizing the theocratic nature of Puritan and Indian societies, we hope to restore to the study of colonial history an understanding of the way in which the conflict between Puritans and Indians arose out of the unity and conviction of hostile, but similar, cultures.

The conclusion of the book argues that the dynamic of Puritan-Indian conflict in New England provides a model for understanding the later conflict between white Americans and other Indian tribes during the westward movement in America. The period of "Manifest Destiny," commonly associated with Anglo-Saxon attitudes in the nineteenth century, finds its genesis in the Puritan mind. And the survival of other Indian cultures into the twentieth century finds its paradigm in the endurance of New England tribes during and since the days of Puritan-Indian conflict.

Our thanks for their cooperation in the writing of this book go to many people, particularly our families for their continual interest and patience. Professors Michael Dorris and James Cox at Dartmouth College provided crucial conceptual advice at early stages of the manuscript; Dr. Wilcomb Washburn, of the Smithsonian Institution, made valuable comments on an early version of the Introduction; and Professor Sacvan Bercovitch at Columbia University gave us helpful editorial assistance in the book's final stages. We are indebted, too, to the staffs of Baker Library, Dartmouth College, Hanover, N.H., the New York State Library,

Albany, N.Y., and Schaffer Library, Union College, Schenectady, N.Y., for their help in locating hard-to-find documents. We also wish to express our appreciation of research assistance provided by Dr. Robert W. Funk, New York State archaeologist, and Dr. Morris Miller, of Toronto. For difficult and invaluable typing assistance, our thanks to Doris Nicholas, Martha Mann, Luci Minsk, and Sandy Goolsby. The following institutions have cooperated in the provision of important documents: Rhode Island Historical Society, New-York Historical Society, and the American Antiquarian Society.

Finally, we voice our thanks to Shari Segal, who first suggested that we do a book about the Puritans and Indians.

Once the documents for this book were selected, we modernized spelling and capitalization and altered punctuation in a few instances where the meanings of particular passages were unclear as they stood. We have, however, made no grammatical changes.

Foreword

"The discovery of America": no phrase more clearly conveys the assumptions and illusions of our culture than does this textbook commonplace. "The discovery of America" expresses the exuberance, the imperialist drive, and the primitive ethnocentrism that attended the growth of the country; it is at once a tribute to the enterprise of the Europeans who conquered a "new world," and an indictment of their willful blindness to native Indian rights. It reminds us of the power of rhetoric (in the service of ideology) to shape our view of history, and by extension to shape history itself. It reminds us, too, of the way a culture can use myth to circumvent the most obvious contradictions—in this case, the contradiction between our ideals of property, liberty, and "the people," and our *de facto* robbery of Indian land and massacre of the native inhabitants. Finally, "the discovery of America" recalls the Puritan roots of our concept of national identity. For though the seventeenth-century New England Puritans did not coin the phrase, it was they who gave it the high visionary meaning it has carried, for the United States, through the eighteenth and nineteenth centuries into our own time.

I am speaking, of course, of what we have come to call the American dream: the "discovery of America" as prophecy and promise, as *God's country, redeemer nation,* and *manifest destiny.**

* Needless to say, I don't mean to attribute the American dream solely to the Puritans. To speak of continuity is not at all to forget discontinuities, or to preclude a diversity of influences, or to deny the significant transformations of Puritan thought in the course of several hundred years. Indeed, my argument rests precisely upon the indisputable fact of discontinuity, diversity, and transformation. Taking that for granted, it seems to me all

15

Other Renaissance explorers and emigrants discovered America as a geographical entity; they put it on the European map of the world. The Puritans discovered America in scripture, precisely as a biblical scholar discovers the meaning of some hitherto obscure text, and they proceeded to put it on the map of sacred history. America, they explained, was nothing less than the new promised land, held in reserve by God for His latter-day saints. It was the wilderness that was to blossom as the rose, the refuge (predicted by Isaiah, Micah, and John the Divine) for the new chosen people that would usher in the millennium. To be sure, they found little or no support for all this from their contemporaries, but their sense of isolation only strengthened them in their conviction. Invoking the principles of exegesis, they pointed out that it was not enough to read scripture; one had to read it with the true spirit. Only the believer could *discern* the tenets of faith in the Old Testament, only the Christian could truly *find* Christ in the New, and only the new American people of God could *discover* the sacred meaning of America. Other (profane) emigrants might exult in the secular benefits of America. The New England Puritans alone could discern in these benefits a great historic destiny, and, by declaring this to the world, make visible their own crucial role in God's plan for mankind.

I need not discuss the influence of their outlook on later generations. David Stineback and Charles Segal have traced the Puritan legacy in this respect in its broad outlines. More important, they have given us a vivid picture of the Puritan outlook in its own right. For perhaps nowhere else does the Puritans' "discovery" show itself more plainly—in all its transparent self-interest, self-deception, and imaginative force—than in their dealings with the Indians. We have often been told that the European invasion of America entailed a clash between two cultures, and that the European triumph was augmented, if not inspired, by a process of cultural misinterpretation. The misnomer *Indian* is emblematic of the way language could be used, in defiance of historical fact, to denigrate a host of native peoples, each with distinctive traditions and institu-

---

the more striking that certain forms of Puritan rhetoric should have persisted, *mutatis mutandis,* into the twentieth century, as a basic framework for understanding the meaning of America.

tions, as *primitives, savages, childlike innocents,* and so on. This was the way of all the emigrant groups, including the Puritans. But the Puritans went one crucial step further. They *discovered* in the Indians the antagonists to the new chosen people. For other emigrants, the Indians were cultural inferiors, requiring the white gifts of religion and civilization. For the Puritans they were primarily * the villains in a sacred drama, counterpart of the heathen tribes that Joshua conquered, children of the Devil who tempted Christ in the desert, forerunners of the legions of darkness that would gather at Gog and Magog for a last furious but futile battle against the elect.

From this perspective, the documents assembled here reveal something more spectacular and more sinister than a clash of cultures. On the one hand, we see the Indians trying to make sense of the invaders' designs, and often enough (to their own misfortune) misinterpreting them. On the other hand, we see the Puritans bent on imposing upon the native peoples their own sacral view of America. The Indian documents, we might say, show the tragic limit of common sense. The Puritan documents show the astonishing capacity of myth not only to obscure but to invert reality. What they tell us, in effect, is that there are two parties in the new world, God's and the Devil's; and that God's party is white, Puritan, and entrusted with a world-redeeming errand, while Satan's party is dark-skinned, heathen, and doomed. Other emigrants—Spanish, French, Dutch, Quakers, and Anglicans—thought that to discover America was to discover a new continent, with an alien, secular culture. For the American Puritans, on the contrary, it was to leap from secular into sacred history. They taught us that to discover America was to see, as only a "true American" could, that the New World had its past and present in prophecy, and that its future lay with an emigrant people destined to be a beacon to mankind.

---

* There were some differences among the Puritans in this respect, as the selections show. The missionary John Eliot, for example, held to the belief (first promulgated by Spanish missionaries) that the Indians might be descendants of the lost tribes of Israel, and Roger Williams angrily objected to New England's Indian policy. But it seems clear that they, and others like them, were exceptions that proved the rule.

This is not the place to discuss how the Puritan view took hold and why it persisted. Briefly, I believe that the answer must be sought in the usefulness of that view to a burgeoning middle-class country, with particular needs for expansion and for a certain kind of ideological consensus. And if so, it seems significant that the recent flowering of American Indian studies has been accompanied by a widespread criticism of American expansionism and a rising interest in ethnicity, class conflict, and cultural pluralism. Indeed, it's safe to say that for our time "the discovery of America" means the discovery of the mundane facts that nourished the assertions of the myth. The authors of this book have made full use of recent scholarship. But unlike some scholars they have not substituted a secular for a sacred myth. They have resisted, that is, the current tendency to invert the Puritan vision into some romantic drama of satanic Puritans versus naturally angelic (or angelically natural) Indians. Instead they present the struggle of two cultures in its broad historical, ideological, and rhetorical complexities—partly through their lucid and very suggestive commentaries, mainly through the documents that reveal those complexities in the voices of the antagonists themselves: Indians both friendly and hostile to the colonists; Puritans representative of virtually the entire spectrum of their society; enemies and critics of the Puritans, like Thomas Lechford, George Cartwright, and Roger Williams; and representatives from other colonies, like Governor William Berkeley of Virginia. This is the first such gathering of these documents, and it makes for fascinating reading. Above all, it offers a vivid and multifaceted account of what it meant to "discover America" in seventeenth-century Puritan New England.

SACVAN BERCOVITCH
Columbia University

Chronology of Important Events
in the History of Puritan-Indian Relations

1616–19   Violent epidemic among southern New England Indians (repeated in 1633–34).

1620   Pilgrims arrive in Plymouth via Holland.

1621   Pilgrims form mutual assistance pact with Massasoit, sachem of the Wampanoags.

1622   Wessagusset founded by Thomas Weston's adventurers on the south side of Massachusetts Bay.

1623   Collapse of Wessagusset venture and retaliation by Miles Standish of Plymouth against Massachuset Indians.

1625   Charles I becomes King of England (dissolves Parliament in 1629); his foremost advisers—Wentworth and Laud—increase persecution of English Puritans.

1629   Charter granted for the settlement of Massachusetts Bay.

1630   John Cotton gives farewell address, "God's Promise to His Plantations," to John Winthrop, Sr., and his Puritan followers on the *Arbella*.
Settlement of Boston by Puritans under Winthrop.

1633   Land sales from Indians to whites required to have governmental approval in Massachusetts Bay (in other colonies by 1663).

1634   Pequot treaty with Massachusetts Puritans.

1635   Thomas Hooker takes his Cambridge congregation to
           Connecticut lands bought from Pequot enemies.
           Hartford founded.
           Fort Saybrook founded by Massachusetts Puritans.
           Roger Williams banished from Massachusetts Bay.

1636   Roger Williams founds Providence.
           Pequot War begins with Endecott expedition to Block
           Island and Connecticut.
           Narragansett treaty with Massachusetts Puritans.

1637   Massacres of Pequot Indians at Mystic Fort and Sadqua
           Swamp.

1642   Civil war in England (1642–49); Parliament and Puritans
           in power.

1643   United Colonies of New England (the New England
           Confederation) established.
           Miantonomo executed by Uncas on orders from the
           governors of the United Colonies.
           Roger Williams publishes *A Key into the Language of
           America* in England.
           Thomas Mayhew, Jr., begins missionary work to the
           Indians on Martha's Vineyard.

1644   Roger Williams obtains colonial charter for the Provi-
           dence Plantations from Parliament.
           Massachuset Indians under Cutshamoquin declare sub-
           mission to Massachusetts Bay.
           Narragansetts declare submission to the King of England.

1645   "A Declaration of Former Passages" issued by John
           Winthrop and the governors of the United Colonies.

1646   John Eliot begins missionary work to Massachuset
           Indians.
           Massachusetts commits itself as a colony to missionary
           work and punishes Indian blasphemy of Christianity with
           death.

1649   In England, the Society for the Propagation of the
           Gospel in New England established to provide funds to

support Puritan missionary efforts to the Indians.
Charles I beheaded by Puritans in England.

1650 Father Drouillette visits Puritan colonies on mission from the French government in Canada.

1660 First Indian church established at Natick by John Eliot.
Monarchy restored in England under Charles II.

1662 John Winthrop, Jr., obtains royal charter for Connecticut.

1663 Roger Williams obtains royal charter for Rhode Island.
First translation of the Bible by Eliot into Algonquian.

1664 Metacom (King Philip) becomes sachem of the Wampanoags.
Royal Commissioners arrive from England to investigate Puritan rule in New England.

1671 Metacom twice brought before Plymouth magistrates on rumors of a plot to overthrow the English in New England.

1675 King Philip's War (1675-76) begins in southern New England.
Massachusetts conducts surprise attack on the Narragansetts.

1677 All Indians in Massachusetts confined to four Indian towns (reduced to three in 1681).

1682 Uncas and the Mohegans officially submit to the political jurisdiction of Connecticut.
Narrative of Mary Rowlandson's captivity among Metacom's followers in King Philip's War published.

1684 Massachusetts charter revoked by the King of England.

1685 James II becomes King of England.

1689 William and Mary replace James II on the throne.

1691 New provincial charter for Massachusetts issued in England.

Map showing (1) the original locations of the five Indian tribes (Massachusets, Wampanoags, Narragansetts, Pequots, and Mohegans) in continual contact with English settlers in southern New England; and (2) the extent of English expansion on the eve of King Philip's War (1675–76). Dates indicate the beginnings of representative English settlements.

Area settled by English

Indian territory within English settlements

Indian territory outside English settlements

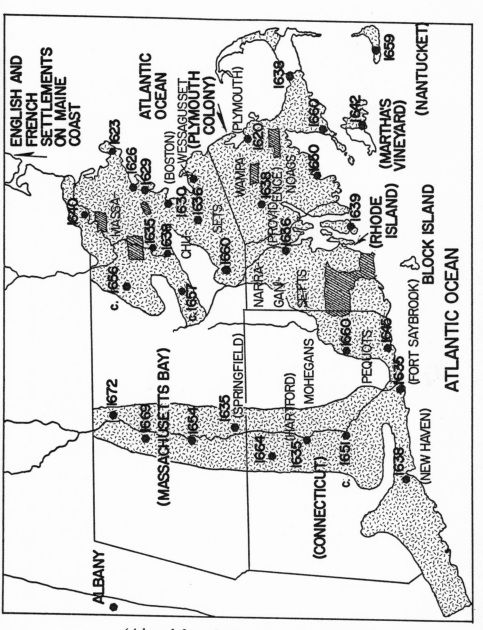

(Adapted from S. G. Curtis; drawn by Jeff Webster from a sketch by David Stineback)

Introduction

"For the Sake of Our Religion"

I

It is impossible for today's scholar or student to understand the attitudes of Indians and whites toward each other in the United States after 1776 without having a clear grasp of colonial interracial relations. This requires, for the most part, an analysis of the impact of English settlement on native cultures during the seventeenth and eighteenth centuries, although other European powers were asserting their interests in North America at the same time. In all, four invading nations dominated Indian-white relations on this continent prior to the American Revolution: Spain, north of Mexico and along the Gulf Coast to Florida, from the 1550s to 1763 (when it relinquished its claims east of the Mississippi River); France, in Canada and south through what is now the Midwest to Louisiana, from 1604 to 1763; England, from New England to Georgia, between 1607 and 1776; and Holland, in the New York-New Jersey area, from 1614 to 1664. As Gary B. Nash has demonstrated, these four nations had essentially the same attitudes toward the natives they encountered in North America. Without exception, the European powers regarded Indians as morally inferior to themselves; the mere fact that Spain, France, England, and Holland felt free to claim inhabited areas of North America as extensions of their empires reflects their sense of superiority.[1] Despite this similarity of attitudes, however, certain noticeable differences in behavior toward Indians developed among the four powers as a consequence of varying demographic and ecological conditions in North America and their own varying definitions of what is now called imperialism.

All four nations claimed New World territory for economic purposes, if one includes in the term "economic" the settlement of new towns and cities. But English colonists, after arriving from the most crowded European country, quickly became more interested in the expansion of their population into Indian territory than settlers from the other three nations. This is perhaps least true of the Puritans in New England; nor was settlement the only important motive of Englishmen in places like Virginia, where, for example, the profitable exportation of tobacco to the mother country was a crucial reason for their continued presence. Nevertheless, the eventual ascendancy of England to the position of the most powerful European nation in the New World by the 1760s was a direct consequence of its physical investment of immigrants in the future of the continent, compared to the more limited imperialistic goals of Spain, France, and Holland.

The land holdings of these latter countries were not relinquished to England willingly; the maintenance of conquered or purchased territory still had great importance for England's periodic enemies beyond the need or desire for population expansion. Until the loss of Canada in 1763, France maintained a thriving fur trade with the Indians north of New York and along the Mississippi River, which greatly profited French society. Holland traded in furs in upstate New York until its claimed territory was conquered by England in the 1660s. Spain sought gold and the establishment of agriculturally based missions, and in the process natives usually became both converts and slaves (which was not quite as bad as the wholesale slaughter of millions of Caribbean natives by Spanish conquistadors in the early sixteenth century).[2] Conversion of natives to the Catholic faith was a primary concern of the French as well, but the nature of the fur trade, the small numbers and military weakness of French colonists (compared to the Spanish), and the greater strength of Indian tribes in their vicinity (compared to those conquered by Spain) prevented the concerted use of slavery for economic purposes.

Wherever European nations in the New World needed Indians as a source of furs, voluntary labor, or religious conversions, race relations were less ugly and genocidal than in areas of the continent, such as Virginia and the Carolinas, where Indians were meaningless to Europeans except as occupants of coveted land or as non-Christian slaves (prior to the eighteenth century). If Europeans found themselves at a numerical or military disadvantage, Indian-white relations remained cautiously respectful, as in the initial years of the English settlements at Jamestown, Plymouth, and Massachusetts Bay.

When one assesses their destructive impact on North American Indian cultures in the sixteenth, seventeenth, and eighteenth centuries, France fares best, followed by Holland and Spain, with England last. Of course, in the New World history of each nation, there are exceptions to this ranking: France decimated the Natchez Indians in the lower Mississippi region in the 1720s and 1730s because it had no economic need for their services; Holland was far more aggressive toward the Indians surrounding New Amsterdam (Manhattan) with whom it had no trading commitment; Spain employed the slavery of Indians far less in Florida than in the southwest; and English Quakers and, to some extent, English Puritans in other areas were less committed to the forcible acquisition of land than their countrymen along the mid-Atlantic coast. Yet, despite these important distinctions it must be emphasized again that, in Nash's words, "Europeans of all nationalities took what they could get in North America and adapted their methods to the circumstances that pertained to any particular area."[3]

In all New World colonies, whether French, Dutch, Spanish, or English, there were always some settlers who were interested in Indians only for the land they occupied; and these individuals inevitably did the greatest damage to Native American cultures. For all the horrors of slavery, Indians conquered by Spain and made nominal Christians seldom were displaced from the lands they had always considered their own. They were oppressed, to be sure, sometimes at great loss of life, but they were not physically separated as tribes from their most prized possession. And if mutually profitable trading relationships could be established with the Europeans, Indian lands were further protected from usurpation. If, on the other hand, a New World colony were sufficiently populous and did not feel the need to convert the Indians to Christianity or to compensate them for their services in money, then the native land base was imperiled and war was the order of the day.

Nothing was, or is to this day, as important to Native Americans as the land itself. In a way that few colonial Europeans could understand, the land *was* Indian culture: it provided Native Americans with their sense of a fixed place in the order of the world, with their religious observances, and with their lasting faith in the importance of the struggling but united community as opposed to the ambitious, acquisitive individual that seemed to them to characterize Europeans in the New World. In colonial times, to maintain their land base, Indians made major cultural adaptations, short of national suicide, to the presence of European powers. Many tribes sought clothing, axes, knives, guns, horses, and liquor; submitted to Christian conversion and military control; set aside traditional tribal rivalries to form military confederacies; even relinquished a portion of land for a written guarantee of no further white encroachment. Though adaptations such as these did not prevent the extinction of more than one third of the original three hundred Indian nations in North America, the survival of the Indian community on the land that had sustained it for generations was the primary goal of Native Americans after the arrival of white settlers. Some individual Indians, to be sure, could be persuaded to sell land that the community alone was entitled to part with. And at first glance, one can even argue that Native Americans, in a larger sense, hastened their own destruction, since the primary cause of dispossession was their unwillingness to set aside the welfare of the community and deal with expansion-minded colonists on their own terms. But for natives to have perceived their land as something that could be fenced by the individual and owned with a piece of paper would have been a surer form of suicide than refusal to submit to a European value system that emphasized personal property and profit. As long as the land remained in the possession of the tribe, the individual Indian could retain the essence of his culture, though disease, war, liquor, and slavery might take their toll.

The history of Virginia's relations with the Indians of Powhatan's Confederacy during the seventeenth century seems to be a classic example of the dynamics of Indian-white conflict throughout American history. It certainly is a clear case of a technologically superior white society destroying the culture of Native Americans.[4] Especially revealing is the colonists' unwillingness to perceive Powhatan's generous provision of food when they needed his assistance in 1607 as anything but an act of fear or a devious form of hostility. Like Custer two centuries later, John Smith could not accept the possibility that the Indians he encountered were capable of acting in their own, rational self-interest. Thus the saving of Smith by Pocahontas, Powhatan's daughter, at the moment he seemed about to die (probably a mock execution designed to impress the English with Powhatan's power) was taken by the English as an act of love for them; Custer insisted that the marriage Mahwissa attempted to arrange between him and her daughter, moments after he had attacked Mahwissa's brother and most of his village, was "unmistakeable proof of confidence and esteem" toward Custer himself.[5] Such naïveté could be the result only of an inveterate refusal to see Indians as rational beings.

However, the best colonial analogy to the period of Manifest Destiny is, in fact, the Puritan-Indian experience, though the similarities may at first glance seem obscure. Puritan leaders, after all, were opposed to the rapid expansion of their population into Indian territory, which they regarded as the realm of nature under Satan's control.[6] Moreover, individual acquisitiveness for material possessions and land was an unintentional by-product of the ethic that Puritans brought to North America, not a human quality they admired. Even as late as 1700, three generations after their culture's arrival, Puritan leaders such as Cotton Mather were decrying the Indianization and materialism of colonists who staked out new ground in the interior of Connecticut, Massachusetts, and Maine; for the orthodox Puritan, the united community was of greater value than individual, material success.[7] This conviction, above all, might suggest that Puritans could appreciate, better than their aggressive countrymen in Virginia, the value put on community survival as against individual acquisition that characterized New England tribes like the Pequots and Narragansetts. And finally, any parallel between Puritan-Indian relations and the conflicts on the American frontier might seem to be invalidated by the intense religiosity of Puritan society.

All of these qualities existed in Puritan society and served to distinguish their colonies from other English settlements, with the partial exception of the Quaker villages in Pennsylvania. Yet there are some overriding similarities between the Puritan experience in the New World (compared to that of other colonies) and the

westward movement in the nineteenth century: The weak missionary effort on the nineteenth-century frontier is akin to the modest
Puritan effort to convert New England Indians to Christianity and
unlike the strong French and Spanish emphasis on conversion or
the virtual absence of concern with converting Indians in other
English and Dutch colonies. Part of the nineteenth-century attitude
toward the Indians was a desire to save them which inadvertently
destroyed them. Liberals in Congress and the federal government
often joined with straightfoward Indian-haters and speculators to
pass measures that removed Indians forcibly from their tribal lands,
with the intention of saving them from land-hungry whites. In 1830
liberal members of Congress voted to coerce eastern Indians to
move west of the Mississippi, and in 1887 the federal government
passed the Dawes Act, which divided up tribal territory among
Indians and whites. These saviors, despite their good intentions,
were destroying Indian culture with its tribal land base. Just so, the
sincere Puritan desire to save Indians from the Devil was insepara-
ble from the requirement that they abandon their own culture and
capitulate to the colonial government. The other seventeenth-
century settlers either destroyed the Indians physically or saved
their souls and allowed their culture to survive.

Most important, there was a secular religiosity—a national zealousness—in nineteenth-century attitudes toward Indians that has a
great deal in common with the Puritans' zealousness and very little
in common with Dutch Albany, English Virginia, or Spanish
Florida. Even though economic forces had more influence on the
rapid westward movement in America after 1800 than on the slower
expansion of Puritan communities in the 1600s, the fervor that
motivated the "taming" of the western frontier is very similar to the
fervor of the Puritan farmer wresting the "howling" wilderness from
the clutches of the Devil.

The common ground between Puritan-Indian relations and white-
Indian relations two hundred years later is a reminder that the
nature of cultural interaction on the American frontier was more
than a matter of two different economic systems at odds with each
other. Two alien philosophies clashed in America: a white code of
behavior that was more self-righteous and self-protective than its
adversary's and therefore more powerful; and an Indian code of

behavior that was more assimilative than its adversary's and, in certain important ways, more enduring.

II

The one hundred Pilgrims who came to North America from England in 1620 and the fifteen hundred Puritans who settled ten years later a few miles above the Pilgrim colony at Plymouth were occupants of an already inhabited land.[8] The latest estimates of native population in 1600 range from 70,000 to 90,000 for the area that is now southern New England: Massachusetts, Connecticut, and Rhode Island.[9] But the epidemics of 1616-19 and 1633-34 drastically reduced the strength and numbers of the four major Indian nations in the area: Wampanoag (in Plymouth Colony); Massachuset (in Massachusetts Bay); Narragansett (in present-day Rhode Island); and Pequot (in present-day Connecticut). To the Pilgrims and Puritans, these epidemics seemed to be the hand of God making room for His followers in the "New World." To the Indians, they appeared to be both a cause and an effect of white occupation. How else could one explain the fact that white colonists during the second epidemic were "not in the least measure tainted" by the disease?[10] From our vantage point in the twentieth century, it is clear that Europeans had already developed an immunity to smallpox; the Indians had not.

These early reductions of native population enabled the colonists at Plymouth and Boston to avoid military confrontations with the Wampanoag and Massachuset Indians of the kind that occurred in the Virginia Colony in 1622, when Powhatan retaliated against Jamestown land encroachments. Yet, for New England Indians, avoidance of warfare with whites was no great advantage. The epidemics reinforced a standard Christian argument—*vacuum domicilium*—used by Europeans to justify the occupation of native lands. In the words of John Cotton, one of the leading Puritan ministers, "where there is a vacant place, there is liberty for the son of *Adam* or *Noah* to come and inhabit, though they neither buy it, nor ask their leaves. ... In a vacant soil, he that taketh possession of it, and bestoweth culture and husbandry upon it, his right it is.

And the ground of this is from the Grand Charter given to *Adam* and his posterity in Paradise, Genesis 1:28. Multiply and replenish the earth, and subdue it." [11] Without the epidemics, this theological argument would have been drastically weakened and the Puritans would have been thrown back on their other justifications for occupation: (1) purchase or gift from the inhabitants, and (2) "lawful war," in which God would "commission" the Puritans to "drive them [the Indians] out without provocation." [12]

Massachusetts Bay and Plymouth seldom had to resort to purchasing territory in their early years of existence. As a means to coexistence, land was used in trade by the Indians, and there seemed, at least in the initial stages of white settlement, room enough for all cultures to coexist as they wished. Like the Plymouth Pilgrims before them, the Puritans met no resistance when they settled in the Boston area. The Massachuset Indians in that particular region were one of the weakest and most widely distributed tribes in all New England, a condition only aggravated by the 1633-34 epidemic. Thus, until the Pequot War began in 1636—and it was conducted far from the center of Puritan strength—there was little friction to justify the fears of either Puritans or Indians. English assumptions to the contrary, tribes like the Massachusets had territorial concepts of land that included even those areas that the Puritans called "vacant," [13] but the issue of purchase or war was postponed until the late 1630s. From then on, the story is one of contention more than cooperation.

Pilgrims and Puritans alike were seeking a geographical area where they could worship God unharassed by competing Christian sects. The prospect of competing native religions, however, was not a serious problem in Pilgrim and Puritan minds, since the European image of native life hardly included the possibility of spirituality, much less the possibility of a rival to the revealed truths of the Christian Bible. The Bible was placed by European Puritans at the center of the Christian faith following the Protestant Reformation begun in the early 1500s by Martin Luther in Germany and John Calvin in Switzerland. And the Bible made it perfectly clear that Satan had been allowed by God to rule the world's wilderness area after Adam's and Eve's original disobedience to God in the Garden of Eden. American Puritans, therefore, left England not only in revulsion against the Anglican Church's corruption of the Reformation but also in full anticipation that they were entering a region of pure unchallenged evil.

Whatever Puritans and Pilgrims had read of the few earlier exploratory contacts between Europeans and New World natives hardly dispelled either their enthusiasm or their fears. For the twentieth-century reader, the published narratives of those earlier contacts on the whole create an image of Indians as friendly; awed by European boats, armor, and guns; resentful of dishonesty and injury (Indians, for example, were occasionally kidnapped for display in Europe); and happy with their considerable crafts and semi-agrarian economies. However, they often portray Indians as initially curious and peaceful yet resentful and violent as time goes by.[14] The reasons for this shift in native attitudes are not explained in the narratives, other than by the suggestion in some that the awed natives plotted from the beginning to deceive whites into dropping their guard. To the modern reader it appears that natives were duped by shrewd and unscrupulous ship captains and crewmen and ultimately resorted to retaliation with good reason.

The transatlantic emigrants to New England, fleeing the religious persecution of the Old World, had an extreme sense of their own physical and mental suffering before and during their journey, a deep appreciation of their cultural ties to England (despite its corruption), and a profound fear of the boundless wilderness and of the potentially hostile and unconverted people who hunted, fished, and farmed that territory. If one keeps these factors in mind, then William Bradford's description of the terror of his fellow Pilgrims is understandable: "what could they see [on landing] but a hideous and desolate wilderness, full of wild beasts and wild men—and what multitudes there might be of them they knew not." [15] Yet, despite these fears, Pilgrims and Puritans did not think that Indians were a race apart. Adam and Eve were their parents, too, but the sin of the original parents had given Satan the territorial domain he needed to oppose God in centuries to come. And if Satan, as Cotton Mather later said, had "decoyed" Indians to North America in the hope of evading Jesus Christ (Satan's principal antagonist and God's last hope for man), then sincere Puritans and Pilgrims could hardly deny themselves the challenge of confronting the "Lost People" of North America with the reality of God's will in the form of their own model societies.[16]

At the heart of the model Christian societies that the Pilgrims and Puritans tried to establish in New England as a shining example to the rest of Christendom was a spirit of exclusivity that bound their members in love and loyalty even as it disenfranchised and excluded a host of heretics: Catholics, Anglicans, Anabaptists (Baptists), Quakers, and Puritans—like Anne Hutchinson in 1636— who advocated private communication with God in preference to ministerial and community authority. The Indian inhabitants of New England were given the benefit in Puritan minds of not being wayward Christians abusing the revealed word of God, but this was more than offset by their being further from the Christian institutions that embodied the word of God. The charter of 1629 that the Massachusetts Bay Puritans brought with them spoke highly of converting the Indians as a final test of Christian purity and purpose—but it was to be conversion by example, not conversion by evangelism. The rigid self-containment of the Puritans' congregations, towns, and colonies in the New World would, the Puritans hoped, both drive out troublemakers from the Christian fold and reform troublemakers outside it. To accomplish both purposes, the Puritans set up communities in which ministers would preach the truth and magistrates would protect it, though spiritual and civil functions would be kept carefully separated in administration to insure purity of thinking and judgment. If this was not a theocratic form of government, it was at least a theocentric one. But the very intensity with which Puritans in Massachusetts Bay and, after 1635, in the colonies of Connecticut and New Haven (later absorbed by Connecticut) strove to establish a society where all functions— spiritual, political, and economic—would be mutually reinforcing made them unable to appreciate the fact that interrelated functions pervaded native cultures in New England, too. The obstacle between Puritans and Indians was literal belief in the Bible. Thoroughly dominated by this belief, the Puritans were forced to think that Indian society was poles apart from their own, but the differences between the two groups were not as great as they thought.

III

New England tribes, as acknowledged by Protestant ministers like Roger Williams and John Eliot, deliberately structured their societies according to their natural environment.[17] Their existence was so nature-based that it became, in their minds, suffused with spirits, or gods, that controlled their physical destiny as nations. Thus, their religious observances, founded as they were upon an intimate relationship between man and nature, were extensive and thoroughly relevant to their lives.

Puritan religion was likewise sensitive to the totality of the natural world. A plague "meant something" to a Puritan as surely as it "meant something" to a Narragansett: everything in nature, from the point of view of both cultures, was to be noted and respected. Yet the notation systems that Puritans and Indians employed were alien to each other, since Englishmen found the meanings of natural events in the Bible, not in acceptance of the natural world as a limited environment in which spirits and man interacted. For the Indian, civilized behavior was an acknowledged relationship with one's own natural world that necessitated respect, fear, and gratitude; men could live in different circumstances and, therefore, have different civilizations. But for the Puritan, there was only one environment—God's—which left no room for the idea of different societies in different circumstances of equal moral value.

In other words, like his American descendants on the moving frontier, the Puritan could not reasonably imagine the existence of native societies that were physically distinct from his own without being morally inferior. To him, nature was not another environment; it was a psychic realm which God allowed Satan to inhabit in order to demonstrate to His chosen people, who had turned nature into fields and cities, how difficult and fortunate their task was. From this point of view, the native inhabitants of the "wilderness" were both enemies of God's people and pawns in God's plan to remind His people of their superiority to the natives. Only if the Indians' dual purpose in Puritan eyes is understood—children of Satan and instruments of God—will the student of Puritan-Indian experience comprehend how desire to convert natives and readiness to kill them could be part and parcel of a single view of reality.

The final lines of William Hubbard's *History of the Indian Wars in New England* (1677) put the issue succinctly:

> For though a great number that are implacable and embittered against us in their spirits, *may be, for the sake of our religion, found hardened to their own destruction;* yet a remnant may be reserved, and afterward called forth, by the power of the Gospel, to give glory to the God of all the earth. (emphasis added) [18]

Nothing will happen to Indians (or Puritans) that is not intended by God to strengthen the position of His chosen followers. Early Puritan leaders were convinced not only that Indians were the dregs of mankind, living without God and therefore without culture, but also that God would make the Indians recognize their own moral inferiority to Puritan settlers and forsake their superstitions for true civilization. When this did not occur spontaneously and God permitted the Indians to remain "proud and insolent," the Puritans had one alternative: for those natives who were belligerent, lawful war and death; for those who were passive, civil and religious instruction. But both ways were a victory for God's people over Satan, since the Indian would be conceding, in violence or submission, his cultural nonexistence.

This thinking accounts for the relatively modest missionary effort Puritans directed toward Indians, maintaining at the same time a staunch image of themselves as a deeply religious people. Since they could not imagine themselves as causing Indians to respond violently to their presence, there was no question of having provoked Indian hostility. On the contrary, their presence was obviously intended by God to provoke Indian admiration and apostasy. Missionaries like Eliot and Thomas Mayhew were primarily facilitators of Indian self-effacement, who offered the natives, through catechism, a slightly clearer image of the already apparent virtue of Puritan society. If that moral superiority was fundamentally self-evident for the Puritan, and ought to have been for the Indian, then why should one adopt a formal process of education and conversion? The children of Satan, when faced with the chosen people, would choose to join; if they did not, then God apparently had other plans for them—i.e., "their own destruction." Thus Hubbard could say, in all sincerity, that the Puritans had been "officious with" (kind to) the Indians by simply coming into their land.[19] Imperialism was salvation.

But New England natives did not feel that they needed saving, and this only reinforced the Puritans' conviction that Indians lived in the clutches of Satan. Puritan writers constantly contended that ordinary Indians were tyrannized by their sachems (political leaders) and powwows (priests), yet many of the documents that argue this theory also present a clear picture of the active and seemingly uncoerced participation of Indians in the politics and religions of their cultures: just the kind of tribal agreement and support the Puritans strove for in Massachusetts Bay.[20] Indians worshipped many gods and the Puritans only one; nevertheless, each group was trying to perpetuate a theocratic way of life in which material aspirations took a back seat to religious piety. Indeed, as the documents in Chapters II and IV suggest, the close relationship between sachems and powwows in native New England societies was similar to the relationship between civil adminstrators and ministers in Puritan society. It is not surprising, therefore, that the opposition among natives to the belated government-sponsored missionary effort to the Indians (a decade and a half after Puritan settlement) came almost equally from sachems and powwows.

Perhaps the tribal unity of Indian society was inadvertently acknowledged by Puritan writers because it reminded them of their own goals, or because Puritan faith presumed that nothing could or should be concealed from God, since He created all reality for the benefit of His followers. In any case, Puritans were not able to draw the most obvious conclusion from their observation of native cultures: that Indians in New England maintained a different spiritual view of life which satisfied, through a similar political organization, the same human needs as the Puritans themselves were attempting to satisfy.

The Puritans' God, in the end, demanded of every other culture the same allegiance that He demanded of His particular favorites. This made it next to impossible for Puritans to accept Indian willingness to trade with them, fight with them, even submit politically to them, without expecting Indians to reject, at the same time, their cultural values and loyalties. No halfway measures were tolerated. If God demanded total allegiance to the social, economic, and political tenets of Puritan faith, then a modified form of

Puritan-Indian interaction could not alter Puritan conviction that Satan ultimately controlled Indian behavior (though God, of course, permitted him to do so for His own reasons). The terrible truth of Puritan-Indian relations in seventeenth-century New England is that Puritan acquaintance with Indians in economic, political, and military matters did not lead to greater understanding and appreciation of native culture. Rather, it confirmed the image of self-satisfied barbarians who denied God's commandment to live exactly as the Puritans lived. There was no middle ground for Indians between total opposition and total imitation.

Years later, during the westward movement of American society, other Indian tribes would be faced with the same ultimatum: sacrifice your own culture and adopt the life-style of Anglo-Americans, or die in the act of resistance. Indeed, even the most liberal legislative acts of the nineteenth century attempted to coerce American Indians into subduing and replenishing the earth, as explicitly commanded in the Old Testament.[21]

IV

If the dominant Puritan attitude toward Indians can be characterized as a biblical interpretation of reality in the wilderness, what was the Indian attitude toward Puritan behavior? As many of the following documents will show, New England natives evaluated Puritan conduct by a more practical yardstick than the Puritans used on them. Both sides in the cultural struggle made comparisons and passed moral judgments; but the judgments of articulate Indians appear to have a consistent common-sense quality about them. Often, natives compared Puritan behavior not to their own way of life, but to the Christian standards that Puritans expected natives to admire; they pointed out that the Puritans were not good Puritans, that they—the Indians—might even take a serious look at the Puritan faith if it produced a society of good examples. On the whole, their attitude can best be described as live and let live. Yet many documents also picture Indians as recalcitrant and shrewd, qualities that seemed, from the Puritan point of view, to express the natives' spiritual degradation. If one realizes, however, that the New England tribes had governmental and religious systems as complex as those of Massachusetts Bay, then qualities such as recalcitrance and shrewdness can also be considered expressions of enlightened self-interest and true leadership, as they are in any culture that is threatened.

After the devastation of numerous epidemics (others struck New England after 1650) and two wars, the Indians who survived into the late 1600s and early 1700s retained an outraged pride in their own land and cultures—despite the white settlers' continual encroachments and contemptuous behavior—and an ironic sense that the Puritan faith had failed to produce models worthy of Indian imitation. Perhaps the ultimate irony is that Puritan culture in New England may have damaged itself more than it damaged the culture of its enemies. While Puritan vitality waned as the natives themselves died, native culture has not suffered the same fate to the same degree. Thousands of Indians in southern New England today survive with cultures that owe a greater debt to their own forebears than to the colonists who arrived from Europe in the seventeenth century.[22]

Chapter I

"If Thy Belly Be Thy God"

Land and Trade

Richard Baxter, the English Puritan theologian and staunch Calvinist, maintained in the latter half of the seventeenth century that wealth was no evidence of God's favor, nor was poverty a mark of His displeasure. Said Baxter:

> Take heed that you judge not God's love, or of your happiness or misery, by your riches or poverty, prosperity or adversity, as knowing that they come alike to all, and love or hatred is not to be discerned by them.... A carnal mind will judge of its own happiness and the love of God by carnal things because it savoreth not spiritual mercies, but grace giveth a Christian another judgment.[1]

Furthermore, said Baxter, it was Satan, and not the Lord, who was "exceeding diligent to get the wealth and prosperity of the world on his side that he may not seem to flatter his servants with empty promises but to reward them with real felicity and wealth."[2] According to Baxter, he who craved wealth was.

> like a foolish traveler who, having a day's journey to go, doth spend all the day in gathering together a load of meat and clothes and money, more than he can carry, for fear of wanting by the way; or

like the foolish runner that hath a race to run for his life and spends the time in which he should be running gathering a burden of pretended necessaries. You have all the while God's work to do and your souls to mind and judgment to prepare for, and you are tiring and vexing yourselves for unnecessary things, as if it were the top of your ambition to be able to say, in hell, that you died rich.[3]

In New England, Roger Williams, the anti-establishment Puritan, agreed: he believed that adversity was not necessarily a sign of God's disfavor since so many of His saints endured it. From a typological position, Williams was able to argue that insofar as prosperity was concerned, "such a temporal prosperity [as the Israelites were given] of outward peace and plenty of all things, of increase of children, of cattle, of honor, of health, of success, of victory, suits not temporally with the afflicted and persecuted estate of God's people now. And therefore spiritual and soul blessedness must be the antitype, viz. in the midst of revilings, and all manner of evil speeches for Christ's sake, soul blessedness." [4] To Williams, it was only spiritual affluence that was worthwhile; this was the sign of the Lord's favor. It could be achieved through grace.

The clergy of the Massachusetts Bay Colony agreed with this position in general. But they made a distinction when it came to their colony as a whole. In New England, they maintained—in God's specially chosen New Canaan—the case was different. There, prosperity was God-given and He rewarded Puritan virtue with worldly successes. It was difficult, therefore, for the clergy to oppose the individual quest for capital in New England, especially since the acquisition of wealth was considered as legitimate a calling for a saint as was clergyman or magistrate.[5] Though a true Calvinist like Baxter could teach that "If thy belly be thy god and the world be thy heaven, then serve and seek them (and pretend not to be a Christian)," [6] it did not follow that it was un-Christian to make money if one worshipped the true God and sought heaven. Puritanism and capitalism—the amassing of riches through private enterprises—were not mutually exclusive.

In the society the Puritans carved out for themselves in New England, their allegiance, first and foremost, was to God. For their professed, overriding purpose was to establish in the New World a New Canaan, according to the Bible, where the "true Christians" could worship God without fear of persecution, and where they could devote every living moment to His glorification without the importunities of Satan. As the self-styled stewards of God, they would have to account to Him for their time on earth and for the possessions they accumulated. They were taught to abhor idleness and to believe that diligence and thrift were religious obligations that must be uppermost in their minds as they engaged in various pursuits in God's name. Foremost of all these pursuits for first-generation Puritans was trade with the Indians, the principal means by which they could acquire wealth and advance their condition in New England. Politically, it was also the most effective means of securing control over territory, thereby eliminating the Satanic influence of the savages and fortifying the Bible Commonwealth against other anti-Christian intrusions.

In the decade following the Great Migration of 1630, some twenty thousand Englishmen settled in New England. They came from diverse backgrounds and training. Some had had commercial experience in Old England; others had been farmers and looked forward to embarking upon their first ventures as tradesmen in the New World. Many were victims of economic distress, and a number of them fled to the New World in fear of religious intolerance. Here in New England, they would be able to participate in what they conceived to be the providential mission of creating a theocratic society patterned after that of Moses, David, and Solomon. And here, within the tenets of Puritanism, they would be able to meet their commitment "to manipulate material life for spiritual ends." [7]

The Puritan who became a merchant, farmer, or trader literally placed his soul within reach of dangerous temptations, since he was in a position of exercising control over goods that were vital to other people. Puritanism had its own fair trade standards, as defined by the Reverend John Cotton: "A man may not sell above the current price, i.e., such a price as is usual in the time and place, and as another (who knows the worth of the commodity) would give for it, if he had occasion to use it...." Prices must not be increased to reflect personal losses, "but where there is a scarcity of the commodity," Cotton declared, "there men may raise their price; for now it is a hand of God upon the commodity, and not the person." Where there was disagreement over what constitutes a "just price," a determination would be made by "the Governor, with one or more of the council" or by "certain select men." [8]

Furthermore, the businessman's control of available cash and credit placed his soul in double jeopardy, as he increasingly acquired a power that might threaten the economy. These were difficult rules by which to live, especially for the merchant and trader, and there were numerous instances of commercial malpractice, overcharging, and usury. When such violations were discovered, the accused were exposed to public censure, as in the case of Robert Keayne who, in 1639, was haled before the General Court in Boston and charged with "taking above six-pence in the shilling profit; in some above eight-pence; and in some small things, above two for one." [9] But Englishmen's commercial transgressions against Indians went unpunished.

Even before the English set foot on the shores of New England, the Indians practiced division of labor and traded with one another. This in turn facilitated commercial relations between English and Indians, which induced various changes in both societies. For the English, trade with the Indians was a means of acquiring wealth and power in New England. For the Indian, trade with the English augmented intertribal divisiveness and transformed the native into a producer for the white man. Indian crafts were gradually eliminated, except for those required for trade with the English, and subsistence hunting was lessened. In his new relationship with the English, the Indian became a commercial hunter, providing furs in exchange for such commodities as iron hoes, steel hatchets and knives, articles of clothing, and a variety of other items that testified to the great magic of the English God and English technology.

In describing the impact of English technology upon the Indians, William Wood wrote in 1634:

> ... The first plowman was counted little better than a juggler: the *Indians* seeing the plow tear up more ground in a day, than their clamshells could scrape up in a month, desired to see the workmanship of it, and viewing well the coulter and share, perceiving it to be iron, told the plowman, he was almost *Hobomok,* almost as cunning as the Devil.... [10]

Yet the Indians were as anxious as the English to engage in trade and soon discovered that by providing furs, corn, and venison to the colonists they could acquire all sorts of wares, including guns and ammunition. Iron agricultural implements were especially desired by the Indians; with these they could improve the corn yield per acre and have enough surplus for trade.[11]

While he could not match the shrewdness of the Englishman, the Indian had a business sense of his own. Wood recorded that

> ... Since the English came, they have employed most of their time in catching beavers, otters, and musquashes, which they bring down into the bay, returning back loaded with English commodities, of which they make a double profit, by selling them to more remote Indians, who are ignorant at what cheap rates they obtain them, in comparison of what they make them pay.... [12]

Nevertheless, the Indians never accumulated the wealth—in the European sense—of many of their English neighbors, who were able to repay their backers in Old England and develop flourishing enterprises. Amassing property had no meaning in the Indian's culture. Even his tribute to the sachem was used to assist the indigent and as a reserve for times of need.

While the trade brought the Indian and the Englishman into greater contact with one another, the Puritan magistrates acted to restrict the items that could be bartered between them. For example, the government prohibited the use of money, "either silver or gold," in trading with the Indians, nor could "strong water" be used in trade.[13] In 1656, Plymouth banned the sale of "barques or boats, sails or other rigging to any Indian or Indians on pain of forfeiting that which is sold and ten times the value thereof." That year, the sale of horses—now a valuable economic asset—was prohibited to Indians in Plymouth and Massachusetts Bay "on penalty of one hundred pounds." [14]

In the early years of settlement, the regulation of Indian economic affairs was coupled with unfounded Puritan fears for their own survival. The Puritans were terrified of arming the Indians, as Richard Hopkins discovered in 1632 when he was "severely whipped, & branded with a hot iron on one of his cheeks, for selling pieces & powder & shot to the Indians." After Hopkins's sentence had been handed down, the magistrates wondered whether "this offense should not be punished hereafter by death," but left the decision to a subsequent court.[15] This regulation was suspended at times during the 1660s, although it was meticulously enforced on the whole, and during King Philip's War, providing arms to the Indians not surprisingly became a capital crime.

Two principal items of exchange used in trade were furs—especially beaver—and wampum. The fur trading enterprises of the Pilgrim monopolists and the Massachusetts Bay Company were unable to keep abreast of, let alone surpass, their French and Dutch competitors, who conducted flourishing operations. Nevertheless, individuals such as William Pynchon, of Springfield, Theophilus Eaton and Captain Nathaniel Turner, of Quinnipiac (New Haven), Richard Collecot, of Dorchester, Edward Hopkins, Thomas Stanton, and William Whiting, of Hartford, and Simon Willard, of Concord, amassed great wealth through the fur trade. For the Euroamerican, the best way of getting at the beaver—in great demand in European markets—was not by hunting himself, but by establishing a relationship with the Indians.[16] As one contemporary Englishman put it, the beaver were "too cunning for the English, who seldom or never catch any of them, therefore we leave them to these skillful hunters whose time is not so precious, whose experience-bought skill hath made them practical and useful in that particular." [17]

Wampum was manufactured from seashells and became an important native industry, especially for those Indians who were unable to participate directly in commercial hunting. Adopted as legal tender by the Puritans in New England but of no value in the old country, wampum was highly prized by the Indians and was redeemable in beaver and other articles as long as the natives were able to maintain its circulation as viable currency. The value of wampum, regulated by the Puritans, was directly related to the price of beaver in England. Generally, wampum beads were rated at four to six to the penny, and a "fathom" of wampum, comprising 240 to 260 beads, bought five shillings or sixty pence worth of merchandise.[18] In the symbiotic relationship that existed between the Indians and the Puritans, wampum and English manufactures bought more than peltry or fish or corn. They also bought what, to the Bay Puritan, was the most precious commodity the Indian had to offer: land.

Of course, on the basis of the concept of *vacuum domicilium,* all the land in New England not being farmed or lived on by the

Indians was considered vacant and awaiting occupation by the Puritans. Nevertheless, as earnestly as the Puritans sought to justify their invasion of the territory that rightfully belonged to the Indian, they found it difficult to ignore the realities of the situation. It would have been ridiculous for John Winthrop and his fellow immigrants to proclaim to the world that they had settled in a vacant land inhabited by Indians. Thus the Indians were a fact the Puritans had to face, although three years passed before Winthrop and his settlers purchased any native lands.[19]

Once begun, purchasing land from the Indians became a complex process that meant one thing to the Puritans and another to the Indians. The head sachem of each New England tribe in the seventeenth century had jurisdiction over his nation's territory. Hunting grounds and fishing areas were controlled by subordinate sachems. While croplands at one time were held in common, with a sachem assigning sections to be cultivated by each family each year, by then the assigned lands remained in the possession of the families who had traditionally cultivated them. Still, no individual Indian could sell any portion of his land without the full sanction of his sachem, acting on behalf of the tribal government.[20]

When such a sale was made to an Englishman, he demanded not only that the seller's rights to the property be extinguished but also that it be placed under the jurisdiction of his own government, which would protect his right to the property. In Puritan New England, no Indian could have jurisdiction over property owned by an Englishman. All sales were final unless provision was made for the Indian seller to continue to hunt and fish on the property. And unless authorized by the Puritan government, no Indian lands could be purchased privately; this control over land purchases prevented complicated legal actions over fraudulent titles and made certain that government objectives were adhered to.

The Massachusetts Bay Colony felt it had a legal claim to certain Indian lands by virtue of the king's charter, which Winthrop carried with him to the New World. New Plymouth, however, had no charter and therefore was unable to assert any legal claim to Indian territory. Thus it became necessary for the Pilgrims to enter into a mutual assistance pact with the Wampanoags. To the Pilgrims, this became their "deed of cession," authorizing them to seize unspecified acreage. For their part, the Wampanoags had no desire to test the effectiveness of English military technology in a struggle over an area that had been depopulated by a devastating epidemic.[21]

The Puritan justification for seizing Indian lands was disputed by Roger Williams, who asserted that "we have not our land by patent from the King, but that the natives are the true owners of it, and that we ought to repent of such a receiving it by patent." [22] He challenged the Puritan government to fulfill "a national duty" and "renounce the patent." But the magistrates felt, on the contrary, that to have acceded to Williams's demand would have "subverted the fundamental state and government of the country." [23] They also were fearful of Williams's challenge as a challenge to the authority of the crown, and they already were in plenty of trouble on that account for their own beliefs. For his radical ideas Williams was expelled from the Massachusetts Bay Colony in 1635.

New England colonists used a number of methods for acquiring Indian lands without coming into conflict with the natives. By far the most popular device was to allow one's cattle to trample an Indian's crops until he became completely unnerved and fled the premises. If he put up a fence to protect his crops, it would mysteriously be torn down. And if he dared harm any of the marauding animals, he would be haled into court to face hostile magistrates. Other techniques, used occasionally, were filling the Indian up with "strong water" and making him sign a deed he could not read; getting a corrupt Indian to lay claim to a piece of land, then recognizing his claim and "buying" it from him; and simply threatening the Indian with violence. A somewhat popular device was to have an Indian charged with a variety of offenses— some of them probably true at times—ranging from riding an Englishman's horse without permission to conspiring against the English. Fines would be imposed that the accused could not pay. At this point, the friendly Englishman would appear and offer to pay the fine in return for a short-term mortgage on the Indian's land. Later, the Englishman would foreclose.[24]

Without official confirmation in government records, it is extremely difficult to determine how frequently these tactics were used. English cattle destroying Indian corn appears to be the principal offense, but only because English courts regularly attempted to curb it. Scholars have established that the other devices were used, and this raises the question of how this kind of behavior could be reconciled with the Puritan abhorrence, in Baxter's words, of "the base and sordid spirit of worldliness." [25] Put another way, the question can be asked: Did not the Puritans in fact behave counter to the moral principles they so loudly espoused when they dealt with the Indians? The Puritans would have answered with a resounding "No."

The fact is that to the Puritan, the Native American was the instrument of Satan. For Cotton Mather the Indians were "doleful creatures who were the veriest ruins of mankind, who were to be found anywhere on the face of the earth"; and even Roger Williams, the great friend of the Indians, said they were devil-worshippers.[26] Ultimately, Mather considered them as chief antagonists to the Puritan errand: "The wilderness through which we are passing to the Promised Land is all over fill'd with fiery flying serpents," he wrote. "But, blessed be God, none of them have hitherto so fastened upon us to confound us utterly! All our way to heaven lies by *dens of lions* and the *mounts of leopards;* there are incredible droves of *devils in our way.*" [27]

The Puritan struggle against sin was, in part, a struggle against Satan as personified by the Indian. It was a life-and-death struggle and the Lord directed the Puritan forces in New England. Therefore, what the Puritan did, he did because God urged him to do it. Since the Puritan's relations with the Indians were dominated by his own importance as a messenger of God, his gain in a transaction with an Indian was a commensurate victory for God over Satan. While New Plymouth authorities declared that "there was no dealing with the Indians above board," [28] these dealings were justified because they were carried out according to the dictates of God. In the very same manner, the Jews had fought the Canaanites for possession of the Promised Land.[29]

1. "Abraham ... Among the Sodomites"

John Winthrop, the founder of the Massachusetts Bay Colony, did not approach the prospect of settling in New England with alacrity. Even though his personal fortunes were in decline by 1629 and he feared that "God will bring some heavy affliction upon this land [England], and that speedily," Winthrop had to convince himself that it was God's will for him to leave his homeland—by now a dangerous and uncomfortable place for Puritans—and for the wilds of the New World, there to build a New Canaan in accordance with divine sanction.[1] One of Winthrop's concerns was justification for Puritan appropriation of Indian lands. Winthrop dealt with this issue, raising the objection to dispossessing the Indians and then responding to it:[2]

Obj. 5. But what warrant have we to take that land, which is and hath been of long time possessed of others the sons of Adam?

Ans. That which is common to all is proper to none. This savage people ruleth over many lands without title or property; for they enclose no ground, neither have they cattle to maintain it, but remove their dwellings as they have occasion, or as they can prevail against their neighbors. And why may not Christians have liberty to go and dwell amongst them in their wastelands and woods (leaving them such places as they have manured for their corn) as lawfully as Abraham did among the Sodomites? For God hath given to the sons of men a twofold right to the earth; there is a natural right and a civil right. The first right was natural when men held the earth in common, every man sowing and feeding where he pleased: then, as men and cattle increased, they appropriated some parcels of ground by enclosing and peculiar manurance, and this in time got them a civil right. Such was the right which Ephron the Hittite had to the field of Machpelah, wherein Abraham could not bury a dead corpse without leave, though for the out parts of the country which lay common, he dwelt upon them and took the fruit of them at his pleasure. This appears also in Jacob and his sons, who fed their flocks as boldly in the Canaanites' land, for he is said to be lord of the country; and at Dotham and all other places men accounted nothing their own, but that which they had appropriated by their own industry, as appears plainly by Abimelech's servants, who in their own country did often contend with Isaac's servants about wells which they had digged; but never about the lands which they occupied. So likewise between Jacob and Laban; he would not take a kid of Laban's without special contract; but he makes no bargain with him for the land where he fed. And it is probable that if the country had not been as free for Jacob as for Laban, that covetous wretch would have made his advantage of him, and have upbraided Jacob with it as he did with the rest. 2dly, There is more than enough for them and us. 3dly, God hath consumed the natives with a miraculous plague, whereby the greater part of the country is left void of inhabitants. 4thly, We shall come in with good leave of the natives.

2. "The Son of Adam or Noah"

John Cotton, the greatest preacher of the Puritan era, was at Southampton to deliver a farewell sermon to John Winthrop and his group as they made ready for their departure for New England aboard the *Arbella* in 1630. The Reverend Cotton took as his text II Samuel 7:10: "Moreover I will appoint a place for my people Israel, and will plant them, that they may dwell in a place of their own, and move no more; neither shall the children of wickedness afflict them any more, as beforetime." Cotton, who was to come to America in 1633, sought to strengthen the faith and fire the enthusiasm of the colonists as he addressed himself to *God's Promise to His Plantations:*[1]

The placing of a people in this or that country is from the appointment of the Lord.

This is evident in the text, and the Apostle speaks of it as grounded in nature, *Acts* 17. 26. *God hath determined the times before appointed, and the bounds of our habitation. Deut. 2 chap. 5. 9.* God would not have the *Israelites* meddle with the *Edomites,* or the *Moabites,* because He had given them their land for a possession. God assigned out such a land for such a posterity, and for such a time.

Quest. Wherein doth this work of God stand in appointing a place for a people?

Answ. First, when God espies or discovers a land for a people, as in *Ezek.* 20. 6. He brought them into a land that He had espied for them: and that is, when either He gives them to discover it themselves, or hear of it discovered by others, and fitting them.

Secondly, after He had espied it, when He carrieth them along to it, so that they plainly see a providence of God leading them from one country to another: as in *Exod.* 19. 4. *You have seen how I have borne you as an eagle's wings, and brought you unto my self.* So that though they meet with many difficulties, yet He carried them high above them all, like an eagle, flying over seas and rocks, and all hindrances.

Thirdly, when He makes room for a people to dwell there, as in *Psal.* 80. 9. *Thou preparedst room for them.* When *Isaac* sojourned among the *Philistines,* he digged one well, and the *Philistines* strove for it, and he called it *Esek.* And he digged another well, and for that they strove also, therefore he called it *Sitnah:* and he removed thence, and digged another well, and for that they strove not, and he called it *Rehoboth,* and said, *For now the Lord hath made room for us, and we shall be fruitful in the Land.* Now no *Esek,* no *Sitnah,* no quarrel or contention, but now he sits down in *Rehoboth* in a peaceable room.

Now God makes room for a people 3 ways:

First, when He casts out the enemies of a people before them by lawful war with the inhabitants, which God calls them unto: as in *Psal.* 44. 2. *Thou didst drive out the heathen before them.* But this course of warring against others, & driving them out without provocation, depends upon special commission from God, or else it is not imitable.

Secondly, when He gives a foreign people favor in the eyes of any native people to come and sit down with them either by way of purchase, as *Abraham* did obtain the field of *Machpelah;* or else when they give it in courtesy, as *Pharaoh* did the Land of *Goshen* unto the sons of *Jacob.*

Thirdly, when He makes a country though not altogether void of inhabitants, yet void in that place where they reside. Where there is a vacant place, there is liberty for the son of *Adam* or *Noah* to come and inhabit, though they neither buy it, nor ask their leaves. *Abraham* and *Isaac,* when they sojourned amongst the Philistines, they did not buy that land to feed their cattle, because they said There is room enough. And so did *Jacob* pitch his tent by *Sechem, Gen.* 34. 21. There was *room enough* as *Hamor* said, *Let them sit down amongst us.* And in this case if the people who were former inhabitants did disturb them in their possessions, they complained to the King, as of wrong done unto them: As *Abraham* did because they took away his well, in *Gen.* 21. 25. For his right whereto he pleaded not his immediate calling from God, (for that would have seemed frivolous amongst the heathen) but his own industry and culture in digging the well, verse 30. Nor doth the King reject his plea, with what had he to do to dig wells in their soil? but admitteth it as a principle in Nature, that in a vacant soil, he that taketh possession of it, and bestoweth culture and husbandry upon it, his right it is. And the ground of this is from the Grand Charter given to *Adam* and his posterity in Paradise, *Gen.* 1. 28. *Multiply, and replenish the earth,* and subdue it. If therefore any son of *Adam* come and find a place empty, he hath liberty to come, and fill, and subdue the earth there. This Charter was renewed to *Noah, Gen.* 9. 1. *Fulfill the earth and multiply:* so that it is free from that common grant for any to take possession of vacant countries. Indeed no nation is to drive out another without special Commission from heaven, such as the Israelites had, unless the natives do unjustly wrong them, and will not recompense the wrongs done in peaceable sort, & then they may right themselves by lawful war, and subdue the country unto themselves.

This placing of people in this or that company, is from God's sovereignty over all the earth, and the inhabitants thereof: as in *Psal.* 24. 1. *The earth is the Lord's, and the fulness thereof.* And in *Jer.* 10. 7. God is there called, *The King of Nations:* and in *Deut.* 10. 14. Therefore it is meet He should provide a place for all nations to inhabit, and have all the earth replenished. Only in the text here is meant some more special appointment, because God tells them it by His own mouth; He doth not so with other people, He doth not tell the children of *Sier,* that He hath appointed a place for them: that is, He gives them the land by promise; others take the land by His providence, but God's people take the land by promise. And therefore the *Land* of *Canaan* is called a Land of Promise, which they discern, first, by discerning themselves to be in Christ, in whom all the promises are yea, and amen.

3. "No Time to Pamper the Flesh"

The prime objective of the Pilgrims in 1621 was survival, and survival depended upon an amicable relationship with the Indians, who taught the English how to overcome the rigors of New England. Robert Cushman, who helped facilitate the Pilgrims' immigration to America and served as their agent in England for many years, spent three weeks in New Plymouth that year. On his return to England, he published a pamphlet entitled, *Of the State of the Colony, and the need of Public Spirit in the Colonists.*[1] In his description of the uncertain early days of the Pilgrims, Cushman conspicuously fails to mention the fact that the Pilgrims survived the first year only through the assistance of the "helpless and idle" Wampanoags.[2]

And whoso rightly considereth what manner of entrance, abiding, and proceedings we have had among these poor heathens since we came hither, will easily think that God hath some great work to do towards them.

They were wont to be the most cruel and treacherous people in all these parts, even like lions; but to us they have been like lambs, so kind, so submissive, and trusty, as a man may truly say, many Christians are not so kind nor sincere.

They were very much wasted of late, by reason of a great mortality that fell amongst them three years since; which, together with their own civil dissensions and bloody wars, hath so wasted them, as I think the twentieth person is scarce left alive; and those that are left, have their courage much abated, and their countenance is dejected, and they seem as a people affrighted. And though when we first came into the country, we were few, and many of us were sick, and many died by reason of the cold and wet, it being the depth of winter, and we having no houses nor shelter, yet when there was not six able persons among us, and that they came daily to us by hundreds, with their sachems or kings, and might in one hour have made a dispatch of us, yet such fear was upon them, as that they never offered us the least injury in word or deed. And by reason of one Squanto, that lives amongst us, that can speak English, we have daily commerce with their kings, and can know what is done or intended towards us among the savages; also we can acquaint them with our courses and purposes, both human and religious. And the greatest commander of the country, called Massasoit, cometh often to visit us, though he lives fifty miles from us, often sends us presents, he having with many other of their governors promised, yea, subscribed obedience to our Sovereign Lord King James, and for his cause to spend both strength and life. And we, for our parts, through God's grace, have with that equity, justice, and compassion carried ourselves towards them, as that they have received much favor, help, and aid from us, but never the least injury or wrong by us. We found the place where we live empty, the people being all dead and gone away, and none living near by eight or ten miles; and though in the time of some hardship, we found, travelling abroad, some eight bushels of corn hid up in a cave, and knew no owners of it, yet afterwards hearing of the owners of it, we gave them (in their estimation) double the value of it. Our care also hath been to maintain peace amongst them, and have always set ourselves against such of them as used any rebellion or treachery against their governors; and not only threatened such, but in some sort paid them their due deserts. And when any of them are in want, as often they are in the winter, when their corn is done, we supply them to our power, and have them in our houses eating and drinking, and warming themselves; which thing, though it be something a trouble to us, yet because they should see and take knowledge of our labors, orders and diligence, both for this life and a better, we are content to bear it; and we find in many of them, especially of the younger sort, such a tractable disposition, both to religion and humanity, as that if we had means to apparel them, and wholly to retain them with us (as their desire is), they would doubtless in time prove serviceable to God and man; and if ever God send us means, we will bring up hundreds of their children both to labor and learning. . . .

The country is yet raw; the land untilled; the cities not builded, the cattle not settled. We are compassed about with a helpless and idle people, the natives of the country, which cannot, in any comely or comfortable manner, help themselves, much less us. We also have been very chargeable to many of our living friends, which helped us hither, and now again supplied us; so that before we think of gathering riches, we must even in conscience think of requiting their charge, love, and labor; and cursed be that profit and gain which aimeth not at this. Besides, how many of our dear friends did here die at our first entrance; many of them, no doubt, for want of good lodging, shelter, and comfortable things; and many more may go after them quickly, if care be not taken. Is this then a time for men to begin to seek themselves? Paul saith, that men in the last days shall be lovers of themselves; but it is here yet the *first* days, and, as it were, the dawning of this new world. It is now, therefore, no time for men to look to get riches, brave clothes, dainty fare; but to look to present necessities. It is now no time to pamper the flesh, live at ease, snatch, catch, scrape, and pill, and hoard up; but rather to open the doors, the chests, and vessels, and say, brother, neighbor, friend, what want ye? Any thing that I have? Make bold with it; it is yours. . . .

4. "The Governor Hath Sent Him a Coat"

Of major importance to the Pilgrims in the summer of 1621 was the establishment of trade relations with the Indians. The key Indian leader in the Plymouth area through whom this could be accomplished was Massasoit, sachem of the Wampanoags, who lived some forty miles southwest of the colony, on the shores of Narragansett Bay. Governor William Bradford, therefore, sent Stephen Hopkins, probably as Assistant Governor, and Edward Winslow, later Governor of Plymouth, on a diplomatic mission to Massasoit, bearing a special message and gifts including "a horseman's coat of red cotton, and laced with a slight lace." [1] What happened during this expedition was recorded in a journal, probably by Winslow:[2]

The message was as follows: that forasmuch as his [Massasoit's] subjects came often and without fear upon all occasions amongst us, so we were now come unto him; and in witness of the love and good-will the English bear unto him, the Governor hath sent him a coat, desiring that the peace and amity that was between them and us might be continued; not that we feared them, but because we intended not to injure any, desiring to live peaceably, and as with all men, so especially with them, our nearest neighbors. But whereas his people came very often, and very many together unto us, bringing for the most part their wives and children with them, they were welcome; yet we being but strangers as yet at Patuxet, alias New Plymouth, and not knowing how our corn might prosper, we could no longer give them such entertainment as we had done, and as we desired still to do. Yet if he would be pleased to come himself, or any special friend of his desired to see us, coming from him they should be welcome. And to the end we might know them from others, our governor had sent him a copper chain; desiring if any messenger should come from him to us, we might know him by bringing it with him, and hearken and give credit to his message accordingly; also requesting him that such as have skins should bring them to us, and that he would hinder the multitude from oppressing us with them. And whereas, at our first arrival at Pamet, called by us Cape Cod, we found there corn buried in the ground, and finding no inhabitants, but some graves of dead new buried, took the corn, resolving, if ever we could hear of any that had right thereunto, to make satisfaction to the full for it; yet since we understand the owners thereof were fled for fear of us, our desire was either to pay them with the like quantity of corn, English meal, or any other commodities we had, to pleasure them withal; requesting him that some one of his men might signify so much unto them, as we would content him for his pains. And last of all, our Governor requested one favor of him, which was that he would exchange some of their corn for seed with us, that we might make trial which best agreed with the soil where we live.

With these presents and message we set forward the 10th June, about nine o'clock in the morning, our guide resolving that night to rest at Nemasket, a town under Massasoit, and conceived by us to be very near, because the inhabitants flocked so thick upon every slight occasion amongst us; but we found it to be some fifteen English miles. On the way we found some ten or twelve men, women, and children, which had pestered us till we were weary of them, perceiving that (as the manner of them all is) where victual is easiest to be got, there they live, especially in the summer; by reason whereof, our bay affording many lobsters, they resort every spring-tide thither; and now return with us to Nemasket. Thither we came about three o'clock after noon, the inhabitants entertaining us with joy, in the best manner they could, giving us a kind of bread called by them *maizium* [maize] and the spawn of shads, which then they got in abundance, insomuch as they gave us spoons to eat them. With these they boiled musty acorns; but of the shads we eat heartily. After this they desired one of our men to shoot at a crow, complaining what damage they sustained in their corn by them; who shooting some fourscore off and killing, they much admired at it, as other shots on other occasions.

After this, Squanto told us we should hardly in one day reach Pakanokick, moving us to go some eight miles further, where we should find more store and better victuals than there. Being willing to hasten our journey, we went and came thither at sunsetting, where we found many of the Nemaskeucks (they so calling the men of Nemasket) fishing upon a weir which they had made on a river which belonged to them, where they caught abundance of bass. These welcomed us also, gave us of their fish, and we them of our victuals, not doubting but we should have enough where'er we came. There we lodged in the open fields, for houses they had none, though they spent the most of the summer there....

The next morning we brake our fast, took our leave, and departed; being accompanied with some six savages....

After we came to a town of Massasoit's, where we eat oysters and other fish. From thence we went to Pakanokick; but Massasoit was not at home. There we stayed, he being sent for. When news was brought of his coming, our guide Squanto requested that at our meeting we would discharge our pieces. But one of us going about to charge his piece, the women and children, through fear to see him take up his piece, ran away, and could not be pacified till he laid it down again; who afterward were better informed by our interpreter. Massasoit being come, we discharged our pieces and saluted him; who, after their manner, kindly welcomed us, and took us into his house, and set us down by him; where, having delivered our foresaid message and presents, and having put the coat on his back and the chain about his neck, he was not a little proud to behold himself, and his men also to see their king so bravely attired.

This being done, his men gathered near him, to whom he turned himself and made a great speech; they sometimes interposing, and, as it were, confirming and applauding him in that he said. The meaning whereof was, as far as we could learn, thus: Was not he, Massasoit, commander of the country about them? Was not such a town his, and the people of it? And should they not bring their skins unto us? To which they answered, they were his, and would be at peace with us, and bring their skins to us. . . .

5. "Some of You Steal Our Corn"

Phineas Pratt, who arrived in Massachusetts from Old England in 1622, was one of the founders of Thomas Weston's ill-fated economic enterprise at Wessagusset (Weymouth), outside Wampanoag territory. The colonists began "with little provision" and "neither applied themselves to planting of corn, nor taking of fish, more than for their present use; but went about to build castles in the air, and making of forts, neglecting the plentiful time of fishing." Without provisions or powder and shot with which to hunt, many starved to death when winter came in 1623, and the rest "hardly escaped." [1] Those who survived were no match for the Massachuset Indians, who, following the theft of their own provisions by the English, seemed to be plotting the destruction of the English at Wessagusset and Plymouth. Hearing of an impending massacre, Pratt was determined to warn Plymouth of the danger. The following passage is his account of the rumored conspiracy, his escape to Plymouth, and that colony's pre-emptive strike against some of the Massachuset Indians.[2]

But after this, when they saw famine prevail, Pecksuot said, "why do your men & your dogs die?" I said, "I had corn for a time of need. Then I filled a chest, but not with corn & spread corn [on top for] him [to see. When he] opened the cover and when I was sure he saw it, I put [the cover] dow[n] ... as if I would not have him see it." Then he said, "No Indian sow.... You have much corn & English men die for want." Then they h[ave] ... intent to make war. They removed some of their houses to ... a great swamp near to the pale of our plantation. After this, [one] morning I saw a man going into one of their houses, weary with travelling.... Then I said to Mr. Salisbury, our surgeon, ["]surely their sachem hath employed him for some intent to make war upon us.["] Then I took a bag with gunpowder and put it in my pocket, with the top of the bag hanging out, & went to the house where the man was laid upon a mat. The woman of the house took hold of the bag, saying, ["]what is this so big?["] I said, ["]it is good for savages to eat,["] and struck her on the arm as hard as I could. Then she said, ["]Machit powder English men, much Machit. By and by Abordicis bring much men, much sanups, & kill you & all English men at Wessagusset & Patuxet.["] The man that lay upon the mats, seeing this, was angry and in a great rage, and the woman seemed to be sore afraid. Then I went out of the house, and said to a young man that could best understand their language, ["]go ask the woman, but not in the man's hearing, why the man was angry, & she afraid?["] Our interpreter, coming to me said, "these are the words of the woman—[']the man will [tell?] ... Abordicis what I said & he & all Indians will be angry with me ... [' "] ...

Some time after this their sachem came suddenly upon us with a great number of armed men; but their spies, seeing us in a readiness, he & some of his chief men, turned into one of their houses a quarter of an hour. Then we met them without the pale of our plantation & brought them in. Then said I to a young man that could best speak their language, "Ask Pecksuot why they come thus armed." He answered, "Our sachem is angry with you." I said, "Tell him if he be angry with us, we be angry with him." Then said their sachem, "English men, when you come into the country, we gave you gifts and you gave us gifts; we bought and sold with you and we were friends; and now tell me if I or any of my men have done you wrong." We answered, "First tell us if we have done you any wrong." He answered, "Some of you steal our corn & I have sent you word times without number & yet our corn is stolen. I come to see what you will do." We answered, "It is one man which hath done it. Your men have seen us whip him divers times, besides other manner of punishments, & now here he is bound. We give him unto you to do with him what you please." He answered, "It is not just dealing. If my men wrong my neighbor sachem, or his men, he sends me word & I beat or kill my men, according to the offense. If his men wrong me or my men, I send him word & he beats or kills his men according to the offense. All sachems do justice by their own men. If not we say they are all agreed & then we fight, & now I say you all steal my corn."

At this time, some of them, seeing some of our men upon our fort, began to start, saying, "Machit Pesconk," that is, naughty guns. Then looking around about them went away in a great rage. At this time we strengthened our watch until we had no food left. In these times the savages oftentimes did creep upon the snow, starting behind bushes & trees to see whether we keep watch or not . . . ; then in the night, going into our court of guard, I saw one man dead before me & another at my right hand & another at my left for want of food. . . .

The offender being bound, we let him loose, because we had no food to give him. Charging him to gather ground nuts, clams & mussels, as other men did, & steal no more. One or two days after this, the savages brought him, leading him by the arm, saying "Here is the corn. Come see the place where he stole it." Then we kept him bound some few days. After this, two of our company said "we have been at the sachem's house & they have near finished their last canoe that they may encounter with our ship. Their greatest care is how to send their armies to Plymouth because of the snow.["] Then we prepared to meet them there. One of our company said, "They have killed one of our hogs." Another said, "One of them struck at me with his knife;" & others say, "They threw dust in our faces." Then said Pecksuot to me, "Give me powder & guns & I will give you much corn." I said, "By & by men bring ships & victuals." But when we understood that their plot was to kill all English people in one day when the snow was gone, I would have sent a man to Plymouth, but none were willing to go. Then I said ["]If Plymouth men know not of this treacherous plot,

they & we are all dead men; therefore if God willing, tomorrow I
will go.["] That night a young man, wanting wit, told Pecksuot early
in the morning. Pecksuot came to me & said in English, "Me hear
you go to Patuxet; you will lose yourself: the bears and the wolves
will eat you; but because I love you I will send my boy Nahamit
with you; & I will give you victuals to eat by the way & to be
merry with your friends when you come there." I said, "Who told
you so great a lie that I may kill him." He said, "It is no lie, you
shall not know." Then he went home to his house. Then came 5
men armed. We said, "Why come you thus armed?" They said,
"We are friends; you carry guns where we dwell & we carry bow &
arrows where you dwell." These attended me 7 or 8 days & nights.
Then they supposing it was a lie, were careless of their watch near
two hours on the morning. Then said I to our company, "Now is
the time to run to Plymouth. Is there any compass to be found?"
They said, "No, but them that belong to the ship." I said, "They
are too big. I have borne no arms of defense this 7 or 8 days. Now
if I take my arms they will mistrust me.["] Then they said, "The
savages will pursue after you & kill you & we shall never see you
again." Thus with other words of great lamentation, we parted.
Then I took a hoe & went to the Long Swamp near by their houses
& digged on the edge thereof as if I had been looking for ground
nuts, but seeing no man I went in & ran through it. Then looking
around about me, I ran southward 'till 3 of the clock, but the snow
being in many places, I was the more distressed because of my
footsteps. The sun being beclouded, I wandered, not knowing my
way; but at the going down of the sun, it appeared red; then
hearing a great howling of wolves, I came to a river; the water
being deep & cold & [with] many rocks, I passed through with
much ado. Then was I in great distress—faint for want of food,
weary with running, fearing to make a fire because of them that
pursued me. Then I came to a deep dell or hole, there being much
wood fallen into it. Then I said in my thoughts, this is God's
providence that here I may make a fire. Then, having made a fire,
the stars began to appear.... The day following, I began to travel
... but being unable, I went back to the fire ... & about three of
the clock I came to that part ... Plymouth Bay, where there is a
town of later time ... Duxbury. Then, passing by the water on my
left hand ... [I] came to a brook & there was a path. Having but a

short time to consider ... fearing to go beyond the plantation, I kept running in the path.... Then running down a hill ... [I saw] an Englishman coming in the path before me. Then I sat down on a tree & rising up to salute him, said, "Mr. [John] Hamden, I am glad to see you alive." He said, "I am glad & full of wonder to see you alive: let us sit down, I see you are weary." I said, "Let ... [us] eat some parched corn." Then he said, "I know the cause ... Massasoit hath sent word to the governor ... that Abordicis & his confederates have contrived a plot hoping [to kill?] all English people in one day here as men [are] hard by [ma]king canoe ... stay, & we will go with you. The next day a young ... [man] named Hugh Stacey went forth to fell a tree & saw two ... [Indians?] rising from the ground. They said Abordicis had sent ... [them to] the Governor, that he might send men to truck for such beaver, but they would not go, but said, "Was not there an English[man] ... come from Wessagusset." He answered, "He came.".... They said he was their friend ... but they turned another way....

Two or 3 days after my coming to Plymouth, 10 or 11 men [under Captain Miles Standish] went in a boat to our plantation, but I being faint was not able to go with them. They first gave warning to the master of the ship & then contrived how to make sure of the lives of two of their chief men, Wittiwamut, of whom they boasted no gun could kill, and Pecksuot, a subtle man. These being slain, they fell upon others where they could find them....

6. "They Saw ... a Walking Island"

New England Indians viewed English technology as a manifestation of the great power of the English God and as evidence of His alliance with the colonists. The English had brought with them all sorts of strange and fascinating things that could make life easier in New England for the white man and the red man. The following passage from William Wood, who sought to promote immigration to the Massachusetts Bay Colony, also reveals some of the inadvertent trading and unforeseen influences that transpired in the early years of English settlement.[1]

These Indians being strangers to arts and sciences, and being unacquainted with the inventions that are common to a civilized people, are ravished with admiration at the first view of such sight: They took the first ship they saw for a walking island, the mast to be a tree, the sail white clouds, and the discharging of ordnance for lightning and thunder, which did much trouble them, but this thunder being over, and this moving island steadied with an anchor, they manned out their canoes to go and pick strawberries there, but being saluted by the way with a broadside, they cried out, what much hoggery, so big walk, and so big speak, and by and by kill; which caused them to turn back, not daring to approach till they were sent for. They do much extol and wonder at the *English* for their strange inventions, especially for a windmill, which in their esteem was little less than the world's wonder, for the strangeness of his whisking motion, and the sharp teeth biting the corn (as they term it) into such final pieces; they were loath at the first to come near to his long arms, or to abide in so tottering a tabernacle, though now they dare go anywhere so far as they have an English guide. The first plowman was counted little better than a juggler: the *Indians* seeing the plow tear up more ground in a day, than their clamshells could scrape up in a month, desired to see the workmanship of it, and viewing well the coulter and share, perceiving it to be iron, told the plowman, he was almost *Hobomok,* almost as cunning as the Devil; but the fresh supplies of new and strange objects hath lessened their admiration, and quickened their inventions, and desire of practicing such things as they see, wherein they express no small ingenuity, and dexterity of wit, being neither furthered by art, or long experience. It is thought they would soon learn any mechanical trades, having quick wits, understanding apprehensions, strong memories, with nimble inventions, and a quick hand in using of the axe or hatchet, or such like tools: much good might they receive from the *English,* and much might they benefit themselves, if they were not strongly fettered in the chains of idleness; so as that they had rather starve than work, following no employments, saving such as are sweetened with more pleasures and profit than pains or care, and this is indeed one of the greatest accusations that can be laid against them, which lies but upon the men (the women being very industrious), but it may be hoped that good example and good instructions may bring them to a more industrious and provident course of life. For already, as they have learned much subtlety & cunning by bargaining with the *English,* so have they a little degenerated from some of their lazy customs, and show themselves more industrious. In a word, to set them out in their best colors, they be wise in their carriage, subtle in their dealings, true in their promise, honest in defraying of their debts, though poverty constrain them to be something long before; some having died in the *English* debt, have left beaver by order of will for their satisfaction: they be constant in friendship, merrily conceited in discourse, not luxuriously abounding in youth, nor dotingly forward in old age, many of them being much civilized since the *English* colonies were planted, though but little edified in religion: they frequent often the *English* churches, where they will sit soberly, though they understand not such hidden mysteries. They do easily believe some of the history of the Bible, as the creation of the world, the making of man, with his fall: but come to tell them of a Savior, with all the passages of the Gospel, and it exceeds so far their *Indian* beliefs, that they will cry out *(Pocatnie) id est,* is it possible? Yet such is their conviction of the right way, that when some *English* have come to their houses, victuals being offered them, forgetting to crave God's blessing upon the creatures received, they have been reproved by these, which formerly never knew what calling upon God meant: thus far for their natural disposition and qualities.

7. "For a Little Profit"

John Josselyn, a non-Puritan who visited America twice, recorded various aspects of the life-style of the New England Indians. His account of his second voyage in 1663 included the following report of the different items the Indians use for trade and what they received in exchange for them:[1]

... Their drink they fetch from the spring, and were not acquainted with other, until the *French* and *English* traded with that cursed liquor called *rum, rumbullion,* or kill-devil, which is stronger than spirit of wine, and is drawn from the dross of sugar and sugar canes. This they love dearly, and will part with all they have to their bare skins for it, being perpetually drunk with it, as long as it is to be had. It hath killed many of them, especially old women who have died when dead drunk. Thus instead of bringing of them to the knowledge of Christianity, we have taught them to commit the beastly and crying sins of our nation, for a little profit. When the *Indians* have stuffed their paunches, if it be fair weather and about midday they venture forth again, but if it be foul and far spent, they betake themselves to their field-bed at the sign of the star, expecting the opening of the eastern window, which if it promise serenity, they truss up their fardels, and away for another *moose.* This course they continue for six weeks or two months, making their *webs* their *mules* to carry their luggage. They do not trouble themselves with the horns of *moose* or other *deer,* unless it be near an *English* plantation because they are weighty and cumbersome. If the *English* could procure them to bring them in, they would be worth the pains and charge, being sold in *England* after the rate of forty or fifty pounds a ton. The red heads of *deer* are the fairest and fullest of marrow, and lightest; the black heads are heavy and have less marrow; the white are the worst, and the worst nourished. When the *Indians* are gone, there gathers to the carcass of the *moose* thousands of *mattrises,* of which there are but few or none near the seacoasts to be seen. These devour the remainder in a quarter of the time that they were hunting of it....

Their merchandise are their beads [wampum], which are their money. Of these there are two sorts: blue beads and white beads. The first is their gold, the last their silver. These they work out of certain shells so cunning that neither *Jew* nor devil can counterfeit. They drill them and string them, and make many curious works with them to adorn the persons of their *sagamores* and principal men and young women, as belts, girdles, tablets, borders for their women's hair, bracelets, necklaces, and links to hang in their ears. Prince *Philip* [Metacom] a little before I came for England, coming to *Boston* had a coat on and buskins set thick with these beads in pleasant wild works and a broad belt of the same. His accoutrements were valued at twenty pounds. The *English* merchant giveth them ten shillings a fathom for their white, and as much more or near upon for their blue beads. Delicate sweet dishes too they make of *birch-bark,* sewn with threads drawn from *spruce* or white cedar-roots, and garnished on the outside with flourished works, and on the brims with glistering quills taken from the *porcupine,* and dyed, some black, others red, the white are natural. These they make of all sizes from a dram cup to a dish containing a pottle. Likewise buckets to carry water or the like, large boxes too of the same materials, dishes, spoons and trays wrought very smooth and neatly out of the knots of wood, baskets, bags, and mats woven with *spark,* bark of the *linetree* and *rushes* of several kinds, dyed as before, some black, blue, red, yellow; bags of *porcupine* quills woven and dyed also; coats woven of *turkey* feathers for their children, tobacco pipes of stone with their imagery upon them, kettles of *birch-bark* which they used before they traded with the *French* for copper kettles, by all which you may apparently see that necessity was at first the mother of all inventions. The women are the workers of most of these, and are now, here and there one excellent needle woman, and will milk a cow neatly. Their richest trade are furs of divers sorts, black *fox, beaver, otter, bear, sable, mattrises, fox, wildcats, rattons, martins, musquash, moose-skins.*

8. "That All Interlopers ... Be Restrained"

For the Puritans, now organized into a confederation of colonies, 1644 was a critical year that demanded crucial decisions if they were to achieve commercial viability. The Dutch, the prime competitors of the English, French, and Swedes, for a number of years had been amassing great wealth in beaver and other pelts. But that year, their monopoly at Renssalaerwyck went bankrupt, out-traded by private individuals who were acquiring the best furs the Indians had to offer.[1] As a matter of self-preservation, the commissioners of the United Colonies proposed the following scheme, to be considered and acted on by the general courts of the individual Puritan colonies, with the exception of Rhode Island, which was not included in the confederation:[2]

Whereas the trade with the Indians in these parts is or may be of great concernment, but withall subject to many questions and differences as whether each jurisdiction shall be limited and restrained to their own known and allowed bounds, whether in each jurisdiction each particular person shall have liberty at his discretion to manage a particular trade according to his opportunity, or whether the trade shall be rented out to some other at certain yearly rate, or such proportion by the hundred or skin, or whether as the colonies are now united so a general stock be raised for, and throughout them all, unto which each man shall have liberty to put in as he is able and willing. The Commission[ers] conceived this latter more profitable and honorable and accordingly agreed to commend it to their general courts in their several jurisdictions with these following considerations.

1. It is conceived that a stock of five or six thousand pounds may begin such a trade, but ten thousand or more may comfortably, and to good advantage be employed in it.

2. That in each plantation every man may either put in his proportion under his own name ... provided he put not in less than 20 shillings, or divers may put in under the name of some one whom they generally trust and are satisfied in, and in such case he whose name is used, to be called an undertaker or feoffee, and all the rest adventurers.

3. That in each jurisdiction two or three be chosen by the undertakers to manage this joint stock, by providing commodities for trade, settling trading houses, hiring factors or servants to trade with the Indians, receiving the beaver or other proceed of the trade from them with accounts from time to time and what else may be necessary and ordered as proper to their place and these to be called committees.

4. That if the several general courts approve this course of trading by a joint stock every man may have time within three months after to underwrite what he will furnish for the trade, and six months after to pay it in. Provided that whatever any man underwrites no more shall be accounted or expected than what he payeth in within the aforesaid six months.

5. For the payment of every man's proportion, either money, English commodities fit for trade, wampum, beaver, English corn,

or cattle fit for the butcher or market shall be accepted: so that by the committees they be duly and indifferently rated, that they may equal to the payment of others that no man be wronged.

6. That this way of trading with due privileges be established by each general court for ten years and that all interlopers both our own and others be restrained as much as may be.

7. That the accounts of this joint stock be made by the aforesaid committees every year and tendered to the view of the Commissioners in each jurisdiction before this yearly meeting in September. And that after the first year so much of the gain and profits (if it please God to prosper the trade) be divided as the Commissioners for the colonies with the aforesaid committees shall think meet.

8. The aforesaid committees to have such allowance and consideration for their care and pains in managing this joint stock as the undertakers shall think meet.

9. Whereas it is conceived there will be a general court in each jurisdiction this next ensuing month or the beginning of November, where these propositions may be seriously considered, the Commissioners promise mutually to certify each other what entertainment they find that accordingly each jurisdiction and trader may order their own occasions.

9. "Till the English Taught Them"

In 1664, a Royal Commission, appointed by Charles II, arrived in New England, headed by Colonel Richard Nicolls, and comprised of Sir Robert Carr, Colonel George Cartwright, and Samuel Maverick. Nicolls's squadron brought the Dutch government to its knees at Manhattan, and New Amsterdam became New York. Far more complicated was the commission's second objective: evaluating and regulating New England's Puritan colonies. Cartwright was biased against Massachusetts, but even so his devastating case against it was justified:[1]

...the Indians never knew what selling of land, or mortgaging meant, till the English taught them, yet it was proved before the Commission that the Indians sent to know where they would have the money paid, before the time in the mortgage was expired; and answer was returned, they could not receive it now, because Mr. [John] Winthrop [Jr.] was in England, yet after that seized upon the country as forfeited.

...It was proved before the Commission that Cachanaquand (of whom they pretended to have bought land) was younger brother to Pessicus, & by custom of those Indians had not power to sell land. For there the chief sachem only sold land, and disposed of the under-sachems; as Miantonomo had sold Rhode Island, Connecticut, & Prudence Isles, the Township of Warwick, and Providence, & had disposed of those under-sachems. But besides it was proved, that Cachanaquand is simple, and that he was seduced, being made drunk, & kept so for some days, & carried to Boston, where this sale was made, about 6000 acres of the best in that province for about 25£ (300 fathom of peage). In this purchase, & in another pretended to by Mr. Brown, as also in the mortgage, Mr. Winthrop, governor of Connecticut, Major [Josiah] Winslow of New Plymouth Colony were joined together with these of the Massachusetts; Mr. Winthrop being by, at the hearing of the cause, did openly declare, that he knew nothing of it, & that his name was made use of without his consent, & without his knowledge; which made it look like a combination (as it was afterwards confessed to be) that the Commissioners of the United Colonies, being always the chief men of those 3 colonies, & New Haven, (for Rhode Island was excluded) might always make orders in favor of the purchasers against Rhode Island, and so they did. But besides all this, there was an order made by the General Court of Rhode Island, that none should buy land in that province of the Indians without consent of the court upon penalty of forfeiting what they bought; it was openly proved, that this order was made before these purchases. Such an order had been long before made in all the other colonies, & executed against Mr. [Jahleel?] Brenton eleven years after possession, & 7 years after having built an house upon some purchased land in the Massachusetts Colony, as he complained in a petition. The Commissioners did not think themselves bound to express all these particulars in their declaration. That all these things, & more had been proved might have appeared, if the papers had not been lost at sea.

That declaration there mentioned was also made by the Commissioners. The case this. The Massachusetts give away a tract of land, on the eastern side of Pawcatuck River, within the Colony of Rhode Island, pretending, they had conquered it from the Pequot Indians. Betwixt their conquest & their donation of land, by their own relation, there are about 20 years. The Commissioners could not perceive where in their charter their own militia was so much put into their own hands as to make an invasive [invasion?]. To defend themselves is permitted them; but to make an offensive war, & so far out of their own bounds, to conquer nations, & to dispose of the conquered lands is not to be found there. And as this prerogative was not granted to any one colony; so neither was it granted to them all jointly. For they never had any such charter.

They had made a combination amongst themselves (but left out Rhode Island) in imitation of the states of the united provinces, & styled themselves, the United Colonies. By this they took more power than was ever given, or intended them, as by the copy, if not lost, might have seen. That there should be an agreement amongst all the several colonies, for assisting of each other, & for keeping a good correspondence betwixt each other, as that servants, debtors, & murderers, or thieves might not be defended against their just prosecutors, is absolutely necessary. But then it ought to be under a head, so long as there is a king, neither then are they to exercise the king's prerogative without his leave & consent.

But it was proved before the Commission: that Miantonomo, the Narragansett sachem, had conquered that very tract of land on the east side of Pawcatuck from the Pequots, some years before that the English war [had] begun, & had given it Soso, & that Miantonomo with 500 Indians did assist in that war against the Pequots, & so did Uncas another sachem. Yet these had no share of the conquest. Pessicus & Ninigret, the present Narragansett sachem, acknowledged this to be true also. Of this Soso the Rhode Islanders bought it. Notwithstanding divers protected by the Massachusetts, build there; and authorized thereto by violence seized on, & carried away the persons of the Rhode Islanders, prisoners to Boston, kept them there several months; they beat the constable & took away his staff, and committed many other outrages, whereby the purchasers were very much damnified; all this was proved, & to have been done since His Majesty's happy return into England. Unless violence, & expression be a good title, the Massachusetts had no reason to complain of that order.

The Pequots' country lay chiefly betwixt the rivers of Pawcatuck & Mohegan. That country is now given by His Majesty to the Colony of Connecticut, as conquered by them (& so indeed it seemed to be by a relation of that war made to the Commissioners). Some of these Pequots were ordered by the United Colonies, or the Massachusetts to plant on the east side of that river. Those of the Massachusetts party would then plant on that land the Rhode Islanders held, the Rhode Islanders, on that land which the Massachusetts held, so that betwixt both the Indians were denied, or hindered to plant at all. Now the Commissioners had prevailed with Mr. Winthrop, the Governor of Connecticut, to provide a place for those Indians in that which had been their own country, against the next planting season, & he promised to see it done. Upon this reason the Commissioners made that part of the order not to hinder the Indians from planting there this summer....

If cheating of the Indians by a mortgage, & a fraudulent purchase; if pretending a conquest where they made none, & selling the lands pretended to be conquered without their own limits; if oppressing of their neighbors be to be justified by magna charta, then their title to those lands claimed are good; and their combination to destroy Rhode Island is effectual. For all those lands they speak of are the only lands which the Narragansett sachems submitted to His Majesty in 1664, and the only lands now granted Rhode Island by His Majesty's charter, & before the Lords & commons.

The Commissioners are also blamed by some for doing another piece of injustice which, these gentlemen having overslipped, shall be here set down.

Tocomano (a petty sachem) gives to Mr. Brown a tract of land about 1652, whether Mr. Brown did accept of it then or no, is uncertain, but it is certain Mr. Brown did not draw any writing for it then, as afterwards he did; but goes that year to Old England, & was Sir Henry Vane's steward at Raby. In 1660, when he saw that the King was to return into Old England, he returned into New England. But before he came thither, though in the same year,

Tocomano sells that tract of land to trustees for Rhode Island, and they, before they bought it, sent to New Plymouth, in whose jurisdiction Mr. Brown's family was, to know if they had any obligation upon that land. They returned answer, Tocomano might sell it to whom he pleased. Thereupon writings are made, and sealed by Tocomano, & his son, & his grandson and 40£ paid the same day, and 20£ next day, both to Tocomano himself. Then in the year 1661 Mr. Brown makes a writing, & gets the same 3 men to seal it, which says thus, Whereas I Tocomano about 9 years since gave such a tract of land to Mr. Brown to make an English town on, but then he could not because he was to go to Old England. But now being returned, and having a mind to make an English town, and having taken for his associates Mr. [John] Winthrop of Connecticut, Major [Humphrey] Atherton of Boston, Major [Josiah] Winslow & Mr. [Thomas] Willet of New Plymouth & all whom I approve well of, I do confirm unto the said Mr. Brown the said tract of land &c. Presently after this Mr. Brown dies, & Mr. Willet (his son-in-law) says that Tocomano came to him, and asked if his grandchild could sell to Rhode Island men that land which he had given Mr. Brown. Mr. Willet answered, No. Tocomano replies, but he hath sold it, & gotten a great deal of peage [wampum]. What must be done? Mr. Willet answered, take the peage from him, lest he spend it. Upon this Tocomano goes away, & within a short time returns with a bag of peage, which Mr. Willet kept ever since, & when this case was heard at Warwick in Rhode Island province, where the land lies, he delivered the peage to the Commissioners. Since then Tocomano is dead. But his son appeared before the Commissioners and when he saw both the writings, he said, he had sealed them, and showed which was his father's, and which was his son's seal, at each deed; and that his father had received 60£ of Rhode Island men; but that neither he, nor his son had received any of it.

The deeds, both were seen and so dated. The answer returned from Plymouth was proved on oath, the sealing of the deed, and the paying of the money then to Tocomano himself was proved by 3 oaths. The Commissioners judged the purchase of Rhode Island good, if Mr. Brown's deed had been before the other; yet buying it without the consent of the court would have barred him by the practice of all the other colonies....

The judgments which the Commissioners gave concerning those lands in the Narragansett country were grounded upon those evidences which were produced before them, and are set down in each particular case. . . .

That there was a design to ruin the Colony of Rhode Island may appear by the Massachusetts refusing them ammunition, in a time of very great danger; and by the inserting of the names of some of the principal men of Connecticut, & New Plymouth into all their pretended purchases, and mortgage of Narragansett lands as will appear by their deeds.

That the United Colonies did usurp authority is certainly plain in that, that the authority of disposing of lands, without the limits of their respective limits, which they exercised, was not given them by the King; if that act be justified, they may dispose of all New England both when and as they please.

Chapter II

"God Wraps Us in His Ordinances"

Government Relations

The record of government relations in seventeenth-century New England is a succession of clashes between similar political systems: Indian tribes against Puritan colonies; colonies against each other; and tribes against each other. Often, all three kinds of conflict occurred simultaneously. But tribal rivalries and wars were relatively infrequent prior to Puritan settlement (compared to the number of wars in Europe), and political rifts in the Protestant ranks developed after 1630, for the most part. Neither would have increased if it were not that a colonizing European nation was asserting political jurisdiction, in the name of God, over indigenous New England societies.

Once again, the three justifications put forward by Puritans for their right to native land were "lawful war" specially commissioned by God against heathen Indians who proudly resisted the political control of Puritan society; purchase or gift from the natives; and, most frequently, *vacuum domicilium*—the freedom to claim untilled or vacated land. Throughout the seventeenth century, the Puritans asserted all three claims when the need arose. However, once the Pequot War (1636–37) and King Philip's War (1675–76) were behind them, Puritan apologists dropped the justification of "lawful war" and defended themselves against the King of England's attempt to turn Massachusetts Bay into a dependent royal province by emphasizing the second and third justifications, which were not based on the colony's messianic orientation or the original patent the colony had received from an earlier English king in 1629. As John Higginson put the case in 1689, Massachusetts

> had the possession and use of [its lands] by a twofold right warranted by the Word of God. 1) By a right of just occupation from the Grand Charter in Genesis 1st and 9th Chapters, whereby God gave the earth to the sons of Adam and Noah, to be subdued and replenished. 2) By a right of purchase from the Indians, who were native inhabitants, and had possession of the land before the English came hither, and that having lived here sixty years, I did certainly know that from the beginning of these plantations our fathers entered upon the land, partly as a wilderness and *vacuum domicilium*, and partly by the consent of the Indians, and therefore care was taken to treat with them, and to gain their consent, giving them such a valuable consideration as was to their satisfaction.[1]

When thus threatened with the usurpation of their own rights, as the native tribes had been threatened years before by them, Puritans came to the defense of a system of government that was similar, in important ways, to the native governments that they had always defined as savage and uncivilized.

Indian cultures in New England and Puritan culture in Massachusetts Bay and Connecticut were more democratic than European society. The hereditary ruling sachems of Indian tribes, whom the English incorrectly identified as kings, governed their people with a modified system of advice and consent in which subordinate sachems could rebel with a dissatisfied portion of the population if the chief administrative sachem ignored the wishes of his tribe.[2] Consequently, as several English leaders perceived, sachems usually ruled through a tribal council that was more broadly representative than the sachems themselves. Close at hand in important tribal decisions were native priests—powwows—who functioned as medicine men, spiritual leaders, and cultural custodians.

In practice, Puritan leadership was also hereditary, with dominant families among the "elect" or "saved" members of Puritan society providing a chain of governors that stretched through several generations. Nevertheless, these men were subject to annual election and possible removal from office and were advised by a representative General Court that functioned like a tribal council. Technically, Puritan society practiced separation of church and state, which prevented ministers from becoming administrators and vice versa. But this separation of powers (as, apparently, in native societies) was less a matter of varying abilities and spirituality than an efficient way of broadening group accountability and insuring group unity. In native cultures and Puritan culture, all leaders—political and religious—shared the philosophical assumptions of their society; and within each system, the voting franchise was distributed to individuals who believed in the religious tenets of the culture.

However, similarities between Puritan and native cultures did not prevent serious conflict. One group was settling on the other's land as if God had ordained that land for its own way of life: "God's people take the land by promise," said John Cotton, not by "providence" or convenience. "When God wraps us in his ordinances, and warms us with the life and power of them as with wings, there is a land of promise." If this were not made clear in the Bible, Cotton concluded, then Puritans would be "but intruders upon God" (and upon the Indians, presumably).[3] The promise from God was confirmed in the minds of Puritans by their observation that Indians in New England lived a less agrarian life than they, though the Bible commanded the descendants of Adam (including Indians) to bestow "culture and husbandry" upon the earth. Thus the lands that the Indians did not farm but used for hunting instead became the *vacuum domicilium* that the Puritans could claim as their own.

The early laws of Massachusetts Bay and Connecticut (settled in 1635) asserted political jurisdiction over neighboring Indians and limited their cultural autonomy. Land sales by Indians to whites had to be licensed by the Massachusetts General Court as early as 1633, a policy that became standard in all the colonies by 1663. Selling guns and powder to Indians was quickly forbidden (Massachusetts: 1633, Connecticut: 1642), but the sale of liquor was not penalized until the 1650s. Living amidst Indians in Connecticut after 1642 meant a three-year imprisonment. To restrain Indians from "whatever may be a means to disturb our peace and quiet," individuals in Massachusetts Bay were even punished, after 1656, for selling boats and skiffs to natives. Far more aggressive than these measures were laws, beginning in 1633, against Indians worshipping "their false Gods" and working on Sundays. And if an Indian in the jurisdiction of Massachusetts Bay were publicly to assert his own religion as the equal of Puritan faith, he could be executed as of November 4, 1646. All Indian offenders had to be tried in a white court; but a white offender against an Indian could not be tried in an Indian court.

Puritans had to be more careful, however, about offending or resisting native governments outside their particular jurisdiction. Some of this caution was mere expediency: for most of the 1630s, Puritans were outnumbered by Indians, who were able to maintain positions of neutrality on occasions when Puritans sought to pit one tribe against another. But the English massacres of Pequot Indians in 1637 and the state-ordered execution in 1643 of Miantonomo, a paramount Narragansett sachem, painted a picture of political submission or death that few Indians could ignore.[4] For decades after, the Narragansetts tried to limit their English "alliance" with the United Colonies of Massachusetts, Connecticut, Plymouth, and New Haven to nonresistance, while the Mohegan Indians, under their sachem Uncas, became willing military allies of the Puritans, who nevertheless remained wary of all tribes. The additional fact that Uncas had executed Miantonomo for the United Colonies did nothing to induce the Narragansetts to join the Mohegans in a Puritan alliance. So the inevitable cycle began: the Narragansetts insisted on retaliation against Uncas and neutrality with the English, who replied, in turn, with repeated threats of war if the "proud and insolent" Narragansetts did not submit to their litigation of all complaints (no matter how justified) against any Indians that cooperated with the English.

As an additional complication, the Narragansetts' home lay within the recently chartered Colony of Rhode Island, founded by Roger Williams after his banishment from Massachusetts Bay. The more Williams insisted from Providence that Massachusetts had no right to claim Indian land without a bill of sale, the more Massachusetts imagined a military conspiracy between Rhode Island and the Narragansetts. Since such an alliance was unthinkable in Rhode Island and Puritans would not, in fact, attack another Christian colony (even if it were not Puritan), the Narragansetts were sure to be the only losers. Thus, in exchange for Williams's advocacy of their rights, the Indians in Rhode Island became the special object of Puritan wrath. Years later, when the Narragansetts were nearly exterminated by a surprise Puritan attack during King Philip's War, the aggressors had only the flimsiest reasons for their conduct.

If Narragansett neutrality could not prevent Puritan retaliation and Mohegan alliance could not prevent continued Puritan suspicion, and if native and Puritan political systems were not, in fact, alien to each other, how is the clash of cultures in New England best explained? The answer seems to lie in each culture's spiritual perception of itself and its economic relationship to the land. The Europeans, with a faith in private land ownership, were settling a mysterious "New World" as God's last hope for Christianity; the Indians, with no such faith, were secure in their spiritual home and saw no reason to fear the consequences of a live-and-let-live attitude toward the newcomers. The technologically superior whites were, in fact, more fearful of the natives than the numerically superior natives were of them, a situation in which occasional but extreme violence was more likely than if the Indians had been the more fearful party.

10. "To Return the Patent Back Again to the King"

The basis for much of the racial conflict between Puritans and Indians in New England was the religious conflict between English Puritans in Massachusetts and English dissenters in Rhode Island. If the European colonists had presented a united front to the natives after 1635, the Narragansett Indians might have been spared being made the scapegoat between 1637 and 1675, when Puritan fury toward non-Puritan Englishmen in New England reached virulent proportions and required the elimination, by negotiation or war, of the native proprietors who were permitting the continued existence of Rhode Island as a colony.

Banished from Massachusetts in 1635, Roger Williams became the leading political and theological opponent of Puritan dominance in New England. His lengthy debates in print with John Cotton, the foremost Puritan theoretician, show clearly that theological disagreements could be examined in a gentlemanly fashion by disputing Christians.[1] But Williams's primary sin in Puritan eyes could not be countenanced (or punished, for that matter): he gave aid and comfort to the enemy. Behind Cotton's dismissal of Williams's attitude to purchasing land from Indians (printed below) is the recognition, on the one hand, that Williams was entitled to his mistaken point of view and, on the other hand, that such sentimentality about Indian rights might be fatal to Puritan survival in New England.[2] Thus Puritans were faced with the irony of having created a new threat to their hegemony by driving Williams and the Narragansetts into each other's arms.

By the patent it is, that we [the settlers of Massachusetts Bay] received allowance from the King to depart his kingdom, and to carry our goods with us, without offense to his officers, and without paying custom to himself.

By the patent, certain select men (as magistrates, and freemen) have power to make laws, and the magistrates to execute justice, and judgment amongst the people, according to such laws.

By the patent we have power to erect such a government of the church, as is most agreeable to the Word, to the estate of the people, and to the gaining of natives (in God's time) first to civility, and then to Christianity.

To this authority established by this patent, *Englishmen* do readily submit themselves: and foreign plantations (the *French,* the *Dutch,* and *Swedish)* do willingly transact their negotiations with us, as with a colony established by the royal authority of the state of *England.*

This patent, Mr. *Williams* publicly, and vehemently preached against, as containing matter of falsehood, and injustice: falsehood in making the King the first Christian prince who had discovered these parts: and injustice, in giving the country to his *English* subjects, which belonged to the native Indians. This therefore he pressed upon the magistrates and people, to be humbled for from time to time in days of solemn humiliation, and to return the patent back again to the King. It was answered to him, first, that it was neither the King's intendment, nor the *English* planters' to take possession of the country by murder of the natives, or by robbery; but either to take possession of the void places of the country by the law of nature, (for *vacuum domicilium cedit occupanti:)* or if we took any lands from the natives, it was by way of purchase, and free consent.

A little before our coming, God had by pestilence, and other contagious diseases, swept away many thousands of the natives, who had inhabited the Bay of *Massachusetts,* for which the patent was granted. Such few of them as survived were glad of the coming of the *English,* who might preserve them from the oppression of the *Narragansetts.* For it is the manner of the natives, the stronger nations to oppress the weaker.

This answer did not satisfy Mr. *Williams,* who pleaded, the natives, though they did not, nor could subdue the country, (but left it *vacuum domicilium)* yet they hunted all the country over, and for the expedition of their hunting voyages, they burnt up all the underwoods in the country, once or twice a year, and therefore as noble men in *England* possessed great parks, and the King great forests in *England* only for their game, and no man might lawfully invade their propriety: so might the natives challenge the like propriety of the country here.

It was replied unto him.

1. That the King, and noble men in *England,* as they possessed greater territories than other men, so they did greater service to church, and commonwealth.

2. That they employed their parks, and forests, not for hunting only, but for timber, and for the nourishment of tame beasts, as well as wild, and also for habitation to sundry tenants.

3. That our towns here did not disturb the huntings of the natives, but did rather keep their game fitter for their taking; for they take their deer by traps, and not by hounds.

4. That if they complained of any straits we put upon them, we gave satisfaction in some payments, or other, to their content.

5. We did not conceive that it is a just title to so vast a continent, to make no other improvement of millions of acres in it, but only to burn it up for pastime.

But these answers not satisfying him, this was still pressed by him as a national sin, to hold to the patent, yea, and a national duty to renounce the patent: which to have done, had subverted the fundamental state and government of the country.

11. "Thanks to the People"

Edward Winslow's trustworthiness as an observer of native behavior has been seriously questioned recently by one Puritan scholar.[1] However, the following description by Winslow contains an authenticity of perception not found in many Pilgrim/Puritan documents.[2] Its image of Massasoit's Wampanoag government flies in the face of the European myth that New World natives either had no tribal governments to speak of or were dominated by tyrannical rulers who bore a striking resemblance to the Satan of Christian theology who controlled his legions through cunning and terror.

Massasoit's tribal government was complex and relatively republican in its distribution of power and influence. There is no available evidence, moreover, that other New England tribes were any less sophisticated politically than the Wampanoags, or that the Wampanoag system had decayed by 1675 under the leadership of Massasoit's youngest son, Metacom (King Philip).

Their sachems cannot be all called kings, but only some few of them, to whom the rest resort for protection, and pay homage unto them; neither may they war without their knowledge and approbation; yet to be commanded by the greater, as occasion serveth. Of this sort is Massasoit, our friend, and Canonicus, of Narragansett, our supposed enemy. Every sachem taketh care for the widow and fatherless, also for such as are aged and any way maimed, if their friends be dead, or not able to provide for them. A sachem will not take any to wife, but such an one as is equal to him in birth; otherwise, they say, their seed would in time become ignoble; and though they have many other wives, yet they are no other than concubines or servants, and yield a kind of obedience to the principal, who ordereth the family and them in it. The like their men observe also, and will adhere to the first during their lives; but put away the other at their pleasure. This government is successive, and not by choice. If the father die before the son or daughter be of age, then the child is committed to the protection and tuition of some one amongst them, who ruleth in his stead till he be of age; but when that is, I know not.

Every sachem knoweth how far the bounds and limits of his own country extendeth; and that is his own proper inheritance. Out of that, if any of his men desire land to set their corn, he giveth them as much as they can use, and sets them their bounds. In this circuit whosoever hunteth, if they kill any venison, bring him his fee; which is the fore parts of the same, if it be killed on the land, but if in the water, then the skin thereof. The great sachems or kings know their own bounds or limits of land, as well as the rest. All travellers or strangers for the most part lodge at the sachem's. When they come, they tell them how long they will stay, and to what place they go; during which time they receive entertainment, according to their persons, but want not. Once a year the pnieses [a

lesser rank of leaders] use to provoke the people to bestow much
corn on the sachem. To that end, they appoint a certain time and
place, near the sachem's dwelling, where the people bring many
baskets of corn, and make a great stack thereof. There the pnieses
stand ready to give thanks to the people, on the sachem's behalf;
and after [they] acquaint the sachem therewith, who fetcheth the
same, and is no less thankful, bestowing many gifts on them. . . .

12. "How Solidly and Wisely These
Savage People Did Consider"

Even as early as 1636, the Narragansetts were a pivotal force in
Indian-Puritan relations. In *Wonder-Working Providence* (1654), Edward Johnson gives a graphic picture of the attempt by Massachusetts authorities to gain the support of this tribe against
another—the Pequots—both of which occupied territory desired by the
Puritans.[1] Johnson's description of this treaty council is interesting for
the evidence it provides of delegated and shared authority among the
Narragansetts, and also for its clear image of Narragansett shrewdness in analyzing Pequot and Puritan strengths and Narragansett
subtlety in elaborating their own neutral position between the two
warring parties.

Eventually, the Narragansetts allied themselves with the English in
the Pequot War and watched in horror as Puritans massacred the
Pequot inhabitants of Mystic Fort. After the war, Narragansett
difficulties with the Puritans were partly a consequence of their own
insistence on the justice of adopting Pequot survivors into their own
tribe.

Lastly, for the frontispiece of their present distress, namely, the
Indian war, they with much meekness and great deliberation, wisely
contrived how they might best help their fellow brethren; hereupon
they resolved to send a solemn embassage to old Canonicus, chief

sachem of the Narragansett Indians, who being then well stricken in years had caused his nephew Miantonomo to take the government upon him, who was a very stern man, and of a great stature, of a cruel nature, causing all his nobility and such as were his attendance to tremble at his speech. The people under his government were very numerous, besides the Eastern Niantic Indians, whose prince was of near alliance unto him; they were able to set forth, as was then supposed, 30,000 fighting men. The English sought by all means to keep these at least from confederating with the Pequots, and understanding by intelligence, that the Pequots would send to them for that end, endeavored to prevent them. Fit and able men being chosen by the English, they haste them to Canonicus' court, which was about forescore miles from Boston.

The Indian king hearing of their coming, gathered together his chief counsellors, and a great number of his subjects to give them entertainment, resolving as then that the young king should receive their message, yet in his hearing. They arriving, were entertained royally, with respect to the Indian manner. Boiled chestnuts is their white-bread, which are very sweet, as if they were mixed with sugar; and because they would be extraordinary in their feasting, they strive for variety after the English manner, boiling puddings made of beaten corn, putting therein great store of black berries somewhat like currants. They having thus nobly feasted them, afterward give them audience, in a state-house, round, about fifty foot wide, made of long poles stuck in the ground, like your summer-houses in England, and covered round about, and on the top with mats, save a small place in the middle of the roof, to give light, and let out the smoke.

In this place sat their sachem, with very great attendance; the English coming to deliver their message, to manifest the greater state, the Indian sachem lay along upon the ground, on a mat, and his nobility sat on the ground, with their legs doubled up, their knees touching their chin; with much sober gravity they attend the interpreter's speech. It was matter of much wonderment to the English, to see how solidly and wisely these savage people did consider of the weighty undertaking of a war; especially old Canonicus, who was very discreet in his answers. The young sachem was indeed of a more lofty spirit, which wrought his ruin, as you may hear, after the decease of the old king. But at this time his answer was, that he did willingly embrace peace with the English, considering right well, that although their number was but small in comparison of his people, and that they were but strangers to the woods, swamps, and advantageous places of this wilderness, yet withal he knew the English were advantaged by their weapons of war, and especially their guns, which were of great terror to his people, and also he had heard they came of a more populous nation by far than all the Indians were, could they be joined together. Also on the other hand, with mature deliberation, he was well advised of the Pequots' cruel disposition and aptness to make war, as also their near neighborhood to his people, who though they were more numerous, yet were they withal more effeminate, and less able to defend themselves from the sudden incursions of the Pequots, should they fall out with them. Hereupon he deems it most conducing to his own and his people's safety to direct his course in a middle way, holding amity with both. . . .

13. "However His Death May Be Grievous"

Though the Narragansetts were forbidden to adopt Pequot war survivors, other Indian allies of the Puritans—the Mohegans—were not. This double standard was the result of two factors: (1) the Mohegans had fought more fiercely than the Narragansetts against the Pequots; and (2) the Mohegans were a much smaller and weaker tribe than the Narragansetts.

The Narragansetts were hardly impressed by Puritan reasoning in this matter; and the situation was aggravated further by the intense personal rivalry between Miantonomo, the powerful and respected Narragansett sachem, and Uncas, the leader of the Mohegans. In 1636, Miantonomo had agreed that he would not retaliate against Uncas for Mohegan raids on the Narragansetts without first receiving Puritan approval. When he obtained John Winthrop's acquiescence in 1643, but was unexpectedly captured by the weaker Mohegan forces, the United Colonies of New England in their first organizational decision decreed his execution. Of particular interest in the execution order, printed below, is the Puritans' fear that Uncas might not hate Miantonomo enough to carry out Puritan wishes.[1] Uncas knew, however, that without Puritan support his own tribe's survival was in doubt, and Miantonomo died as ordered.

At a meeting of the Commissioners for the United Colonies at Boston the seventh September 1643

It was agreed that the government of the Massachusetts in the behalf of the United Colonies of New England give Canonicus and the Narragansetts to understand that from time to time we have taken notice of the violation of that league between the Massachusetts and themselves, (notwithstanding the manifestations of love & integrity towards them by the English) which they have discovered as by other ways, so lately by their concurrence with Miantonomo their sachem in his mischievous plots to root out the body of the English nation purchasing the aid of all the Indians by gifts, threats and other allurements to their party (except a few viz. Uncas and his men, whom they have not spared to invade notwithstanding a tripartite covenant to the contrary, between the government of Connecticut, Miantonomo & Uncas, sagamore of the Mohegan, under their hands & marks): but understanding how peaceable Canonicus & Mascus the late father of Miantonomo governed that great people, we rather ascribe these late tumults, outbreakings & malicious plots to the rash and ambitious spirit of Miantonomo than any effected way of their own. And therefore once more notwithstanding all those former unworthy passages so well known unto us, as a people inclining to peace & desiring their good, we do in our own names and in the behalf, & with the consent of the United Colonies tender them peace & such loving correspondency as hath formerly been ever observed on our parts viz. the several Governments of the Massachusetts, Plymouth, Connecticut, & New Haven with all such as are in combination & confederation with them, both English and Indians, as Uncas sagamore of the Mohegans & his people, Massasoit and his people, Sacononoco & his people, Pumham and his people, whose peace and lawful liberties we may not suffer to be violated. And if the Narragansetts be desirous of peace as formerly we shall be as careful to preserve their peace & liberties from violation: but shall expect more faithful observance than we have formerly found from Miantonomo in the time of his government, requiring answer with as much expedition as the weight of the case requireth. And whereas Uncas was advised to take away the life of Miantonomo whose lawful captive he was, they may well understand that this is without violation of any covenant between them & us for Uncas being in confederation with us, and one that hath diligently observed his covenants before mentioned for aught we know, & requiring advice from us upon serious consideration of the promise, viz. his treacherous & murderous disposition against Uncas and how great a disturber he hath been of the common peace of the whole country, we could not in respect of the justice of the case, safety of the country, and faithfulness of our friend do otherwise than approve of the lawfulness of his death, which agreeing so well with the Indians' own manners and concurring with the practice of other nations with whom we are acquainted, we persuade ourselves however his death may be grievous at present, yet the peaceable fruits of it will yield not only matter of safety to the Indians but profit to all that inhabit this continent.

That as soon as the Commissioners for Connecticut and New Haven shall return into those parts that then Uncas be sent for to Hartford with some considerable number of his best & trustiest men, and that then he being made acquainted with the advice of the Commissioners, Miantonomo be delivered unto him that so execution may be done according to justice & prudence, Uncas carrying him into the next part of his own government and there put him to death provided that some discreet & faithful persons of the English accompany them and see the execution for our more full satisfaction, and that the English meddle not with the head or body at all: and this being done that notice be given to all the confederates by letters that so the Massachusetts Government may thereupon send to Narragansett, & Plymouth may take due course with Massasoit as after is advised.

That Hartford furnish Uncas with a competent strength of English to defend him against any present fury or assault of the Narragansetts or any other.

That in case Uncas shall refuse to execute justice upon Miantonomo, that then Miantonomo be sent by sea to the Massachusetts, there to be kept in safe durance till the Commissioners may consider further how to dispose of him.

That Plymouth labor by all due means to restore Massasoit to his full liberties in respect of any encroachments by the Narragansetts or any other natives, that so the proprieties of the Indians may be preserved to themselves, and that no one sagamore encroach upon the rest as of late: and that Massasoit be reduced to these former terms and agreements between Plymouth and him.

Jo: WINTHROP Presid   EDW: WINSLOW
THO: DUDLEY   WM COLLIER
GEO: FENWICK   EDWA: HOPKINS
THEOPH EATON   THO: GREGSON.

14. "We Freely Give Over Ourselves"

The following two documents of 1644 should be read together. The first is the calculated submission of weak Massachuset Indians to the Bay government in Boston; the second is the calculated submission of the strong Narragansetts, a month later, to King Charles I in London.[1] Though the difference between the two acts may seem slight, it is not. As they witnessed the gradual weakening of native opposition to Puritan control over New England and the increasing isolation of their own tribe, the Narragansetts chose to go over the heads of local Englishmen and acknowledge the political authority of the mother country. To the leaders of Massachusetts Bay, this gesture seemed exactly what it was intended to be: an assertion of political equality between Puritans and Indians, both of whom the Narragansetts describe as the King's subjects.

A.

Wossamegon, Nashowanon, Cutshamache [Cutshamoquin], Mascanomet, & Squaw Sachem did voluntarily submit themselves to us, as appeareth by their covenant subscribed with their own hands, here following, & other articles to which they consented.

We have & by these presents do voluntarily, & without constraint or persuasion, but of our own free motion, put ourselves, our subjects, lands, & estates under the government & jurisdiction of the Massachusetts, to be governed & protected by them, according to their just laws & orders, so far as we shall be made capable of understanding them; & we do promise for ourselves, & all our subjects, & all our posterity, to be true & faithful to the said government, & aiding to the maintenance thereof, to our best ability, & from time to time to give speedy notice of any conspiracy, attempt, or evil intention of any which we shall know or hear of against the same; & we do promise to be willing from time to time to be instructed in the knowledge & worship of God. In witness whereof we have hereunto put our hands the 8th of the first month [March], anno 1644.

> CUTSHAMACHE,
> NASHOWANON,
> WOSSAMEGON,
> MASCANOMET,
> SQUAW SACHEM.

Certain Questions propounded to the Indians, and Answers.

1. To worship the only true God, which made heaven & earth, & not to blaspheme him.

An: We do desire to reverence the God of the English & to speak well of him, because we see he doth better to the English than other gods do to others.

2. Not to swear falsely. An: They say they know not what swearing is among them.

3. Not to do any unnecessary work on the Sabbath day, especially within the gates of Christian towns. An: It is easy to them; they have not much to do on any day, & they can well take their ease on that day.

4. To honor their parents & all their superiors.

An: It is their custom to do so, for the inferiors to honor their superiors.

5. To kill no man without just cause & just authority.

An: This is good, & they desire to do so.

6. To commit no unclean lust, as fornication, adultery, incest, rape, sodomy, buggery, or bestiality. An: Though sometime some of them do it, yet they count that naught, & do not allow it.

7. Not to steal. An: They say to that as to the 6th query.

[8.] To suffer their children to learn to read God's Word, that they may learn to know God aright, & worship him in his own way.

[An:] They say, as opportunity will serve, & English live among them, they desire to do so.

[9.] That they should not be idle.

To these they consented, acknowledging them to be good.

Being received by us, they presented 26 fathoms of wampum, & the Court directed the Treasurer to give them five coats, two yards in a coat, of red cloth, & a potfull of wine.

B.

The Act and Deed of the voluntary and free submission of the chief Sachem, and the rest of the princes, with the whole people of the Narragansetts, unto the Government and protection of that honorable State of Old England as set down, here, verbatim.

Know all Men, Colonies, Peoples, and Nations, unto whom the fame hereof shall come; that we, the chief sachems, princes or governors of the Narragansetts (in that part of America, now called New England), together with the joint and unanimous consent of all our people and subjects, inhabitants thereof, do upon serious consideration, mature and deliberate advice and counsel, great and weighty grounds and reasons moving us thereunto, whereof one most effectual unto us, is, that noble fame we have heard of that Great and Mighty Prince, Charles, King of Great Britain, in that honorable and princely care he hath of all his servants, and true and loyal subjects, the consideration whereof moveth and bendeth our hearts with one consent, freely, voluntarily, and most humbly to submit, subject, and give over ourselves, peoples, lands, rights, inheritances, and possessions whatsoever, in ourselves and our heirs successively forever, unto the protection, care and government of that Worthy and Royal Prince, Charles, King of Great Britain and Ireland, his heirs and successors forever, to be ruled and governed according to the ancient and honorable laws and customs, established in that so renowned realm and kingdom of Old England; we do, therefore, by these presents, confess, and most willingly and submissively acknowledge ourselves to be the humble, loving and obedient servants and subjects of His Majesty; to be ruled, ordered, and disposed of, in ourselves and ours according to his princely wisdom, counsel and laws of the honorable state of Old England; *upon condition of His Majesty's royal protection,* and righting us of what wrong is, or may be done unto us, according to his honorable laws and customs, exercised amongst his subjects, in their preservation and safety, and in the defeating and overthrow of his, and their enemies; not that we find ourselves necessitated hereunto, in respect of our relation, or occasion we have, or may have, with any of the natives in these parts, knowing ourselves sufficient defense, and able to judge in any matter or cause in that respect; but have just cause of jealousy and suspicion of some of His Majesty's pretended subjects. Therefore our desire is, to have our matters and causes heard and tried according to his just and equal laws, in that way and order His Highness shall please to appoint: *Nor can we yield over ourselves unto any, that are subjects themselves in any case;* having ourselves been the chief sachems, or princes successively, of the country, time out of mind; and for our present and lawful enacting hereof, being so far remote from His Majesty, we have, by joint consent, made choice of four of his loyal and loving subjects, our trusty and well-beloved friends, Samuel Gorton, John Wickes, Randall Holden and John Warner, whom we have deputed, and made our lawful attornies or commissioners, not only for the acting and performing of this our deed, in the behalf of His Highness, but also for the safe custody, careful conveyance, and declaration hereof unto his grace: being done upon the lands of the Narragansett, at a court or general assembly called and assembled together, of purpose, for the public enacting, and manifestation hereof.

And for the further confirmation, and establishing of this our Act and Deed, we, the abovesaid sachems or princes, have, according to that commendable custom of Englishmen, subscribed our names and set our seals hereunto, as so many testimonies of/our faith and truth, our love and loyalty to that our dread Sovereign, and that according to the Englishmen's account. Dated the nineteenth day of April, one thousand six hundred and forty four.

> PESSICUS, his mark, Chief
> Sachem, and successor of that
> late deceased Miantonomo.
> The mark of that ancient CA-
> NONICUS, Protector of that
> late Deceased Miantonomo,

during the time of his nonage.

The mark of MIXAN, son and heir of that abovesaid Canonicus.

Witnessed by two of the chief counsellors to Sachem Pessicus.

AWASHOOSSE, his mark,

Indians.

TOMANICK, his mark,

Sealed and delivered, in the presence of these persons.

CHRISTOPHER HELM,

English.

ROBERT POTTER,

RICHARD CARDER.

15. "There Is a Spirit of Desperation Fallen Upon Them"

Puritans in Massachusetts Bay had a difficult time separating their fears of Narragansett savagery from their fears of Separatist heresy in Rhode Island. Roger Williams had procured a colonial charter for Rhode Island from Parliament in 1644, shortly before the Narragansetts' submission to King Charles (who was at war with Parliament). If one considers Puritan fears of all non-Puritans, it is not surprising that Williams's warning to Massachusetts Bay in 1645 that the Narragansetts were going to war again against the Mohegans, and that Rhode Island had decided to remain neutral, was interpreted by John Winthrop as a tacit declaration of war by Rhode Island against the Puritan colonies.[1] In Winthrop's statement from "A Declaration of Former Passages," the "children of strife" who "dishonor and provoke God" are the whites in Rhode Island.

A.

For his much honored Mr. Governor, John Winthrop
Providence, 25th of June, 1645

MUCH HONORED SIR,—Though I should fear that all the sparks of former love are now extinct, etc., yet I am confident that your large talents of wisdom and experience of the affairs of men will not lightly condemn my endeavor to give information and satisfaction, as now I have done in this poor apology, with all due respects presented to your honor, and the hands of my worthy friends with you.

Sir, for tidings concerning the public, three days since I received a letter from the Dutch Governor reporting some new hopes of peace. For ourselves, the flame of war rageth next door unto us. The Narragansetts and Mohegans, with their respective confederates, have deeply implunged themselves in barbarous slaughters. For myself I have (to my utmost) dissuaded our neighbors, [Narragansetts] high and low, from arms, etc., but there is a spirit of desperation fallen upon them, resolved to revenge the death of their prince [Miantonomo], and recover the ransom for his life, etc., or to perish with him. Sir, I was requested by both parties, yourselves and the Narragansetts, to keep the subscribed league [in 1636] between yourselves and them, and yours and their posterity. Sir, that, and the common bonds of humanity move me to pray yourselves and our friends of Connecticut to improve all interests and opportunities to quench these flames. My humble requests are to the God of Peace that no English blood be further spilt in America: it is one way to prevent it by loving mediation or prudent neutrality. Sir, (excepting the matters of my soul and conscience to God, the Father of Spirits) you have not a truer friend and servant to your worthy person and yours, nor to the peace and welfare of the whole country, than the most despised and most unworthy.

ROGER WILLIAMS

B.

Mr. Williams by the messengers wrote to the Commissioners [of the United Colonies] assuring them that the country would suddenly be all on fire meaning by war, ... that the Narragansetts had been with the plantations combined with Providence and solemnly treated and settled a neutrality with them: which fully shows their counsels and settled resolutions for war.

Thus while the Commissioners in care of the public peace sought to quench the fire kindled amongst the Indians these children of strife breathe out threatenings, provocations and war against: the English themselves: so that unless they should dishonor and provoke God, by violating a just engagement, & expose the colonies to contempt and danger from the barbarians they [the United Colonies] cannot but exercise force when no other means will prevail to reduce the Narragansetts and their confederates to a more just and sober temper.

The eyes of other Indians under the protection of the Massachusetts and not at all engaged in this quarrel are (as they have expressed themselves to the English messengers) fastened upon the English with strict observation, in what manner and measure they provide for Uncas his safety: if he perish they will charge it upon them who might have preserved him, and no Indians will trust the English if they now broke engagements, either in the present or succeeding generations. If Uncas be ruined in such a cause, they foresee their heads upon the next pretence shall be delivered to the will of the Narragansetts, with whom therefore they shall be forced to comply, as they may for their future safety, and the English may not trust an Indian in the whole country. The premise being weighed it clearly appears that God calls the colonies to a war....

[JOHN WINTHROP]

16. "Unnecessary Wars and Cruel Destructions"

The single most eloquent plea for Puritan humanity toward New England natives is found in a letter from Roger Williams to the General Court of Massachusetts on October 5, 1654.[1] While the following passage from the letter is largely self-explanatory, two statements by Williams need some clarification and emphasis:

1. The "seeming occasions for their destructions" that fall on the "body" as well as the "heads of Indians" refers to pre-emptive Puritan attacks on native women and children.

2. Williams's fear that, "for the sake of a few inconsiderable pagans," everything that "the gracious hand of the Lord hath so wonderfully planted in the wilderness should be destroyed" reflects his conviction that unnecessary Puritan attacks on Indians will create a devastating confederacy of angry tribes.

Notice, in addition, that Williams insists that Puritans have never had any reason to fear the Narragansetts. Though he clearly was no admirer of native culture and religion, he did have a deep respect, unlike the Puritans, for the value and feasibility of native neutrality. This may be his greatest contribution to American political thought.

I never was against the righteous use of the civil sword of men or nations, but yet since all men of conscience or prudence ply to windward, to maintain their wars to be defensive (as did both King and Scotch, and English, and Irish too, in the late wars), I humbly pray your consideration, whether it be not only possible, but very easy, to live and die in peace with the natives of this country.

For, secondly, are not all the English of this land, generally, a persecuted people from their native soil? And hath not the God of peace and Father of mercies made these natives more friendly in this, than our native countrymen in our own land to us? Have they not entered leagues of love, and to this day continued peaceable commerce with us? Are not our families grown up in peace amongst them? Upon which I humbly ask, how it can suit with Christian ingenuity to take hold of some seeming occasions for their destructions, which, though the heads be only aimed at, yet, all experience tells us, falls on the body and on the innocent. . . .

Whether I have been and am a friend to the natives turning to civility and Christianity, and whether I have been instrumental, and desire so to be, according to my light, I will not trouble you with; only I beseech you consider, how the name of the most holy and jealous God may be preserved between the clashings of these two viz.: the glorious conversion of the Indians in New England, and the unnecessary wars and cruel destructions of the Indians in New England. . . .

I cannot yet learn, that it ever pleased the Lord to permit the Narragansetts to stain their hands with any English blood, neither in open hostilities nor secret murders, as both Pequots and Long Islanders did, and Mohegans, also, in the Pequot wars. It is true they are barbarians, but their greatest offenses against the English have been matters of money, or petty revenging of themselves on some Indians, upon extreme provocations, but God kept them clear of our blood. . . .

But, I beseech you, say your thoughts and the thoughts of your wives and little ones, and the thoughts of all English, and of God's people in England, and the thoughts of His Highness and Council (tender of these parts), if, for the sake of a few inconsiderable pagans, and beasts, wallowing in idleness, stealing, lying, whoring, treacherous witchcrafts, blasphemies, and idolatries, all that the gracious hand of the Lord hath so wonderfully planted in the wilderness, should be destroyed. . . .

17. "It Was Reasonable to Succor One's Christian Brethren"

In 1650, a French Catholic priest from a missionary outpost in northern Maine paid a visit to Plymouth and Massachusetts Bay. Though Protestants and Catholics in the New World habitually kept their distance from each other, Father Drouillette's appearance had a special political purpose: he was soliciting the United Colonies' participation in declaring war against the aggressive Iroquois Indians in the Dutch Colony of New Netherland (later New York).[1] The Iroquois had been conducting raids on their trading rivals—the Hurons and French—and they had also made life painful for some tribes in western and northern New England with whom Englishmen in Plymouth and Boston had trading arrangements.

The Pilgrims and Puritans treated Drouillette hospitably and sent him on his way with the confident feeling that he had succeeded in his mission for the Governor of Canada and his Indian allies. Once he was gone, however, the leaders of the United Colonies decided that such a war would expose their outlying settlements to successful reprisals from the Iroquois.

Drouillette's mission reveals some important facts about the shifting balance of power in seventeenth-century New England:

1. As much as Puritans and Catholics maligned each other's religious efforts, they were not opposed in principle to fighting together against a heathen enemy.

2. Puritans wanted to control the Indians within their territory, but they were not willing to protect them from external threats (in this case, the Iroquois) in order to earn their submission.

3. Catholic missionaries to the Indians, like their Puritan counterparts, were political agents acting in their own nation's behalf. Indians had no trouble understanding this fact, but the missionaries were unable to perceive the conflict of interest caused by the confusion of their spiritual and temporal roles.

I left [Plymouth] on the twenty-fourth [of December], and returned to Boston by land, in company with the son and nephew of my [blank space], who paid for me during the journey. I arrived at Roxbury, where the minister, named Master [John] Eliot, who was teaching some savages, received me at his house, because night was overtaking me; he treated me with respect and kindness, and begged me to spend the winter with him.

The next day, the twenty-ninth, I arrived at Boston, and proceeded to Major General [Edward] Gibbon's.

On the thirtieth of the said month, I spoke to Mr. [William] Hibbins, one of the magistrates, who assured me that he was very glad that the Governor of Plymouth [William Bradford] was willing to grant aid against the Iroquois. He said that it was very reasonable to succor one's Christian brethren, even if of another religion,—and especially against a pagan persecutor of the Christians. . . .

On the last of the said month, I returned to Roxbury to ask permission from Mr. [Thomas] Dudley, the Governor, that safe conduct might be inserted in the letter for the passage of the French who might wish to go through Boston against the Iroquois; and, grasping my hand, he said to me: "Assure your Governor [of

Canada] that we wish to be his good friends and servants, whatever war there may be between the crowns. I am very glad that the Governor of Plymouth is willing to further the assistance that you desire against the Iroquois: I will aid him with all my power.....

On the ninth of the same month [January], the bad weather detained us at Marblehead, where there are many persons; the minister, named William Walter, received me with kindness. In his company I went to Salem, to converse with Mr. [John] Endecott, who speaks and understands French well; he is a good friend to our nation, and desirous that his children should continue in this friendship. Seeing that I had no money, he paid my expenses, and had me eat with the magistrates, who during eight days gave audience to every one. I left with him, in the form of a letter, a power of attorney which he asked from me, in order to act efficiently during the General Court of Boston, which was to be held on the thirteenth of May. He assured me that he would do his utmost to obtain consent from the Colony of Boston [Massachusetts Bay], which served as a standard for the others,—telling me that the Governor of Plymouth had good reason for seeking to obtain that from the [United] Colonies. At my departure, he told me that he had carefully read what I had left in writing on behalf of our Governor, and of my catechumens [converted Indians], and that he perfectly understood it; that he would despatch a man to carry me a letter at Kennebec [Maine]; and that he would tell me, as soon as he could, what he should have done in this matter, and obtained from the magistrates.....

On the eighth of February, I departed for the river of Kennebec, where I continued my interrupted mission. All the English who are on this river received me with many demonstrations of friendship.

On the thirteenth of April, Mr. John Winslow, my true [blank space], arrived from Plymouth and Boston at Koussinoc. He assured me that all the magistrates [Massachusetts Bay] and the two Commissioners of Plymouth have given their word, and resolved that the other colonies should be urged to join them against the Iroquois in favor of the Abenakis, who are under the protection of this Colony of Plymouth,—which has the proprietorship of Koussinoc, and for its rights of lordship takes the sixth part of what accrues from the trade. He said, moreover, that Mr. Bradford, the Governor,—who is one of the five merchants, or farmers, who furnish everything necessary for the trade,—had already despatched, by the twentieth of March, Captain Thomas Willet,—who is greatly attached to the Abenakis, with whom he had been acquainted at Koussinoc for several years,—with letters presented in behalf of aid against the Iroquois. He carries these to the Governors of Hartford, or Connecticut, which is on the river of the Sokokis, fifty leagues from Plymouth; and of New Haven, or Quinnipiac, which is ten leagues from Hartford; and even to the Governor of Manhattan, in order to prevent him from further trading of arms to the Iroquois, and to urge upon him that he shall not only not oppose those who would attack the Iroquois, but even aid the English in this project, by virtue of the union upon which, some years ago, he entered with New England. . . .

18. "A Kind of Invocation Used Among Them"

Ninigret was a powerful sachem of the Eastern Niantics, a small tribe between the Wampanoags and the Narragansetts and tributary to the latter. In 1664, Metacom had succeeded his brother Wamsutta as leader of the Wampanoags and immediately aroused Pilgrim fears that he was not as friendly as his father Massasoit had been. English theories of a budding conspiracy between Metacom and the leaders of other tribes, including Ninigret, became commonplace.[1] Six years before the actual outbreak of King Philip's War (1675), charges were brought by Puritans in Connecticut that Ninigret had had a secret meeting with emissaries from Metacom to plot the overthrow of the United Colonies; and a hearing was held in Rhode Island that resulted in a dismissal of all charges, owing chiefly to the testimony of Ninigret himself. The following passage is an excerpt from his self-defense:[2]

The sachem Ninigret being brought before the Council, the Governor did require his interpreter to tell him, the said sachem, that there was information to the Governor here, from the Governor of New York and Connecticut, and also from Major Mason, that the said sachem was contriving to cut off all the English; and that he, the said Ninigret, had reported he would draw as many Indians as he could into the combination. . . .

To which the said sachem replied (by his interpreter), that he wondered there should be any such report raised, considering his own innocency, and that ever since himself heard the words by the commissioners, spoken as from King Charles his mouth, and hath since laid it up in his heart that the King did look upon himself and Pessicus and their Indians as his subjects, together with the English; and said he understood that the English of this colony were to help them, if any should be too mighty for them, and they to do the like to the English if any should invade or make war upon the colony. To the other part, he replied that since you cannot inform me who raised this report, I will tell you who it was; it was one Nonaconapoonog; the reason why he did it was this, that in their former war with the Long Island Indians, they having taken the daughter of the sachem of Long Island with divers more upon condition that he released his daughter, that the said sachem did submit himself unto him, and engaged to pay him yearly tribute, even as the Pequots did the like, who paid tribute to the English, being overcome of them; that the sachem and his daughter being dead, the tribute hath not been paid for some years; but lately the Long Island Indians sent him as an acknowledgment by way of tribute five pounds in peage [wampum], at the account of six white peage per penny, with a promise that they would be subject unto him for the future; and that also at the same time they sent him as a present, the barrel of the deceased sachem's gun without either lock or stock to it, and that these presents and messages were sent unto him by an Indian called Manecopungun; who also coming to him a second time upon the same message, the sachem told him that he did forgive them all their offenses, and gave them their lives also, and would look upon them as his friends and subjects; and that now he was making a great dance, and if they would, they might send some women, and some ancient men to see it and to be partakers thereof; and that now he is informed that Nonaconapoonog is forsaken of all his kindred, and is in a very sad condition, laying his hand over his face; and that the said Nonaconapoonog's friends say unto him, it is justly befallen him for the lies he hath made, and for his disturbing the country; and Ninigret in his present dance, also telling him that now his condition was such, there was no place left where he might go to secure himself, for that all people that did hear of his baseness would hate him, and that he desired to die. . . .

The Governor bid his interpreter to ask him, if there were no plot among the Indians, what did seven of Philip, the sachem of Mount Hope's ancient men, do with him ten days together.

He says he sent for two Indians named Cajawottore, a Narragansett Indian, that now lives at Pocasset, and Nattawhahore, formerly a Cononicut [?] Indian, now at Pocasset, because he knew they were formerly his Indians, and had skill to bark cedar trees and to make bark houses, which his men had not good skill in, and that they had got the barks, but being disturbed by these troubles had not used them.

And that another Indian named Pumechecamuck, a bold fellow, that lived formerly on Rhode Island, now above Puncatusett, came to complain to him against one of his Indians, that had taken a white blanket from him and spent it in drink; and that two young men came with him to see the dance; and also saith that there was never a Mount Hope Indian there; but that Philip did send to Cocumscusett for an old man to teach or inform his men in a certain dance, and he wonders that it is not taken for a plot.

He being demanded what was the reason of this great dance, replied; it is known to you it is no unusual thing for us so to do; but that it is often used from the time after the weeding of our corn till such time as we do eat of it; and farther said it was a kind of invocation used among them, that they might have a plentiful harvest. . . .

19. "Rather Minding Gain Than Godliness"

King Philip's War (1675–76) was fought, in part, as a contest between different English aspirants for territory that had been sold by the Narragansetts to non-Puritans like Roger Williams and the territory still held in 1675 by the Narragansetts. Both Connecticut and Massachusetts Bay were willing to expand their domains, first, by somehow eliminating the Indians in Rhode Island and, second, by opposing the English in Rhode Island with contrived counterclaims on their land. Because Connecticut's dubious title to this territory appeared more legitimate than Massachusetts's title (dismissed as invalid in 1665 by commissioners from England), it was not overturned until after the war.[1]

The following passage from Connecticut colonial records reflects not only Connecticut's desire for Rhode Island territory (forty years after the initial English settlement of that colony), but also the extent to which Puritans based their territorial claims on the "heresy" of those already occupying the land in question.[2] The Puritan banishment of Roger Williams in 1635 had precipitated the settlement of Rhode Island. Once he and other English dissenters were out of sight, however, they were not out of mind: the Puritan argument for claiming Indian lands—*vacuum domicilium*—was used to claim dissenters' land after their death. Puritans would not themselves kill white Rhode Islanders over the disputed land; but if Narragansetts killed Rhode Islanders and Puritans could kill Narragansetts, then the heretic colony would be truly vacant.

Forasmuch as all those lands in the Narragansett country do lie and are circumscribed within the known limits of our charter, viz. from Narragansett Bay on the east etc. as is therein graciously expressed by His Majesty to be granted the Colony of Connecticut, which have been and now are recovered out of the hands of the Indian enemies that had victorized over or caused the people totally to desert all those lands which they had possessed themselves of, formerly; and for that sundry of the said people there inhabiting lived dishonorably both to God, our King and nation, and more unsafe for themselves, rather minding gain than godliness, whereby both His Majesty, ourselves and the people have been abused, and the tract or territory more exposed to devastation, and so is now become a *vacuum domicilium;* but this late merciful recovery being obtained by conquest and success of war unto ourselves of this colony and our confederates,—the Council sees cause to declare unto all such person or persons, both English and Indians that have or shall pretend to any right or possession there, upon the said deserted or vanquished lands in that country, that all such shall make their application to the government of this colony, for such grants, leave and liberty to take up and possess such and so much as they shall see cause to grant and allow them; it being both duty to God and our King, and also is our intent and purpose, to have it all so laid and disposed as may best advantage religion and the safety of the inhabitants. And whosoever shall presume otherwise to possess themselves there, may expect to be dealt withal as intruders and condemners of His Majesty's authority in our hands.

Chapter III

"If God Be with Us"

The Pequot War

The overriding objective of the Puritan errand into the wilderness of New England was to establish a "city upon the hill," a new Jerusalem that would be a beacon unto the world, complete the Protestant Reformation, and usher in the millennium. In seeking to fulfill their mission, the Puritans viewed themselves as the chosen people even as the Israelites were formerly the chosen of the Lord. They likened the wilderness of New England to the desert waste-land of Exodus, where the children of Israel sojourned for forty years on their way to the Promised Land. They believed that as the Lord had led the Israelites out of the bondage of Egypt, so had He led the Puritans from the land of iniquity, which was Old England, into the Promised Land, which was New England.

The Puritans knew that this sanctuary was not devoid of sin. In fact, they saw the natural world as Satan's domain and all creatures generic to it as mortal enemies of the Lord. As the Israelites in the desert were tested by trial and tribulation, so would the Puritans be tested in New England. For was it not in the wilderness that the faith of the Israelites was purified and the Lord handed the Ten Commandments to Moses? Was it not in the wilderness that John the Baptist sought to revitalize the faith? And did not Christ overcome temptation in the wilderness?

God did not bring His chosen people to New England's wilderness so that they would be destroyed by the minions of Satan. When the Puritans encountered hardships there, it was Satan bending "his forces against us" and stirring "up his instruments to all kinds of mischiefs," as John Winthrop asserted, "so that I think here are some persons who never showed so much wickedness in England as they have done here." [1] Because the Puritan conceived of himself as the adherent of the only true religion, he also believed himself to be the special target of the Devil, as well as a special threat to the Devil and his emissaries. In any case, God would protect the Puritans because His mission was their mission. Had not John Cotton assured them, as they departed Old England, that the godly "shall enjoy their own place with safety and peace"? And Francis Higginson said: "If God be with us ... who can be against us?" [2]

The New Canaan could be built only after the Puritans had established control over the territory they claimed in New England and after their powerful adversaries had been eliminated. Thus, following their arrival in Massachusetts Bay in 1630, the Puritans embarked upon a campaign to acquire land from the Indians; and, as the colonists became more and more secure in their settlements and additional Englishmen arrived in the Bay Colony, they sought to expand their domain.

The first major conflict with the Indians as a consequence of Puritan expansionism took place in 1636–37, when the Puritans conducted a war of extermination against the Pequots of Connecticut. In only a few months, the Puritans, with their superior firepower, annihilated the Indians, who had not yet been able to acquire arms from the Dutch or French. Captain John Underhill scoffed that the Pequots "might fight seven years and not kill seven men. They came not near one another," said Underhill, "but shot remote, and not point-blank, as we often did with our bullets, but at rovers, and then they gaze up in the sky to see where the arrow falls and not until it has fallen do they shoot again." To Underhill, such fighting was "more for pastime, than to conquer and subdue enemies." [3] However, Lieutenant Lion Gardiner, commander of Fort Saybrook, saw evidence to the contrary. While examining victims of an Indian raid in a nearby field, Gardiner found "the body of one man shot through, the arrow going in at the right side, the head sticking fast, half through a rib on the left side, which I took out and cleansed it, and presumed to send to the [Massachusetts] Bay, because they had said the arrows of the Indians were of no force." There was no question in Gardiner's mind that the Indians could kill Englishmen at will.[4]

Although the Pequots were given to feuding with a number of tribes and sub-tribes, including the Narragansetts, they sought a peaceful relationship with the Massachusetts Bay Colony and other Puritans of New England. And they were prepared to pay a heavy price for peace, but only if it was consistent with their concept of honor and tradition.[5]

In November 1634, a delegation of Pequot chiefs arrived at the Massachusetts Bay Colony with a twofold objective. They sought to negotiate a trade agreement with the Puritans to compensate for commercial losses.[6] In addition, the Pequots solicited Puritan intervention in arranging a peace between themselves and the Narragansetts. The Massachusetts magistrates were amenable to granting the Pequot request, providing their own demands were met. These requirements included four hundred fathoms of wampum, forty beaver skins, and thirty otter skins.[7] But this was a far greater tribute than the amount of wampum, beaver, and otter skins the Pequots were prepared to offer. The English demand, in fact, totaled almost half the taxes levied in the Massachusetts Bay Colony in 1634.[8]

Later, the Pequot tribal council in Connecticut refused to ratify the Massachusetts demands. After all, the Pequots were not at war with the Bay Colony. They had come voluntarily to seek a treaty of trade and peace with the Bay Puritans and believed themselves to be negotiating with equals. Nevertheless, Pequot ambassadors were authorized to make a princely counter-offer to the Puritans at the original meeting. "They offered us also," John Winthrop recorded, "all their right at Connecticut, and to further us what they could, if we would settle a plantation there."[9] Subsequently, the Pequots molested no English settler in Connecticut, nor did they demand payment for the right to settle there, until the outbreak of war in 1636.

The question of submission to the Bay Colony was also raised at the meeting when the Puritan magistrates insisted that the Pequots should "deliver up those who were guilty" in the death two years earlier of Captain John Stone, an unsavory West Indian trader and adulterer who had been banished from the Bay Colony under threat of death if he ever returned.[10] The Pequot ambassadors replied: "The sachem, who then lived, was slain by the Dutch, and all the men, who were guilty, etc., were dead of the pox, except two." [11] Intent upon pressing their trade advantage with the Pequots, the Puritans let the Stone matter rest for two years. However, in 1636, when the Massachusetts magistrates again demanded that the Pequots hand over the two surviving murderers—who were not Pequots but Western Niantics, tributary to the Pequots—it seemed to the Pequots tantamount to an edict that they subject themselves to Massachusetts Bay. For them to yield the two wanted men would have undermined the entire tributary system under which superior tribes were bound to provide protection for tribute. Again the Pequot ambassadors were not authorized to accede to the Puritan demand, although they had agreed in 1634 to bring the matter before the Pequot council and reportedly declared that "if they were worthy of death, they [the Pequot ambassadors] would move their sachem to have them delivered (for they had no commission to do it)." [12]

The Pequot ambassadors had made clear to the magistrates precisely what they were empowered to offer and to what they could not commit their tribe. Nevertheless, the ambassadors undertook to report the Puritan demands to their council. This was the basis for the conclusion of the treaty—an agreement that has never been found and exists only in John Winthrop's brief and cryptic paraphrase of the proceedings. Yet Winthrop made a point of recording the following: "and so [we] should be at peace with them, and *as friends* to trade with them, *but not to defend them,* etc." [13] At the very least, this is evidence that the Pequots were opposed to being a protectorate of Massachusetts.

The Pequot interpretation of the treaty was observed by both sides for more than a year. Ultimately, the problems that led to the outbreak of the Pequot War were generated within the Massachusetts Bay Colony itself and were stimulated by the Puritan desire to control all settlement in New England. In 1634, the authority of the Boston magistrates had been questioned by the Reverend Thomas Hooker and his followers—a challenge that matured in 1635, when the dissenters decided to colonize an area of

Connecticut that was outside the Massachusetts Bay Company patent and comprised a portion of the territory yielded by the Pequots. But this location already had been claimed by the Dutch and by a group of Englishmen known as the Saybrook Company, who were controlled by Massachusetts Bay. While Hooker's dissenters were creating difficulties for the Puritan establishment in Massachusetts, John Winthrop, Sr., informed his son, John, Jr., in England, of the treaty concluded with the Pequots. Quickly, the Saybrook Company instructed the younger Winthrop, whom they appointed Governor of Connecticut, to establish a colony at the mouth of the Connecticut River and to build a fort there against Dutch invasion. Hooker, opposed to the younger Winthrop's jurisdiction over Connecticut, agreed to a compromise under which the colonists accepted subservience to Massachusetts and the Saybrook Company. But in these circumstances, the younger Winthrop, with no constituency, found it virtually impossible to govern.

Connecticut was now a powder keg. While the treaty between the Pequots and Massachusetts facilitated orderly settlement of Connecticut, it did not quell intertribal feuding or arrest the rivalry between Connecticut and the Bay Colony. The success of both Puritan colonies depended upon forcing the Pequots into a degree of subjugation greater than Connecticut's own subservience to Massachusetts Bay.

In 1636, Jonathan Brewster, a Plymouth leader, sent a message to Fort Saybrook—based on information secured from the Mohegan sachem Uncas—that "the Pequots have some mistrust, that the English will shortly come against them (which I take is by indiscreet speeches of some of your people here [in Connecticut] to the natives) and therefore out of desperate madness do threaten shortly to set both upon Indians, and English jointly." [14] Rumors and warnings of this sort invariably fired Puritan suspicions. It was now necessary for the Pequots to be held accountable for provoking those same fears and punished. But if the Connecticut settlers were permitted to punish the Pequots, they might make them tributaries to Connecticut or fight them and claim the territory by right of conquest. Massachusetts could not permit this to happen and issued an ultimatum to the Pequots at a conference at Fort Saybrook between John Winthrop, Jr., the Western Niantic sachem Sassious, and representatives of the Pequots, held in July 1636. The ultimatum required that the Pequots adhere to the earlier treaty terms as interpreted by the Puritans, including giving up Captain Stone's killers to English punishment. Although Sassious personally subordinated himself to John Winthrop, Jr., and relinquished his entire territory to the Governor, Massachusetts continued to persist with this demand after the meeting. A few days later, the Puritans had the last "provocation" they needed. Captain John Oldham, a trusted aide of the Massachusetts government, was murdered by Narragansett Indians at Block Island, and the Puritans insisted that the crime had been committed by the Pequots. A punitive expedition was dispatched under John Endecott, who destroyed Indian villages on Block Island, killing a few inhabitants, and then threatened a Pequot village on the mainland, burning crops and homes. The Pequot War had begun.

The war of 1636-37 is the first instance of total war in New England and comprised only two major battles. One was at Mystic Fort, the other at the Sadqua Swamp, near New Haven. The English brought to bear upon the Pequots the full force of European weaponry and fired Mystic Fort. In this onslaught the English gave the Indians no quarter. The brutality of the English at Mystic outraged even their seasoned allies, the Mohegans. Captain Underhill recorded that after the fight "Our Indians came to us, and much rejoiced at our victories, and greatly admired the manner of Englishmen's fight, but cried mach it, mach it; that is, It is naught, it is naught, because it is too furious, and slays too many men." [15]

To the Puritans, the Pequot enemy was "bloody," "barbarous," "murdering," "insolent," and "proud." There was an unemotional ferocity about the Indian, whose very existence—whatever sex or age—constituted a Satanic threat to the Puritan Army of Christ. Underhill thought of the Pequots as "a warlike nation, a people that spend most of their time in the study of warlike policy." [16] To Philip Vincent they had inherently "barbarous and cruel natures." [17] And William Bradford always remembered how many of the first Pilgrims imagined themselves

> in continual danger of the savage people, who are cruel, barbarous, and most treacherous, being most furious in their rage and merciless where they are overcome; not being content only to kill and take

away life, but delight to torment men in the most bloody manner that may be; flaying some alive with the shells of fishes, cutting off the members and joints of others by piecemeal and broiling on the coals, eat[ing] the collops of their flesh in their sight while they live, with other cruelties [too] horrible to be related.[18]

So conditioned were the English settlers to these characterizations of the Indians that, after the events of 1637, the Puritans were able to picture themselves fighting devils with the same savagery they ascribed to the Indians. Accounts of the Puritan victory over the Pequots are replete with expressions of exultation and relief. John Mason, commander of the Connecticut forces, reported:

Thus were they now at their wits end, who not many hours before exalted themselves in their great pride, threatening and resolving the utter ruin and destruction of all the English, exulting and rejoicing with songs and dances. But God was above them, who laughed his enemies and the enemies of his people to scorn, making them as a fiery oven: Thus were the stout-hearted spoiled, having slept their last sleep, and none of their men could find their hands. Thus did the Lord judge among the heathen, filling the place with dead bodies.[19]

And William Bradford, while no participant in the massacre of the Pequots, recorded Puritan feelings when he wrote:

It was a fearful sight to see them thus frying in the fire and the streams of blood quenching the same, and horrible was the stink thereof. But the victory seemed a sweet sacrifice, and they gave praise thereof to God, who had wrought so wonderfully for them, thus to enclose their enemies in their hands and give them so speedy a victory over so proud and insulting an enemy.[20]

Thus went the war that was described by Edward Johnson as a "quarrel . . . as ancient as Adam's time, propagated from the old enmity between the seed of the woman, and the seed of the serpent, who was the signer of this war." [21]

How could the Puritan man of God justify his slaughter of the Pequots? How could he defend his attack on defenseless men, women, and children? The Puritan answer was simply that God had sanctioned and conducted the war. For in the Old Testament, there was justification of Puritan actions in the Israelites' bloody wars of the Lord against the pagans. It was God who first required and then directed the Puritan destruction of the Pequots. He fought "for us" in the Pequot War, William Pynchon maintained, because He demanded—from the first English settlement—the complete submission of the natives to the true faith.[22] When the Pequots refused to submit—or resist—they signed their own death warrant. They thus provoked their own destruction merely by being themselves.

Word of the English victory reverberated throughout New England and struck fear into the hearts of the natives; fear of English military technology, fear of the English God, and fear of the savagery of English fighting. John Winthrop believed "the Lord's hand appeared in it," and William Hooke explained this by preaching that when "a people are in Covenant with God, and cleave only to Him," He "enters himself presently [as] the General of all their forces, leads their armies, and fights their battles." [23]

20. "By the Sword of the Lord"

In July 1636, Block Island Narragansetts murdered Captain John Oldham. While Oldham had at one point been considered an unsavory character, he had been rehabilitated by the Massachusetts government and entrusted with major responsibilities. At one time, Oldham's friendship had been highly valued by the Narragansetts and his death at their hands is curious. Perhaps the Indians held Oldham responsible for the smallpox epidemic of 1633–34.[1]

Miantonomo and Canonicus were exonerated from any blame in plotting Oldham's death. And Miantonomo himself led a Narragansett expedition of two hundred warriors to avenge Oldham's death on behalf of the Massachusetts government.[2] But this was not justice enough for the Puritans. In August 1636, the Massachusetts magistrates authorized a force of ninety volunteers under Captain John Endecott to go to Block Island "to put to death the men of Block Island, but to spare the women and children, and to bring them away, and to take possession of the island."[3] The Puritan version of Oldham's death, with a firsthand report of the Block Island expedition, was written by Captain Underhill.[4]

... I shall ... begin with a true relation of the New England wars against the Block Islanders, and that insolent and barbarous nation, called the Pequots, whom, by the sword of the Lord, and a few feeble instruments, soldiers not accustomed to war, were drove out of their country, and slain by the sword, to the number of fifteen hundred souls, in the space of two months and less; so as their country is fully subdued and fallen into the hands of the English. And to the end that God's name might have the glory, and His people see His power, and magnify His honor for His great goodness....

The cause of our war against the Block Islanders, was for taking away the life of one Master John Oldham, who made it his common course to trade amongst the Indians. He coming to Block Island to drive trade with them, the islanders came into his boat, and having got a full view of commodities which gave them good content, consulted how they might destroy him and his company, to the end they might clothe their bloody flesh with his lawful garments. The Indians, having laid the plot, into the boat they came to trade, as they pretended; watching their opportunities, knocked him in the head, and martyred him most barbarously, to the great grief of his poor distressed servants, which by the providence of God were saved. This island lying in the road way to Lord Sey and the Lord Brooke's plantation, a certain seaman called to John Gallop, master of the small navigation standing along to the Massachusetts Bay, and seeing a boat under sail aboard the island, and preceiving the sails to be skillfully managed, bred in him a jealousy, whether that the island Indians had not bloodily taken the life of our countrymen, and made themselves master of their goods. Suspecting this, he bore up to them, and approaching near them was confirmed that his jealousy was just. Seeing Indians in the boat, and knowing her to be the vessel of Master Oldham, and not seeing him there, gave fire upon them and slew some; others leaped overboard, besides two of the number which he preserved alive and brought to the Bay. The blood of the innocent called for vengeance. God stirred up the heart of the honored Governor, Master Henry Vane, and the rest of the worthy magistrates, to send forth a hundred well appointed soldiers, under the conduct of Captain John Endecott, and in company with him that had command, Captain John Underhill, Captain Nathan Turner, Captain William Jenyson, besides other inferior officers. I would not have the world wonder at the great number of commanders to so few men, but know that the Indians' fight far differs from the Christian practice; for they most commonly divide themselves into small bodies, so that we are forced to neglect our usual way, and to subdivide our divisions to answer theirs, and not thinking it any disparagement to any captain to go forth against an enemy with a squadron of men, taking the ground from the old and ancient practice, when they chose captains of hundreds and captains of thousands, captains of fifties and captains of tens. We conceive a captain signifieth the chief in way of command of any body committed to his charge for the time being, whether of more or less, it makes no matter in power, though in honor it does. Coming to an anchor before the island, we espied an Indian walking by the shore in a desolate manner, as though he had received intelligence of our coming. Which Indian gave just ground to some to conclude that the body of the people had deserted the island.

But some knowing them for the generality to be a warlike nation, a people that spend most of their time in the study of warlike policy, were not persuaded that they would upon so slender terms forsake the island, but rather suspected they might lie behind a bank, much like a form of a barricado. Myself with others rode a shallop, made towards the shore, having in the boat a dozen armed soldiers. Drawing near to the place of landing, the number that rose from behind the barricado were between fifty or sixty able fighting men, men as straight as arrows, very tall, and of active bodies, having their arrows notched. They drew near to the water side, and let fly at the soldiers, as though they had meant to have made an end of us all in a moment. They shot a young gentleman in the neck through a collar, for stiffness as if it had been an oaken board, and entered his flesh a good depth. Myself received an arrow through my coat sleeve, a second against my helmet on the forehead; so as if God in His providence had not moved the heart of my wife to persuade me to carry it along with me, (which I was unwilling to do), I had been slain.... The arrows flying thick about us, we made haste to the shore; but the surf of the sea being great, hindered us, so as we could scarce discharge a musket, but were forced to make haste to land. Drawing near the shore through the strength of wind, and the hollowness of the sea, we durst not adventure to run ashore, but were forced to wade up to the middle; but once having got up off our legs, we gave fire upon them. They finding our bullets to outreach their arrows, they fled before us. In the meanwhile ... [Captain] Endecott made to the shore, and some of this number also repulsed him at his landing, but hurt none. We thought they would stand it out with us, but they perceiving we were in earnest, fled; and left their wigwams, or houses, and provision to the use of our soldiers. Having set forth our sentinels, and laid out our pardues[?], we betook ourselves to the guard, expecting hourly they would fall upon us; but they observed the old rule, 'Tis good sleeping in a whole skin, and left us free from an alarm.

The next day we set upon our march, the Indians being retired into swamps, so as we could not find them. We burnt and spoiled both houses and corn in great abundance; but they kept themselves in obscurity. Captain Turner stepping aside to a swamp, met with some few Indians, and charged upon them, changing some few bullets for arrows. Himself received a shot upon the breast of his corselet, as if it had been pushed with a pike, and if he had not had it on, he had lost his life.

A pretty passage worthy [of] observation. We had an Indian with us that was an interpreter; being in English clothes, and a gun in his hand, was spied by the islanders, which called out to him. What are you, an Indian or an Englishman? Come hither, saith he, and I will tell you. He pulls up his cock and let fly at one of them, and without question was the death of him. Having spent that day in burning and spoiling the island, we took up the quarter for that night. About midnight myself went out with ten men about two miles from our quarter, and discovered the most eminent plantation they had in the island, where was much corn, many wigwams, and great heaps of mats; but fearing less we should make an alarm by setting fire on them, we left them as we found them, and peacefully departed to our quarter; and the next morning with forty men marched up to the same plantation, burnt their houses, cut down their corn, destroyed some of their dogs instead of men, which they left in their wigwams.

Passing on toward the water side to embark our soldiers, we met with several famous wigwams, with great heaps of pleasant corn ready shelled; but not able to bring it away, we did throw their mats upon it, and set fire and burnt it. Many well-wrought mats our soldiers brought from thence, and several delightful baskets. We being divided into two parts, the rest of the body met with no less, I suppose, than ourselves did. The Indians playing least in sight, we spent our time, and could no more advantage ourselves than we had already done, and set sail for Saybrook Fort, where we lay through distress of weather four days; then we departed.

21. "What Cheer, Englishmen . . .
What Do You Come For?"

After their rather farcical foray against the Block Island Indians, during which Underhill's soldiers became irate when they discovered the Narragansetts had departed the projected battleground, the Puritan warriors left for Fort Saybrook and eventually for Pequot country. There, the Endecott mission was to apprehend the murderers of Captain Walter Norton and Captain John Stone and "seven more of their company," who had been "sailing along the Niantic shore with five vessels" when they were attacked and killed by natives.[1] Underhill picks up the story:[2]

. . . The Indians spying of us came running in multitudes along the water side, crying, What cheer, Englishmen, what cheer, what do you come for? They not thinking we intended war, went on cheerfully until they came to Pequot River. We thinking it the best way, did forbear to answer them; first, that we might the better be able to run through the work; secondly, that by delaying of them, we might drive them in security, to the end we might have the more advantage of them. But they seeing we would make no answer, kept on their course, and cried, What, Englishmen, what cheer, what cheer, are you hoggery, will you cram us? That is, are you angry, will you kill us, and do you come to fight? That night the Western Niantic Indians, and the Pequots, made fire on both sides of the river, fearing we would land in the night. They made most doleful and woeful cries all the night, (so that we could scarce rest) hallooing one to another, and giving the word from place to place, to gather their forces together, fearing the English were come to war against them.

The next morning they sent early aboard an ambassador, a grave senior, a man of good understanding, portly carriage, grave and majestical in his expressions. He demanded of us what the end of our coming was. To which we answered, that the governors of the Bay sent us to demand the heads of those persons that had slain Captain Norton and Captain Stone, and the rest of their company, and that it was not the custom of the English to suffer murderers to live; and therefore, if they desired their own peace and welfare, they will peacefully answer our expectation, and give us the heads of the murderers.

They being a witty and ingenious nation, their ambassador labored to excuse the matter, and answered, We know not that any of ours have slain any English. True it is, saith he, we have slain such a number of men; but consider the ground of it. Not long before the coming of these English into the river, there was a certain vessel that came to us in way of trade. We used them well, and traded with them, and took them to be such as would not wrong us in the least matter. But our sachem or prince coming aboard, they laid a plot how they might destroy him; which plot discovereth itself by the event, as followeth. They keeping their boat aboard, and not desirous of our company, gave us leave to stand hallooing ashore, that they might work their mischievous plot. But as we stood they called to us, and demanded of us a bushel of wampam—peage, which is their money. This they demanded for his ransom. This peal did ring terribly in our ears, to demand so much for the life of our prince, whom we thought was in the hands of honest men, and we had never wronged them. But we saw there was no remedy; their expectation must be granted, or else they would not send him ashore, which they promised they would do, if we would answer their desires. We sent them so much aboard, according to demand, and they, according to their promise, sent him ashore,* but first slew him. This much exasperated our spirits, and made us vow a revenge. Suddenly after came these captains

* This was noways true of the English, but a devised excuse.

with a vessel into the river, and pretended to trade with us, as the former did. We did not discountenance them for the present, but took our opportunity and came aboard. The sachem's son succeeding his father, was the man that came into the cabin of Captain Stone, and Captain Stone having drunk more than did him good, fell backwards on the bed asleep. The sagamore took his opportunity, and having a little hatchet under his garment, therewith knocked him in the head. Some being upon the deck and others under, suspected some such thing; for the rest of the Indians that were aboard had order to proceed against the rest at one time; but the English spying treachery, run immediately into the cook-room, and, with a fire-brand, had thought to have blown up the Indians by setting fire to the powder. These Devil's instruments spying this plot of the English, leaped overboard as the powder was a firing, and saved themselves; but all the English were blown up. This was the manner of their bloody action. Saith the ambassador to us, Could ye blame us for revenging so cruel a murder? For we distinguish not between the Dutch and English, but took them to be one nation, and therefore we do not conceive that we wronged you, for they slew our king; and thinking these captains to be of the same nation and people as those that slew him, made us set upon this course of revenge.

Our answer was, They were able to distinguish between Dutch and English, having had sufficient experience of both nations; and therefore, seeing you have slain the King of England's subjects, we come to demand an account of their blood, for ourselves are liable to account for them. The answer of the ambassador was, We know no difference between the Dutch and the English; they are both strangers to us, we took them to be all one; therefore we crave pardon; we have not wilfully wronged the English. —This excuse will not serve our turns, for we have sufficient testimony that you know the English from the Dutch. We must have the heads of those persons that have slain ours, or else we will fight with you. He answered, Understanding the ground of your coming, I will entreat you to give me liberty to go ashore, and I shall inform the body of the people what your intent and resolution is; and if you will stay aboard, I will bring you a sudden answer.

We did grant him liberty to get ashore, and ourselves followed suddenly after before the war was proclaimed. He seeing us land our forces, came with a message to entreat us to come no nearer, but stand in a valley, which had between us and them an ascent, that took our sight from them; but they might see us to hurt us, to our prejudice. Thus from the first beginning to the end of the action, they carried themselves very subtly; but we, not willing to be at their direction, marched up to the ascent, having set our men in battalia. He came and told us he had inquired for the sachem, that we might come to a parley; but neither of both of the princes were at home; they were gone to Long Island.

Our reply was, We must not be put off thus, we know the sachem is in the plantation, and therefore bring him to us, that we may speak with him, or else we will beat up the drum, and march through the country, and spoil your corn. His answer, if you will but stay a little while, I will step to the plantation and seek for them. We gave them leave to take their own course, and used as much patience as ever men might, considering the gross abuse they offered us, holding us above an hour in vain hopes. They sent an Indian to tell us that Mommenoteck was found, and would appear before us suddenly. This brought us to a new stand the space of an hour more. There came a third Indian persuading us to have a little further patience, and he would not tarry, for he had assembled the body of the Pequots together, to know who the parties were that had slain these Englishmen. But seeing that they did in this interim convey away their wives and children, and bury their chiefest goods, we perceived at length they would fly from us; but we were patient and bore with them, in expectation to have the greater blow upon them. The last messenger brought us this intelligence from the sachem, that if we would lay down our arms, and approach about thirty paces from them, and meet the heathen prince, he would cause his men to do the like, and then we shall come to a parley.

But we seeing this drift was to get our arms, we rather chose to beat up the drum and bid them battle. Marching into a campaign field we displayed our colors; but none would come near us, but standing remotely off did laugh at us for our patience. We suddenly set upon our march, and gave fire to as many as we could come near, firing their wigwams, spoiling their corn, and many other necessaries that they had buried in the ground we raked up, which the soldiers had for booty. Thus we spent the day burning and spoiling the country. Towards night embarked ourselves. The next morning, landing on the Niantic shore, where we were served in like nature, no Indians would come near us, but run from us, as the deer from the dogs. But having burnt and spoiled what we could light on, we embarked our men, and set sail for the Bay. Having ended this exploit, came off, having one man wounded in the leg; but certain numbers of their slain, and many wounded. This was the substance of the first year's service. . . .

22. "They Had Always Loved the English"

On October 21, 1636, Miantonomo (who, with his uncle Canonicus, ruled the powerful Narragansetts of Rhode Island) was in Boston with several other sachems, including Cutshamoquin, of the Massachuset tribe. They had come at the invitation of Governor Henry Vane to conclude a treaty of peace and trade with the Massachusetts Bay Colony.[1] With war pending between the Massachusetts government and the Pequots, Miantonomo knew the English needed him. However, John Winthrop, who recorded the proceedings in his journal, makes no mention of any concessions the Puritans may have made to the Narragansetts in return for their alliance. Nor is there any way of determining this point through the treaty itself, which no longer exists. Nevertheless, strains in the relationship between the Narragansetts and the Bay Colony magistrates during and following the Pequot War suggest that Miantonomo had bargained shrewdly with the Puritans.[2] Winthrop's journal entry follows:[3]

Miantonomo, the sachem of Narragansett, (being sent for by the Governor,) came to Boston with two of Canonicus's sons, and another sachem, and near twenty sanaps. Cutshamoquin gave us notice the day before. The Governor sent twenty musketeers to meet him at Roxbury. He came to Boston about noon. The Governor had called together most of the magistrates and ministers, to give countenance to our proceedings, and to advise with them about the terms of peace. It was dinner time, and the sachems and their council dined by themselves in the same room where the

Governor dined, and their sanaps were sent to the inn. After dinner, Miantonomo declared what he had to say to us in [blank] propositions, which were to this effect: —that they had always loved the English, and desired firm peace with us: that they would continue in war with the Pequots and their confederates, till they were subdued; and desired we should so do: they would deliver our enemies to us, or kill them: that if any of theirs should kill our cattle, that they would not kill them, but cause them to make satisfaction: that they would now make a firm peace, and two months hence they would send us a present.[4]

The Governor told them, they should have answer the next morning.

In the morning we met again, and concluded the peace upon the articles underwritten, which the Governor subscribed, and they also subscribed with their marks, and Cutshamoquin also. But because we could not well make them understand the articles perfectly, we agreed to send a copy of them to Mr. Roger Williams, who could best interpret them to them. So, after dinner, they took leave, and were conveyed out of town by some musketeers, and dismissed with a volley of shot.

THE ARTICLES.

1. A firm peace between us and our friends of other plantations (if they consent) and their confederates (if they will observe the articles, etc.) and our posterities.

2. Neither party to make peace with the Pequots without the other's consent.

3. Not to harbor, etc., the Pequots, etc.

4. To put to death or deliver over murderers, etc.

5. To return our fugitive servants, etc.

6. We to give them notice when we go against the Pequots, and they to send us some guides.

7. Free trade between us.

8. None of them to come near our plantations during the wars with the Pequots, without some Englishman or known Indian.

9. To continue to the posterity of both parties.

23. "They Asked If We Did Use to Kill Women and Children?"

Early 1637 saw Fort Saybrook under siege by the Pequots. The fort had been constructed by Lieutenant Lion Gardiner, "Engineer and Master of Works of Fortification in the legers of the Prince of Orange," on the west bank of the Connecticut River.[1] As commander of Fort Saybrook, Gardiner had anticipated and prepared for the siege, during which the Pequots maintained steady pressure on the defenders, picking off stragglers in the vicinity of the fortification. In February, after curing himself of a wound inflicted only a few days earlier by the Pequots, Gardiner "went out with eight men to get some fowl for our relief."[2] What happened on this foray, he reports in his reminiscence of the Pequot War:[3]

Anthony Dike, master of a bark, having his bark at Rhode Island in the winter, was sent by Mr. Vane, then Governor. Anthony came to Rhode Island by land, and from thence he came with his bark to me with a letter, wherein was desired that I should consider and prescribe the best way I could quell these Pequots, which I also did, and with my letter sent the man's rib as a token. A few days later came Thomas Stanton down the river, and staying for a wind, while he was there came a troop of Indians within musket shot, laying themselves and their arms down behind a little rising hill and two great trees; which I perceiving, called the carpenter whom I had showed how to charge and level a gun, and that he should put two cartridges of musket bullets into two sakers guns that lay about; and we levelled them against the place, and I told him that he must look towards me, and when he saw me wave my hat above my head he should give fire to both the guns; then presently came three Indians, creeping out and calling to us to speak with us: and I was glad that Thomas Stanton was there, and I sent six men down by the Garden Pales to look that none should come under the hill behind us; and having placed the rest in places convenient closely, Thomas and I with my sword, pistol and carbine, went ten or twelve pole without the gate to parley with them. And when the six men came to the Garden Pales, at the corner, they found a great number of Indians creeping behind the fort, or betwixt us and home, but they ran away. Now I had said to Thomas Stanton, Whatsoever they say to you, tell me first, for we will not answer them directly to anything, for I know not the mind of the rest of the English. So they came forth, calling us nearer to them, and we them nearer to us. But I would not let Thomas go any further than the great stump of a tree, and I stood by him; then they asked who we were, and he answered, Thomas and Lieutenant. But they said he lied, for I was shot with many arrows; and so I was, but my buff coat preserved me, only one hurt me. But when I spake to them they knew my voice, for one of them had dwelt three months with us, but ran away when the Bay men came first. Then they asked us if we would fight with Western Niantic Indians, for they were our friends and came to trade with us. We said we knew not the Indians one from another, and therefore would trade with none. Then they said, Have you fought enough? We said we knew not yet. Then they asked if we did use to kill women and children? We said they should see that hereafter. So they were silent a small space, and then they said, We are Pequots, and have killed Englishmen, and can kill them as mosquitoes, and we will take away the horses, cows and hogs. When Thomas Stanton had told me this, he prayed me to shoot that rogue, for, said he, he hath an Englishman's coat on, and saith that he hath killed three, and these other four have their clothes on their backs. I said, No, it is not the manner of a parley, but have patience and I shall fit them ere they go. Nay, now or never, said he; so when he could get no other answer but this last, I bid him tell them that they should go to Connecticut, for if they did kill all the men, and take all the rest as they said, it would do them no good, but hurt, for English women are lazy, and can't do their work; horses and cows will spoil your corn-fields, and the hogs their clam-banks, and so undo them; then I pointed to our great house and bid them tell them there lay twenty pieces of trucking cloth, of Mr. [William] Pynchon's, with hoes, hatchets, and all manner of trade, they were better fight still with us, and so get all that, and then go up the river after they had killed all [of] us. Having heard this, they were mad as dogs, and ran away; then when they came to the place from whence they came, I waved my hat about my head, and the two great guns went off, so that there was a great hubbub amongst them. Then two days after, came down Captain [John] Mason, and Lieutenant [Robert] Seely, with five men more, to see how it was with us; and whilst they were there, came down a Dutch boat, telling us the Indians had killed fourteen English, for by that boat I had sent up letters to Connecticut, what I heard, and what I thought, and how to prevent that threatened danger, and received back again rather a scoff, than any thanks, for my care and pains....

24. "In the Name of the Lord"

John Higginson was twenty-one years old at the outbreak of the Pequot War. Reared in Salem, his education was supervised—following the death of his father, Reverend Francis Higginson—by such Puritan luminaries as John Winthrop, Sr., and John Cotton. He had a knowledge of French and Indian languages. In 1636, he was commissioned to meet with Canonicus for an investigation into the death of John Oldham and, the same year, was named chaplain at Fort Saybrook.[1] About May 1637, young Higginson offered his thoughts about the meaning and implications of the conflict between the Puritans and the Pequots in the following letter to Winthrop.[2]

For the right worshipful and much honored in the Lord Mr. John
Winthrop
Esquire and Deputy Governor these with speed
RIGHT WORSHIPFUL AND MUCH HONORED IN THE LORD, my due

service and respect remembered and having given information to the Governor of the manner of the Lord's proceeding with us here, I spare to write thereof unto yourself. Only I make bold to present you with my weak and feeble thoughts concerning the same which you may be pleased to consider of as you see cause.

First, whether now the Lord begins not to send (as shepherds used to do their dogs to fetch in their straggling sheep so He) the Indians upon His servants, to make them cleave more close together, and prize each other, to prevent contentions of brethren which may prove as hard to break as castle bars, and stop their now beginning breaches before they be as the letting out of many waters that cannot be gathered in again, etc. O that as this is the Lord's meaning so it may be the use that all His servants may make thereof, that He may have the praise in Jesus Christ forever more.

Secondly, whether the Lord intends not in His dealings here with us a gracious warning to all the English in the land that shall ever have to do with Indians again in this kind: For it hath been a common conceit but is in truth a dangerous error, Indians are afraid of pieces, etc. 10 English will make a 100 Indians fly: some dare venture (happily now) with 20, 40, 60 men among a 1000 armed Pequots (for that, if not many more, in probability is their number) etc. etc. but if the passages here be well considered, and the Lord be pleased to sanctify our punishments to be warnings to the wise; I hope it may be a means to root out that deeply-rooted security, and confidence in our own supposed strength (2 English diseases and dangerous worms that used to breed and grow in abused peace or slighted liberties), that so the loss of these, and danger of ourselves may be the safety and preservation of many others.

Thirdly, whether now the Lord calls not by all these and alarms and heavenly warnings from hence, to all His servants louder and louder, etc. more seriously to intend this war than yet they seem to do.

For if that our condition here, to have 10 lusty men out of so little a number as ours is so cruelly slain, others crying and roaring out through extremity of the pain of wounds, others gasping and dying and breathing out their last, ourselves beleaguered by the same bloodthirsty, and hemmed in by those who daily seek our lives, etc. etc. If this I say were the case of the servants of the Lord in the Bay their hearts would be affected, their purses opened and their hands enlarged to defend (not so much their lives and liberties, to say nothing of them) as the glorious Gospel of Jesus Christ, which hath shined amongst us hitherto, and may do yet if it be not our own fault.

And yet this may be the condition of those precious servants of the Lord up this river [the Connecticut settlers] we know not how soon; unless the Lord be pleased as He hath done hitherto and I hope He will make salvation unto them for walls and bulwarks round about. For hath not the Lord in abundant mercy to them, kept the many hundreds of our enemies in a serious and furious beleaguering of us here, and restrained them from attempting anything there as yet as they have upon ourselves, I see not how they could have been preserved without a miracle.

And let not Boston, Roxbury etc. think war is far from them, for this seems to be an universal deluge creeping and encroaching on all the English in the land: The multitudes of our enemies daily increase, by the falling of Mohegans, Nipmucks (who live not many miles from the Bay), Western Niantics at Narragansett and their malice is not to be questioned, their cruelty divers of ours have felt. Their experience in warlike affairs (being men of war from their youth), their advantages against us, in agility and arms, their industrious sedulity plying and attending the war against the English as their mainest business, providing retreats at Long Island, fortifying upon the main, gathering new supplies of forces, confederating with former enemies, giving large rewards to those amongst them, who are most skillful to destroy, etc. (which we hear of from plantations above, and they from Indians) do far exceed the preparations and provisions of the English against them, who yet have far more cause to seek to defend their lives and liberties and Gospel, than such bloodthirsty wretches have to invade, destroy, and take away the same.

And add to the former also this, that now the eyes of all the Indians in the country are upon the English, to see what they will do; and all may be assured of this, that if some serious and very speedy course be not taken to tame the pride and take down the insolency of these now-insulting Pequots though with charge and loss and damage for the present, we are like to have all the Indians in the country about our ears, and then there will be work enough, etc.

In all these respects and many more I desire it may be considered whether the serious and speedy prosecution of this war be not the greatest business New England hath. For it cannot be conceived that either building, planting, fishing, trading, colleges, etc. or, in a word, the good of either Church or Commonwealth can flourish, and go forward, without a timely removing and preventing the wars that now begin. For these are but the beginnings of war, the progress hath been something sad, what the issue will be the Lord, He only knows.

Now the Lord be pleased to raise up the public spirits of His servants (and where they are not to create them) that every heart and head and hand may be stirring and working in this case; for the strength and sinews of these wars I take to lie in the combined abilities and united hearts and hands of all the servants of the Lord etc. (To omit that it cannot be expected that ever wars should prosper abroad, if civil [nay worse and religious] dissensions abound at home) yet all partaking in the good and benefit of peace and in the danger and damage of a common war should also be every way enlarged to their utmost for the procuring and preserving the one, removing and preventing of the other.

Three places and precedents in Scripture I only make bold to present your w[orshi]p with and so I end. Judges 20, 1, 2, 8: Ezra 10, 3, 4: Hag. 2, 4. Hence may be collected this in brief, that (after serious reconciliation with the Lord of armies and Indians Himself) it belongeth firstly and chiefly to you the much honored magistrates that as you have hitherto not been wanting according as the Lord hath called, so now you will arise, be serious, be speedy, be strong, and be courageous in the Lord, etc.

That also our much honored the ministers and watchmen of the Lord will not be wanting to press upon the conscience, charge as a duty, command in the name of the Lord from heaven, etc. the serious and speedy prosecution of this war.

That also all the people of the land should be seriously roused up to open their purses and enlarge their hands, offer their persons etc. to do what service they can to help the Lord against the mighty.

And O that the heavy curse of Merosh may never fall upon any of the Lord's. And O that the disposition of this bearer and others also lately come out of the Bay, who are sensibly affected with things here etc. might run through all the land viz. they would willingly lay down half they have to serve this way, and yet less than a half, a quarter, a tenth would do that now which hereafter all the world cannot recover, etc. But I fear I am too bold; I entreat you therefore pardon my weakness, and consider the things and though I, it may be, am afraid to die, our men here fearful, melancholy, etc. yet the Lord help all His servants to consider what His will and pleasure is in all these sad occurrences hitherto; He be pleased to counsel and direct and bless from heaven all intended enterprises in Jesus Christ. (In great haste) I rest, yours engaged in many bonds in all due service most devoted

JOHN HIGGINSON

[*Ca.* May, 1637]

25. "To Do Execution ... on the Pequots"

In the uneasy time just before the Pequot War, it was important for John Winthrop, Sr., Deputy Governor of the Massachusetts Bay Colony, to prevent the Pequots from forming a military alliance with the Narragansetts. To thwart any such design, Winthrop solicited the services of Roger Williams, who, in 1635, had been banished from Massachusetts and had befriended the Narragansetts. With diplomatic deftness, Williams offered the Narragansetts an alliance with the English against the Pequots, who were then busily courting the Rhode Island tribe. They accepted the offer [see document 22] and began preparing for war. In a letter to Governor Henry Vane and Deputy Governor Winthrop, the banished Williams reports on the kind of strategy proposed by Miantonomo:[1]

NEW PROVIDENCE, this 2d of the week. [May 15, 1637.]

SIR, —The latter end of the last week I gave notice to our neighbor princes of your intentions and preparations against the common enemy, the Pequots. At my first coming to them Canonicus *(morosus aque ac barbarex senex)* was very sour, and accused the English and myself for sending the plague amongst them, and threatening to kill him especially.[2]

Such tidings (it seems) were lately brought to his ears by some of his flatterers and our ill-willers. I discerned cause of bestirring myself, and stayed the longer, and at least (through the mercy of the Most High) I not only sweetened his spirit, but possessed him, that the plague and other sicknesses were alone in the hand of the one God, who made him and us, who being displeased with the English for lying, stealing, idleness and uncleanness, (the natives' epidemical sins), smote many thousands of us ourselves with general and late mortalities.

Miantonomo kept his barbarous court lately at my house, and with him I have far better dealing. He takes some pleasure to visit me, and sent me word of his coming over again some eight days since.

They pass not a week without some skirmishings, though hitherto little loss on either side. They were glad of your preparations, and in much conference with themselves and others, (sifting *de industria* for instructions from them), I gathered these observations, which you may please (as cause may be) to consider and take notice of:

1. They conceive that to do execution to purpose on the Pequots, will require not two or three days and away, but a riding by it and following of the work to and again the space of three weeks or a month, that there be a falling off and a retreat, as if you were departed, and a falling on again within three or four days, when they are returned again to their houses securely from their flight.

2. That if any pinnaces come in ken, they presently prepare for flight, women and old men and children, to a swamp some three or four miles on the back of them, a marvellous great and secure swamp, which they called Ohomowauke, which signifies owl's nest, and by another name, Cuppacommock, which signifies a refuge or hiding place, as I conceive.

3. That therefore Nayantaquit (which is Miantonomo's place of rendezvous,) to be thought on for the riding and retiring to of vessel or vessels, which place is faithful to the Narragansetts and at present enmity with the Pequots.

4. They also conceive it easy for the English, that the provisions and munitions first arrive at Aquidneck, called by us Rhode Island, at the Narragansett's mouth, and then a messenger may be despatched hither, and so to the bay, for the soldiers to march up by land to the vessels, who otherwise might spend long time about the cape and fill more vessels than needs.

5. That the assault would be in the night, when they are commonly more secure and at home, by which advantage the English, being armed, may enter the houses and do what execution they please.

6. That before the assault be given, an ambush be laid behind

them, between them and the swamp, to prevent their flight, etc.

7. That to that purpose such guides as shall be best liked of to be taken along to direct, especially two Pequots, viz.: Wequash and Wuttackquiackommin, valiant men, especially the latter, who have lived these three or four years with the Narragansetts, and know every pass and passage amongst them, who desire armor to enter their houses.

8. That it would be pleasing to all natives, that women and children be spared, etc.

9. That if there be any more land travel to Connecticut, some course would also be taken with the Wunhowatuckoogs, who are confederates with and a refuge to the Pequots.

Sir, if anything be sent to the princes, I find that Canonicus would gladly accept of a box of eight or ten pounds of sugar, and indeed he told me he would thank Mr. Governor for a box full.

Sir, you may please to take notice of a rude view, how the Pequots lie:

River Qunnihticut.

      O a fort of the Nayantaquit men, confederate with the Pequts.

Mohiganic

River.

      Wein O shauks, where   **Ohom | | | owauke,**
the swamp,

      Sasacous the chief Sachim is.   **three or four** miles from

      Mis O tick, where is Mamoho, another chief sachim.

River.

      Nayanta O quit, where is Wepiteammock and our friends.

River.

Thus, with my best salutes to your worthy selves and loving friends with you, and daily cries to the Father of mercies for a merciful issue to all these enterprises, I rest Your worship's unfeignedly respective

                            ROGER WILLIAMS

26. "Every Faithful Soldier of Christ Jesus"

On the eve of the Puritan attack on Mystic Fort, 160 Massachusetts soldiers arrived at Hartford, "where they were encouraged by the reverend ministers there." [1] Edward Johnson, to whom the Pequots were "not only men, but Devils," included this sample speech in his *Wonder-Working Providence* to illustrate what Puritan clergymen said on this occasion:[2]

Fellow soldiers, countrymen, and companions in this wilderness work, who are gathered together this day by the inevitable providence of the great Jehovah, not in a tumultuous manner hurried on by the floating fancy of every high hot-headed brain, whose actions prove abortive, or if any fruit brought forth, it hath been rape, theft, and murder, things inconsisting with nature's light, then much less with a soldier's valor; but you, my dear hearts, purposely picked out by the godly grave fathers of this government, that your prowess may carry on the work, where there justice in her righteous course is obstructed, you need not question your authority to execute those whom God, the righteous Judge of all the world, hath condemned for blaspheming His sacred majesty, and murdering His servants: every common soldier among you is now installed a magistrate; then show yourselves men of courage. I would not draw low the height of your enemies' hatred against you, and so debase your valor. This you may expect, their swelling pride hath laid the foundation of large conceptions against you and all the people of

Christ in this wilderness, even as wide as Babel's bottom but, my brave soldiers, it hath mounted already to the clouds, and therefore it is ripe for confusion; also their cruelty is famously known, yet all true-bred soldiers reserve this as a common maxim, cruelty and cowardice are unseparable companions; and in brief, there is nothing wanting on your enemies' part, that may deprive you of a complete victory, only their nimbleness of foot, and the unaccessible swamps and nut-tree woods, forth of which your small numbers may entice, and industry compel them. And now to you I put the question, who would not fight in such a cause with an agile spirit, and undaunted boldness? yet if you look for further encouragement, I have it for you; riches and honor are the next to a good cause eyed by every soldier, to maintain your own, and spoil your enemies' of theirs; although gold and silver be wanting to either of you, yet have you that to maintain which is far more precious, the lives, liberties, and new purchased freedoms, privileges, and immunities of the endeared servants of our Lord Christ Jesus, and of your second selves, even your affectionated bosom-mates, together with the chief pledges of your love, the comforting contents of harmless prattling and smiling babes; and in a word, all the riches of that goodness and mercy that attends the people of God in the enjoyment of Christ, in His ordinances, even in this life; and as for honor, David was not to be blamed for enquiring after it, as a due recompense of that true value the Lord hath bestowed on him: and now the Lord hath prepared this honor for you, oh you courageous soldiers of His, to execute vengeance upon the heathen, and correction among the people, to bind their kings in chains, and nobles in fetters of iron, that they may execute upon them the judgments that are written: this honor shall be to all His saints. But some of you may suppose death's stroke may cut you short of this: let every faithful soldier of Christ Jesus know, that the cause why some of His endeared servants are taken away by death in a just war (as this assuredly is) it is not because they should fall short of the honors accompanying such noble designs, but rather because earth's honors are too scant for them, and therefore the everlasting crown must be set upon their heads forthwith. Then march on with a cheerful Christian courage in the strength of the Lord and the power of His might, who will forthwith enclose your enemies in your hands, make their multitudes fall under your warlike weapons, and your feet shall soon be set on their proud necks.

27. "Being Bereaved of Pity"

After several months of Puritan-Pequot harassments, Connecticut Puritans declared "offensive war" against the Pequots on May 1, 1637.[1] This act contradicted the Massachusetts government's order that a defensive war only could be conducted by Connecticut against the Pequots. From the point of view of the Connecticut settlers, however, an "offensive war" would enable them to seize Pequot territory by right of conquest and undermine Massachusetts interests in their colony.[2]

Giving command to Captain John Mason, Connecticut proceeded to recruit a contingent of ninety Englishmen and some seventy Mohegans and "River Indians" under Uncas. Their major military objectives were the Pequot sachem Sassacus and his principal village, reported to have been heavily fortified, on the Pequot River. Mason and his troops set out promptly for Fort Saybrook, where Lieutenant Gardiner, upon learning of their mission, concluded "they were not fitted for such a design."[3] Nevertheless, after "five or six days" wrangling over strategy, Mason and his men departed for Narragansett Bay.[4] The military objective now had been changed to Mystic Fort, a Pequot village of less importance, because it was considered a less hazardous operation. Accompanied by five hundred Narragansett warriors, the Puritan troops began their overland journey to the Mystic River and the attack upon Mystic Fort, where the massacre of Pequot men, women, and children began at dawn on May 26, 1637. Underhill, who was Mason's second in command, describes what happened at Mystic Fort:[5]

Having embarked our soldiers, we weighed anchor at Saybrook Fort, and set sail for the Narragansett Bay, deluding the Pequots thereby, for they expected us to fall into the Pequot River; but crossing their expectation, bred in them a security. We landed our men in the Narragansett Bay, and marched overland above two days' journey before we came to Pequot. Quartering the last night's march within two miles of the place, we set forth about one of the clock in the morning, having sufficient intelligence that they knew nothing of our coming. Drawing near to the fort, [we] yielded up ourselves to God, and entreated His assistance in so weighty an enterprise. We set on our march to surround the fort; Captain John Mason, approaching to the west end, where it had an entrance to pass into it; myself marching to the south side, surrounding the fort; placing the Indians, for we had about three hundred of them, without side of our soldiers in a ring battalia, giving a volley of shot upon the fort. So remarkable it appeared to us, as we could not but admire at the providence of God in it, that soldiers so unexpert in the use of their arms, should give so complete a volley, as though the finger of God had touched both match and flint. Which volley being given at break of day, and themselves fast asleep for the most part, bred in them such a terror, that they brake forth into a most doleful cry; so as if God had not fitted the hearts of men for the service, it would have bred in them a commiseration towards them. But every man being bereaved of pity, fell upon the work without compassion, considering the blood they had shed of our native countrymen, and how barbarously they had dealt with them, and slain, first and last, about thirty persons. Having given fire, we approached near to the entrance, which they had stopped full with arms of trees, or brakes. Myself approaching to the entrance, found the work too heavy for me, to draw out all those which were strongly forced in. We gave order to one Master Hedge, and some other soldiers, to pull out those brakes. Having this done, and laid them between me and the entrance, and without order themselves, proceeded first on the south end of the fort.... Having our swords in our right hand, our carbines or muskets in our left hand, we approached the fort, Master Hedge being shot through both arms, and more wounded. Though it be not commendable for a man to make mention of anything that might tend to his own honor, yet because I would have the providence of God observed, and His name magnified, as well for myself as others, I dare not omit, but let the world know, that deliverance was given to us that command, as well as to private soldiers. Captain Mason and myself entering into the wigwams, he was shot, and received many arrows against his head-piece. God preserved him from many wounds. Myself received a shot in the left hip, through a sufficient buff coat, that if I had not been supplied with such a garment, the arrow would have pierced me. Another I received between neck and shoulders, hanging in the linen of my head-piece. Others of our soldiers were shot, some through the shoulders, some in the face, some in the head, some in the legs, Captain Mason and myself losing each of us a man, and had near twenty wounded. Most courageously these Pequots behaved themselves. But seeing the fort was too hot for us, we devised a way how we might save ourselves and prejudice them. Captain Mason entering into a wigwam, brought out a firebrand, after he had wounded many in the house. Then he set fire on the west side, where he entered; myself set fire on the south end with a train of powder. The fires of both meeting in the center of the fort, blazed most terribly, and burnt all in the space of half an hour. Many courageous fellows were unwilling to come out, and fought most desperately through the palisadoes, so as they were scorched and burnt with the very flame, and were deprived of their arms—in regard to the fire burnt their very bowstrings—and so perished valiantly. Mercy did they deserve for their valor, could we have had opportunity to have bestowed it. Many were burnt in the fort, both men, women, and children. Others forced out, and came in troops to the Indians, twenty and thirty at a time, which our soldiers received and entertained with the point of the sword. Down fell men, women, and children; those that scaped us, fell into the hands of the Indians that were in the rear of us. It is reported by themselves, that there were about four hundred souls in this fort, and not above five of them escaped out of our hands. Great and doleful was the bloody sight to the view of young soldiers that never had been in war, to see so many souls lie gasping on the ground, so thick, in some places, that you could hardly pass along. It may be demanded, Why should you be so furious? (as some have said). Should not Christians have more mercy and compassion? But I would refer you to David's war. When a people is grown to such a height of blood, and sin against God and man, and all confederates in the action, there he hath no respect to persons, but harrows them, and saws them, and puts them to the sword, and the most terriblest death that may be. Sometimes the Scripture declareth women and children must perish with their parents. Sometimes the case alters; but we will not dispute it now. We have sufficient light from the Word of God for our proceedings.

28. "So Miraculously Did the Lord Preserve Them"

Pequot casualties at Mystic Fort, according to estimates, ranged from three hundred to seven hundred. So brutal was the plan of attack that when the Narragansetts learned of it, they withdrew from Mason's forces.[1] Now that the fight at Mystic was over, the Pequots were totally decimated and demoralized. Sassacus, the principal sachem of the Pequots, was held responsible for his people's devastating defeat, and only the intercession of his councilors prevented his execution at the hands of his own people. Flight offered the only hope for Pequot safety as their tribespeople were being rounded up by the English virtually everywhere in Pequot country. Sassacus and others who had escaped capture headed for the swamps, with the English in hot pursuit. When a Pequot captive told the English that Sassacus and other fugitives were in hiding at a "hideous swamp" near Quinnipiac (later New Haven), the Puritan soldiers cornered the Indians once more.[2]

On July 14, 1637, shortly before dawn, the Pequots attempted to flee the swamp. Again they were overwhelmed, though Sassacus had already made his escape. Massachusetts Governor John Winthrop describes the swamp fight to William Bradford in a letter dated July 28, 1637:[3]

WORTHY SIR: I received your loving letter and am much provoked to express my affections toward you, but straitness of time forbids me. For my desire is to acquaint you with the Lord's great mercies towards us in our prevailing against His and our enemies, that you may rejoice and praise His name with us. About eighty of our men, having coasted along towards the Dutch Plantation (sometimes by water but most by land) met here and there with some Pequots whom they slew or took prisoners. Two sachems they took and beheaded and not hearing of Sassacus, the chief sachem, they gave a prisoner his life to go and find him out. He went and brought them word where he was; but Sassacus, suspecting him to be a spy, after he was gone, fled away with some twenty more to the Mohawks; so our men missed of him. Yet dividing themselves and ranging up and down as the providence of God guided them (for the Indians were all gone save three or four and they knew not whither to guide them or else would not) upon the 13th of this month they light upon a great company of them; viz. 80 strong men and 200 women and children in a small Indian town fast by a hideous swamp, which they all slipped into before our men could get to them. Our captains were not then come together, but there was Mr. [Roger] Ludlow and Captain Mason, with some ten of their men, and Captain [Daniel] Patrick with some twenty or more of his, who, shooting at the Indians, Captain [William] Trask with fifty more came soon in at the noise. Then they gave order to surround the swamp, it being about a mile long. But Lieutenant [Richard] Davenport and some twelve more, not hearing that command, fell into the swamp among the Indians. The swamp was so thick with shrubwood and so boggy withal that some of them stuck fast and received many shot. Lieutenant Davenport was dangerously wounded about his armhole, and another shot in the head, so as, fainting, they were in great danger to have been taken by the Indians. But Sergeant [Edward] Riggs and [Thomas] Jeffery and two or three more rescued them and slew divers of the Indians with their swords.

After they were drawn out, the Indians desired parley and were offered by Thomas Stanton, our interpreter, that if they would come out and yield themselves, they should have their lives, all that had not their hands in the English blood; whereupon the sachem of the place came forth, and an old man or two and their wives and children, and after that some other women and children. And so they spake two hours, till it was night. Then Thomas Stanton was sent into them again, to call them forth; but they said they would sell their lives there, and so shot at him so thick as if he had not cried out and been presently rescued, they had slain him. Then our men cut off a place of the swamp with their swords, and cooped the Indians into so narrow a compass as they could easier kill them through the thickets. So they continued all the night, standing about twelve foot one from another, and the Indians, coming close up to our men, shot their arrows so thick as they pierced their hat brims and their sleeves and stockings and other parts of their clothes. Yet so miraculously did the Lord preserve them, as not one of them was wounded, save those three who rashly went into the swamp. When it was near day, it grew very dark, so as those of them which were left dropped away between our men, though they stood but twelve or fourteen foot asunder; but were presently discovered and some killed in the pursuit.

Upon searching of the swamp the next morning, they found nine slain, and some they pulled up, whom the Indians had buried in the mire; so as they think that of all this company not twenty did escape, for they after found some who died in their flight of their wounds received. The prisoners were divided, some to those of the River, and the rest to us; to these we sent the male children to Bermuda, by Mr. William Pierce, and the women and maid children are disposed about in the towns. There have been now slain and taken in all, about 700. The rest are dispersed; and the Indians in all quarters so terrified as all their friends are afraid to receive them. Two of the sachems of Long Island came to Mr. [Israel] Stroughton and tendered themselves to be tributaries under our protection. And two of the Nipmuck sachems have been with me to seek our friendship. Among the prisoners we have the wife and children of Mononoto, a woman of a very modest countenance and behavior. It was by her mediation that the two English maids were spared from death, and were kindly used by her; so that I have taken charge of her. One of her first requests was that the English would not abuse her body, and that her children might not be taken from her. Those which were wounded were fetched off soon by John Gallup, who came with his shallop in a happy hour, to bring them victuals, and to carry their wounded men to the pinnace where our chief surgeon was, with Mr. [Rev. John] Wilson, being about eight leagues off. Our people are all in health (the Lord be praised) and although they had marched in their arms all the day and had been in fight all the night, yet they professed they found themselves so fresh as they could willingly have gone to such another business.

This is the substance of that which I received, though I am forced to omit many considerable circumstances. So, being in much straitness of time (the ships being to depart within this four days, and in them the Lord Lee and Mr. Vane) I here break off; and with hearty salutes to, etc., I rest

Yours assured,
JOHN WINTHROP

The 28th of the 5th month, 1637 [4]

The captains report we have slain 13 sachems, but Sassacus and Mononoto are yet living.

Chapter IV

"Hiring Them to Hear Sermons"

Christianizing the Indians

Even before they embarked upon their voyage to New England in 1630, the Puritans had plans for the Indians. They would convert the natives to Christianity as "the work tending to the enlargement of the Kingdom of Jesus Christ." [1] Undoubtedly, the Puritans also saw their projected mission as the planting of "outposts of Protestantism against the Jesuits in Canada." [2] But to John Eliot of Roxbury, who was to become known as the "Apostle to the Indians," the conversion of the red men to Puritan Christianity had even greater ramifications; he believed their turning to the Puritan God was directly related to the advent of the millennium. Eliot was a Fifth Monarchy man and expected glory to be his reward for missionary work among the Indians, which would hasten the coming of Christ's Kingdom on earth and the reign of the saints for a thousand years. (Christ's Kingdom was sometimes called the Fifth Monarchy, being successor to the Assyrian, Babylonian, Persian, and Greek and Roman monarchies.)

In the 1650s, a group of prominent clergymen of Old England held that, according to biblical prophecy, Gentile conversions would both precede and follow the conversion of the Jews to Christianity, and this was the prerequisite for the millennium. Some leading Puritans projected this viewpoint in a public letter published in 1652:

...the Scripture speaks of a *double conversion* of the Gentiles, the first before the conversion of the *Jews,* they being *branches, wild by nature,* grafted into the *true olive tree* instead of the *natural branches,* which are broken off. This fullness of the *Gentiles* shall come in before the conversion of the *Jews,* and till then *blindness hath happened unto Israel, Rom.* 11. 25. The second, after the conversion of the *Jews,* as appears in *Act.* 15, 16, 17. *After this I will return and will build again the Tabernacle of David, which is fallen down, and I will build again the ruins thereof, and I will set it up; that the residue of men might seek after the Lord, and all the Gentiles upon whom my name is called, saith the Lord.* Hence it appears that there are some *Gentiles,* upon whom the Lord's name is called, that are a people to Him, even whilst the *Tabernacle of David* lies in its ruins; and when He hath built again this *Tabernacle of David,* that there are a residue of men, the remainder of the *Gentiles* that shall enquire after the Lord, and worship Him, together with those Gentiles that were formerly converted, and upon whom His name was called. The first conversion of the *Gentiles* in *its fullness* makes way for the coming in of the *Jews,* the *King of the East,* therefore to see this work go on, should cause the people of God to lift up their heads, and expect that the time of the fulfilling that promise is near.[3]

In the same decade, eminent rabbis were having prophetic visions of the coming of the Messiah, and Cromwell was negotiating the return of the Jews to England, where they were surely expected to respond to a revivalist gospel. These developments heightened Eliot's zeal and Edward Johnson exclaimed: "Oh! ye the ancient beloved of Christ ... look here, behind Him whom you have pierced, preparing to pierce your hearts with His *wonder-working providence.*"[4]

As Eliot moved among the natives, he—and other clergymen and intellectuals on both sides of the Atlantic—sought to discover the origin of the Indians and study their customs and habits. The Puritan knew what it was like to live in a land of sin. He had experienced it in Old England, where he was powerless to do anything about it without incurring the wrath of the king or Bishop Laud. It was to escape from that sinful environment—from that sinful government—that the Puritan came to New England, where he could have freedom to practice his religion and to build another

Canaan for the world to emulate. But to live alongside sin in New England—to live alongside the Indian, whom the Puritan considered the corrupt natural man—aroused Puritan apprehensions even as he sought to determine the meaning and significance of the red man. Several theories were current concerning "the original of the savages" in New England, and Daniel Gookin, who served as the first superintendent of all the Indians subservient to the Government of Massachusetts, recorded them. One view was that the Indians were descended from the Tartars or Scythians of northern Asia. Another conjecture was that they were descended from the Moors of Africa. But the prevailing contention at the time was that the Indians were descended from the ten lost tribes of Israel "and that God hath, by some means or other, not yet discovered, brought them into America ... and hath reduced them into such woeful blindness and barbarism, as all these Americans are in." [5] Word from Rabbi Menasseh ben Israel, a famed Jewish scholar living in Amsterdam, that the ten tribes of Israel were definitely transported to America gave even greater impetus to Eliot's determination to save the souls of the Indians. For if the Indians were indeed Jews, their conversion to Puritan Christianity would unquestionably hasten still more the appearance of "Christ's temporal Kingdom here on earth." [6]

Coupled with Puritan interest in the Indians' antecedents was an equally intense curiosity about the red man's religion. This by no means presupposed an interest in cultural relativism or what we now understand as comparative religion. Puritans and other Englishmen sought to interpret the religious mores of the Indians in terms of Christian theology and ritual. They were not equipped to understand the Indian's animistic approach to religion and must have been perplexed by the native's inquiry: "Why have not beasts a soul as man hath, seeing they have love, anger, &c. as man hath?" [7] The Puritan looked for Christian counterparts in Indian religion, and, although they were not present, he insisted upon interpreting what he found in these terms. Hence the Englishman's confusion over the status and function of the native powwow and the comparison of Kiehtan and Hobomok with Jehovah and Satan.[8]

The powwow or medicine man enjoyed great prestige among the Algonquian tribes of southern New England. An intimate of Hobomok, he was both feared and respected as a supernatural being with great powers to preserve and destroy life. He was therefore considered by the Puritans to be in league with the Devil. His principal function was to heal the wounded and cure the sick by invoking the aid of Hobomok, who appeared primarily to the powwow and pnieses, "men of great courage and wisdom." To them Hobomok showed himself "in sundry forms ... as in the shape of a man, a deer, a fawn, an eagle, &c. but most ordinarily a snake." [9] The powwow's power with the supernatural often provided him with a power equal to the political authority of the sachem.[10]

When the powwow succeeded in curing a patient, it was due to the intercession of Hobomok. On the other hand, if the illness was incurable, the powwow blamed it on Kiehtan, the greatest of Indian gods, who created heaven and earth and "all creatures therein." For it was a sign that Kiehtan "is angry" and sends an illness to the Indians that "none can cure." [11]

By 1623, when Edward Winslow wrote about their religion, the Indians' attitude to Kiehtan had begun to cool. Apparently, Hobomok satisfied the needs of the Indians more than Kiehtan. And yet, they believed, in Roger Williams's words, "that the souls of men and women go to the southwest, their great and good men and women to *Cautantouwit* [another name for Kiehtan] His house, where they have hopes (as the Turks have of carnal joys): murderers, thieves and liars, their souls (say they) wander restless abroad." [12]

But Kiehtan and Hobomok were not the only gods the Indians worshipped. Williams advised John Winthrop that the Narragansetts "have plenty of gods or divine powers: the sun, moon, fire, water, snow, earth, the deer, the bear, etc. are divine powers." He reported that he had recorded the names of thirty-eight Indian gods worshipped by the Narragansetts of Rhode Island.[13] And Thomas Mayhew, Jr., the Puritan missionary at Martha's Vineyard, wrote that the Indians there worshipped thirty-seven dieties.[14]

Eliot began his missionary activities among the Indians in 1646. And while Puritan publicists proclaimed him the leader of this movement, he was in fact preceded in this work three years earlier by young Thomas Mayhew in Martha's Vineyard, where he and his father had settled among some three thousand Wampanoags. The Christianizing process there actually was initiated by an Indian,

Hiacoomes, who requested young Mayhew to provide him with Christian indoctrination. Mayhew acceded, and Hiacoomes seems to have undergone a true religious experience. Eventually the effort of the Mayhews and Hiacoomes to propagate the Gospel among the Indians of Martha's Vineyard and Nantucket was by far the most successful of its kind in New England. In 1652, the younger Mayhew was responsible for some 282 Indians at Martha's Vineyard entering into a covenant; seven years later, after his son's death, Thomas Mayhew, Sr., established the first Indian church there.

The Mayhews and Richard Bourne, of New Plymouth, consistently outdid Eliot at every turn; ultimately, Eliot was constrained to admit that the results of his gospelizing had been disappointing. And Gookin noted that the "praying Indians" in Massachusetts had "not yet come so far as to be able or willing to profess their faith in Christ and yield obedience and subjection to Him or His church." [15] But the Mayhews and Bourne never were able to equal the kind of financing Eliot obtained from Old England. Perhaps the fact that Eliot did not hesitate to claim credit for their achievements by implying that he was guiding the total missionary program in New England was largely responsible for their failure to receive significant funding.[16]

For the Puritans, conversion to Christianity was a different matter from the Catholic and orthodox Anglican conversion. No Puritan divine would ever agree that conversion could be accomplished merely by a declaration of faith or a use of sacraments. Puritanism required full church membership. To achieve this, it would be imperative for the Indian—at the very least—to have a recognized conversion experience and a thorough knowledge of the Bible and the Puritan creed.

Until 1663, when Eliot published his Bible in the Algonquian tongue, the most obvious way the Indian could gain a knowledge of the Scriptures and of Puritanism was to learn English. The only alternative was to secure a Puritan clergyman who could speak Algonquian and was willing to embark upon the arduous mission of instructing the Indians in the ways of the Puritan God; but before 1640, Roger Williams was the only Protestant minister able to converse with the Indians in their own language, and he refused to proselytize them. He declared:

...for our *New England* parts, I can speak uprightly and confidently, *I* know it to have been easy for myself, long ere this [1645], to have brought many thousands of these natives, than ever was yet heard of in *America*.... I could have brought the whole country to have observed one day in seven.... Let none wonder at this, for *plausible persuasions* in the mouths of those whom natural men esteem and love: for the power of prevailing forces and armies hath done this in all the *nations* (as men speak) of Christendom.[17]

Any attempt to convert the Indians was against his religious convictions. He believed that only God could "turn a soul from its idols, both of heart, worship, and conversation, before it is capable of worship, to the true and living God." [18]

Nonetheless, as the Puritan clergy in the Bay Colony viewed the situation, there was still another requirement before the Christianization of the Indians could receive Puritan certification. Religious conversion had to be coupled with social conversion. Even if the Indian succeeded in mastering the Bible and the Puritan creed, he would be a long way from full church membership unless his lifestyle conformed to that prescribed by the Puritan God. The natives would have to be converted to Puritan civilization before they could be converted to Puritan Christianity or, at least, both conversions would have to proceed simultaneously. This would be a difficult undertaking, the success of which, many Puritans felt, would be highly doubtful. Furthermore, was it not reasonable to expect that any such program would arouse resentment among many of the English settlers as being "too costly an enterprise for *New England*, that hath expended itself so far in laying the foundation of a commonweal in this wilderness"? [19] Even when Indians wanted to submit to Christianity, they were rarely received into the Puritan church.

Of course there were Indians who were anxious to follow the English God as soon as the Puritan divines began the work of conversion. Some sought to have their children "trained up among the English ... because they would grow rude and wicked at home, and would never come to know God, which they hoped they should do if they were constantly among the English." [20] Others wanted to know what "earthly riches" they would receive for converting to Christianity, and these natives, the elder Mayhew testifies, "have strongly stood for their own meetings, ways and customs, being in their account more profitable than ours, wherein they meet with nothing but talking and praying." [21]

In Massachusetts things were different. Unlike the Mayhew approach in Martha's Vineyard and Nantucket, the Bay Colony government did not wait for Indians to volunteer to become Christians. There, the General Court enacted laws to coerce the Indians into embracing the Puritan God and exploited any Indian dissatisfaction with native institutions and society.[22] And although Eliot believed that he had it in his power to confer upon the red man the greatest gift on earth, namely Christianity, and could not understand why all the Indians did not hasten to embrace the Puritan God and Christ Jesus, he had to make compromises to win converts, as Crown Commissioner George Cartwright reported:

> They convert Indians by hiring them to hear sermons, by teaching them not to obey their heathen princes, & by appointing rulers amongst them over tens, fifties, &c. Those whom they say are converted cannot be distinguished by their lives, manners, or habits from those who are not.[23]

Eliot later verified Cartwright's charge in a communication to the New England Company, in which he admitted that "God put into the heart of the church to send some of their brethren to sundry parts of the country, to call in their countrymen to pray unto God. I foresaw this would be chargeable." Then he added: "Captain Gookin will inform you of some charges in powder and shot for their necessary defences in these times of danger." [24] Eliot's armed "messengers and instruments," who looked "for their pay," were indeed in different parts of the Bay Colony to "teach them [the Nipmucks] the fear of the Lord." [25] So heavily did Eliot count upon the success of his ambassadors that he informed the New England Company that their operations must move forward or "the whole ... will quickly stand still." [26] In 1675, the Nipmucks showed their appreciation of the Gospel by becoming Metacom's first allies in his ill-fated war against the English. And every other "praying town" in the Bay Colony eventually provided some warriors for Metacom.[27]

The missionaries were always quick to declare publicly that they had no motive in converting the natives to Puritan Christianity other than to save Indian souls. Nevertheless, the civil authorities were not averse to exploiting the divisiveness that the Christianization process and intertribal animosities and feuds created among the Indians, since of course these increased the white man's security.

There was no escape for the Indians, who had become deeply conscious of the fact that whenever their life-style conflicted with the ways of the English, the white man's civilization would dominate the red man. Even if they left New England and went west beyond the Hudson, they would only encounter their enemies, the Mohawks. They were caught in the middle between hostile Iroquois power and "the aggressive forces of an expanding English civilization." [28]

Ultimately, the Puritans made no distinction between Christian and heathen Indians during King Philip's War. Both were looked upon with scorn and regarded as treacherous. Metacom had intended the destruction of the white man through this war, but, ironically, it was a major cause of the red man's demise in New England. The Indian "praying towns" were reduced from fourteen to four and the number of "praying Indians" was drastically diminished. By the end of the seventeenth century Eliot was dead, the remaining "praying towns" were being absorbed by the English and incorporated as English towns, and the Indians were beginning to move away to New York and Canada.

29. "Their Gods Made Them"

In 1643, while en route to England to seek a patent that would bring Providence, Portsmouth, and Newport under one colonial government, independent of the Massachusetts Bay Colony, Roger Williams wrote *A Key into the Language of America.* That September, Gregory Dexter displayed it in his London bookshop, and Williams won acclaim as a scholar, Indian linguist, and authority on the morals, religion, and manners of the New England natives. Not only did this work demonstrate to the English Parliament and important religious leaders that he was more interested in the Indian than the Massachusetts Puritans, but also the Warwick Commission granted him the patent he sought. And twelve prominent members of Parliament sent him home with a letter to Massachusetts leaders hailing him as a man "of great industry and travail in his printed Indian labors in your parts, the like whereof we have not seen extant from any part in America." [1]

Williams, who began to study Indian culture shortly after his arrival in the Bay Colony in 1631, and lived among the Narragansetts following his banishment from Massachusetts in 1635, recorded this about their religion:[2]

...He that questions whether God made the world, the *Indians* will teach him. I must acknowledge I have received in my converse with them many confirmations of those two great points, *Heb.* 11. 6. *viz:*

1. That God is.
2. That He is a rewarder of all them that diligently seek Him. They will generally confess that God made all: but then in special, although they deny not that *Englishman's* God made *English* men,

and the heavens and earth there! Yet their gods made them and the heaven, and earth where they dwell.

...I have heard a poor *Indian* lamenting the loss of a child at break of day, call up his wife and children, and all about him to lamentation, and with abundance of tears cry out! O God thou hast taken away my child! Thou art angry with me: O turn thine anger from me, and spare the rest of my children.

If they receive any good in hunting, fishing, harvest &c. they acknowledge God in it.

Yea, if it be but an ordinary accident, a fall, &c. they will say God was angry and did it, *musquántum manit,* God is angry. But herein is their misery.

First, they branch their God-head into many gods.

Secondly, attribute it to creatures.

First, many gods: they have given me the names of thirty-seven, which I have, all which in their solemn worships they invocate: as *Kautántowwit* [Kiehtan], the great *Southwest* God, to ... whose house all souls go, and from whom came their corn, beans, as they say.

...I was once with a native dying of a wound, given him by some murderous *English* ... who robbed him and run him through with a rapier, from whom in the heat of his wound, he at present escaped from them, but dying of his wound, they suffered death at New Plymouth, in *New England,* this *native* dying called much upon *Muckquachuckquànd,* which of other natives I understood (as they believed) had appeared to the dying young man, many years before, and bid him whenever he was in distress [to] call upon him.

Secondly, as they have many of these feigned dieties: so worship they the creatures in whom they conceive doth rest some deity....

When I have argued with them about their Fire-God: can it, say they, be, but this fire must be a god, or divine power, that out of a stone will arise a spark, and when a poor naked *Indian* is ready to starve with cold in the house, and especially in the woods, often saves his life, doth dress all our food for us, and if it be angry will burn the house about us, yea if a spark fall into the dry wood, burns up the country, (though this burning of the wood to them they count a benefit both for destroying vermin, and keeping down the weeds and thickets?)....

Besides there is a general custom amongst them, at the apprehension of any excellency in men, women, birds, beasts, fish, &c. to cry out *Manittôo,* that is, it is a god, as thus if they see one man excel others in wisdom, valor, strength, activity &c. they cry out *Manittôo,* a god: and therefore when they talk amongst themselves of the *English* ships, and great buildings, of the plowing of their fields, and especially of books and letters, they will end thus: *Manittôwock,* they are gods: *Cummanittôo,* you are a god, &c. A strong conviction natural in the soul of man, that God is; filling all things, and places, and that all excellencies dwell in God, and proceed from Him, and that they only are blessed who have that Jehovah their portion. . . .

Of this feast [or dance] they have public, and private and that of two sorts.

First, in sickness, or drought, or war, or famine.

Secondly, after harvest, after hunting, when they enjoy a calm of peace, health, plenty, prosperity, then *Nickòmmo,* a feast, especially in winter, for then (as the Turk saith of the Christian, rather the Antichristian,) they run mad once a year in their kind of Christmas feasting. . . .

These [the powwows] do begin and order their service, and invocation of their gods, and all the people follow, and join interchangeably in a laborious bodily service, unto sweating, especially of the priest, who spends himself in strange antic gestures, and actions even unto fainting.

In sickness, the priest comes close to the sick person, and performs many strange actions about him, and threatens and conjures out the sickness. They [the natives] conceive that there are many gods or divine powers within the body of a man: in his pulse, his heart, his lungs, &c.

I confess to have most of these, their customs, by their own relation, for after once being in their houses and beholding what their worship was, I durst never be an eyewitness, spectator, or looker-on, lest I should have been partaker of Satan's inventions and worships, contrary to *Ephes.* 5. 14. . . .

They have an exact form of king, priest, and prophet, as was in Israel, typical of old in that Holy Land of *Canaan,* and as the Lord *Jesus* ordained in His spiritual Land of *Canaan* His church throughout the whole world: their kings or governors, called *Sachimaüog,* king, and *Atauskowaũg,* rulers do govern: their priests, perform and manage their worship: their wise men and old men, of which number the priests are also, ... whom they call *Taupowaüog.* They make solemn speeches and orations, or lectures to them, concerning religion, peace, or war, and all things. ...

He or she that makes this *Nickòmmo* feast or dance, besides the feasting of sometimes twenty, fifty, an hundred, yea I have seen near a thousand persons at one of these feasts ... they give, I say, a great quantity of money, and all sort of their goods (according to and sometimes beyond their estate) in several small parcels of goods, or money, to the value of eighteen pence, two shillings, or thereabouts, to one person: and that person that receives this gift, upon the receiving of it, goes out, and hollers thrice for the health and prosperity of the party that gave it, the Mr. or Mistress of the feast. ...

By this feasting and gifts, the Devil thrives on their worships pleasantly (as he doth all false worships, by such plausible earthly arguments of uniformities, universalities, antiquities, immunities, dignities, rewards, unto submitters, and the contrary to refusers) so that they run far and near and ask ... [Who makes a feast?]

They have a modest religious persuasion not to disturb any man, either themselves, *English, Dutch,* or any in their conscience, and worship. ...

[Their word for the soul is d]erived from *Cowwene,* to sleep, because say they, it works and operates when the body sleeps. *Michachunck* [is] the soul, in a higher notion, which is of affinity, with a word signifying a looking glass, or clear resemblance, so that it hath its name from a clear sight or discerning, which indeed seems very well to suit with the nature of it. ...

After I had (as far as my language would reach) discoursed (upon a time) before the chief *sachem* or *prince* of the country, with his *archpriests,* and many other in a full assembly; and being night, wearied with travel and discourse, I lay down to rest; and before I slept, I heard this passage:

A *Connecticut* Indian (who had heard our discourse) told the *sachem Miantonomo,* that souls went up to heaven, or downward to hell; for, saith he, our fathers have told us, that our souls go to the *Southwest.*

The *sachem* answered, But how do you know yourself, that your souls go to the *Southwest;* did you ever see a soul go thither?

The native replied; when did he (naming myself) see a soul go to heaven or hell?

The *sachem* again replied: He hath books and writings, and one which God himself made, concerning men's souls, and therefore may well know more than we that have none, but take all upon trust from our forefathers. . . .

30. "We Have Nothing to Do to Censure Indians"

John Cotton published his book, *The Way of Congregational Churches Cleared,* in 1648, as a defense against the Reverend Robert Baillie's charge that Massachusetts Puritans were theological Separatists.[1] Baillie, a major spokesman for the Presbyterian forces in England, also asserted that "of all that ever crossed the American seas," the New England Puritans "are noted as most neglectful of the work of conversion."[2] Cotton defended his career as a non-Separatist minister of the Gospel and credited the Bay Colony with saving the lives of Massachusets Indians following the devastating epidemic that swept the region after the Puritans settled there. He missed no opportunity to criticize Roger Williams—with whom he was engaged in a long-standing debate—for failing to Christianize the natives. Here is Cotton's statement:[3]

. . . there is no principle or allowed practise of ours that doth hinder (much less exceedingly hinder) the work or hope of the conversion of the natives: though we profess we have nothing to do to censure Indians, and so to judge them that are without; yet we think it a principal (though not the only) work and duty of our ministry to attend the work of conversion, both of carnal English, and other nations, whether Christian, or pagan. . . .

I will not speak, what opportunity of reaching forth a blessing to the Indians in this kind, God hath lately begun to open us a door of: in that divers of their sachems, and sagamores, (as they call them, to wit, their governors) have submitted themselves to the government of the English, and have willingly subjected themselves to the acceptance of the Ten Commandments, though some of them do most stick at the Seventh Commandment, as it forbiddeth polygamy. Nevertheless, otherwise they willingly consent to abandon adultery and fornication, and unnatural lusts.

But though the Indians have been slow to learn our language, especially in matters of religion (howsoever in trading they soon understood us) yet we have often offered to bring up their Indian children in our schools, that they might learn to speak to their countrymen in their own language. But because that might prove long, one of our elders (Mr. [John] Eliot, the teacher of the church of Roxbury) hath (with the consent of the natives) preached to them first by an interpreter, but since having with much industry learned their language, he now preacheth to two congregations of them in their own language weekly. One week on the fourth day to one congregation, who sit down near Dorchester Mill, and another week, on the sixth day, to another congregation of them, who sit down in Cambridge, near Watertown Mill. To ease and encourage him in his work, the ministers of neighbor churches take off by turns his weekly lecture on the third day. The fruit hitherto hath been, the Indians resort more and more to these assemblies, bear with reverence and attention, reform (and make laws amongst themselves, for reformation of) sundry abuses, ask sundry questions for their instruction, and among the rest, an old counsellor of one of their sagamores enquired if it might be possible that our God, and our Christ should accept an old sinner such as himself? Mr. Eliot answered him, yes, there was hope, because he never had the means of the knowledge of God offered to him before. And our Savior Christ did sometimes call into His vineyard some to do Him service, even in the last hours of the day, in the last part of their lives. And the old Indian being demanded if he understood this? He answered, yea, saith he, I understand it, and believe it. . . .

. . . Mr. [Roger] Williams his speech doth not so much hold forth the facility of the Indians to any such conversion, as might fit them for church estate, but rather the hypocrisy and formality of the ordinary church members of national churches; which he professeth is so far off from true conversion, that it is the subversion of the souls of many millions in Christendom, from one false worship to another.

It is no unhappiness of any principle of ours, that hath kept Mr. Williams from making use of his great opportunity, and open door, to propagate the Gospel amongst the Indians. For though their facility to such a carnal conversion, as he describeth, gave him no just warrant, to gather them into a church estate: yet it was a just encouragement to provoke him (who understood their language) to have preached the Word of God unto them, which might have been mighty through God (if sincerely dispensed) to have turned them from darkness to light, from the power of Satan unto God, and so have prepared them, both for church fellowship here, and for heaven hereafter.

But if Mr. [Robert] Baillie conceive that either Mr. Williams, or else we were to be blamed, because we do not presently receive Indians into the fellowship of our churches, seeing their facility to conform their outward man to us, and to so much of our religion, as Mr. Williams mentioned: he shall do well to consider beforehand, whether Jacob's children did well to persuade the Schechemites, Gen. XXXIV, to receive circumcision, before they better understood the covenant of Abraham (to which circumcision was a seal) and had made some better profession of taking hold of it.

31. "Preventing the Dishonor ... of the Most High God"

In 1647, one year after Massachusetts launched its missionary effort, John Eliot recorded—with what must have been some embarrassment—a question put to him by Wabbakoxets, reputed to have been an old powwow:

> ... seeing the English had been 27 years (some of them) in this land, why did we never teach them to know God till now? Had you done it sooner, said he, we might have known much of God by this time, and much sin might have been prevented, but now some of us are grown old in sin, &c. ....[1]

Eliot's response, as he wrote it down, was "that we do repent that we did not long ago, as now we do, yet withal we told them, that they were never willing to hear till now, and that seeing God hath bowed their hearts to be willing to hear, we are desirous to take all the pains we can now to teach them." [2]

The fact of the matter is that the Massachusetts Bay Colony dragged its feet when it came to a missionary effort to convert the Indians, though, officially, conversion by example was a major purpose of the Puritan settlement. In Old England, the Bay Colony was being subjected to mounting criticism, as typified by Thomas Lechford: "They have nothing to excuse themselves in this point of not laboring with the Indians to instruct them but their want of a staple trade, and other businesses taking them up." [3] Suddenly, on November 4, 1646, the General Court took several actions. It passed a law against blasphemy, which governed the Indians; forbade Indian worship of their "false gods"; and committed the colony—rather than individual churches—to proselytizing the natives.[4]

A. Against Blasphemy of the Name of God

Albeit faith be not wrought by the sword, but by the Word, & therefore such pagan Indians as have submitted themselves to our government, though we would not neglect any due helps to bring them on to grace, & to the means of it, yet we compel them not to the Christian faith, nor to the profession of it, either by force of arms or by penal laws; nevertheless, seeing the blaspheming of the true God cannot be excused by any ignorance or infirmity of human nature, the eternal power & Godhead being known by the light of nature & the creation of the world, & common reason requireth every state & society of men to be more careful of preventing the dishonor & contempt of the most high God (in whom we all consist) than of any mortal princes & magistrates, it is therefore ordered & decreed, by this Court, for the honor of the eternal God, whom only we worship & serve, that no person within the jurisdiction, whether Christian or pagan, either by wilfull or obstinate denying the true God, or His creation or government of the world, or shall curse God, or reproach the holy religion of God, as if it were but a politic device to keep ignorant men in awe, nor shall utter any other eminent kind of blasphemy, of the like nature & degree; if any person or persons whatsoever, within our jurisdiction, shall break this law they shall be put to death.

[Immediately after the passage of the law against blasphemy, the General Court approved the following:]

It is ordered & decreed by this Court, that no Indian shall at any time powwow, or perform outward worship to their false gods, or to the Devil, in any of our jurisdiction, whether they be such as dwell here, or shall come hither. If any shall transgress this law, the powwower shall pay 5 shillings, the procurer 5 shillings, & every assistant countenancing, by his presence or otherwise, (being of age of discretion) 20 shillings.

B. Indians to Be Instructed in Our Laws and in Religion

Considering that one end in planting these parts was to propagate the true religion unto the Indians, & that divers of them are become subjects to the English, & have engaged themselves to be willing & ready to understand the law of God, it is therefore ordered & decreed, that the necessary & wholesome laws which may be made to reduce them to civility of life shall be once in the year (if the times be safe) made known to them by such fit persons as the Court shall nominate, having the help of some able interpreter with them. Considering, also, that interpretation of tongues is an appointment of God for propagating the truth, & may therefore have a blessed success in the hearts of others in due season, it is therefore further ordered & decreed, that two ministers shall be chosen by the elders of the churches every year, at the Court of Election, & so to be sent, with the consent of their churches, (with whomsoever will freely offer themselves to accompany them in that service,) to make known the heavenly counsel of God among the Indians in most familiar manner, by the help of some able interpreter, as may be most available to bring them to the knowledge of the truth, & their conversion to Jesus Christ; & for the end, that something may be allowed them by the General Court to give away freely unto those Indians whom they shall perceive most willing & ready to be instructed by them.

32. "Such Dry and Rocky Ground"

As he began his missionary effort, John Eliot felt constrained to defend in detail the Massachusetts Bay Colony against charges arising from its delay in Christianizing the Indians. His defense appeared just prior to the popularization of the idea in Europe that Gentiles would precede Jews into Christ's kingdom, a development that greatly encouraged Eliot's efforts:[1]

We are oft upbraided by some of our countrymen that so little good is done by our professing planters upon the hearts of natives; such men have surely more spleen than judgement, and know not the vast distance of natives from common civility, almost humanity itself, and 'tis as if they should reproach us for not making the winds to blow when we list ourselves, it must certainly be a spirit of life from God (not in man's power) which must put flesh and sinews unto these dry bones: if we would force them to baptism (as the Spaniards do about Cusco, Peru, and Mexico, having learnt them a short answer or two to some Popish questions) or if we would hire them to it by giving them coats and shirts, to allure them to it (as some others have done) we could have gathered many hundreds, yea thousands it may be by this time, into the name of churches; but we have not learnt as yet that art of coining Christians, or putting Christ's name and image upon copper mettle. Although I think we have much cause to be humbled that we have not endeavored more than we have done [for] their conversion and peace with God, who enjoy the mercy and peace of God in their land. Three things have made us think (as they once did of building the Temple) it is not yet time for God to work, 1. Because till the Jews come in, there is a seal set upon the hearts of those people, as they think from some apocalyptical places. 2. That as in nature there is no progress *ab extremo ad extremum nisi per media,* so in religion such as are so extremely degenerate, must be brought to some civility before religion can prosper, or the word take place. 3. Because we want miraculous and extraordinary gifts without which no conversion can be expected amongst these; but methinks now that it is with the Indians as it was with our New English ground when we first came over, there was scarce any man that could believe that English grain would grow, or that the plow could do any good in this woody and rocky soil. And thus they continued in this supine unbelief for some years, till experience taught them otherwise, and now all see it to be scarce inferior to Old English tillage, but bears very good burdens; so we have thought of our Indian people, and therefore have been discouraged to put plow to such dry and rocky ground, but God having begun thus with some few it may be they are better soil for the Gospel and we can think: I confess I think no great good will be done till they be more civilized, but why may not God begin with some few, to awaken others by degrees? Nor do I expect any great good will be wrought by the English (leaving secrets to God) (although the English surely begin and lay the first stones of Christ's Kingdom and Temple amongst them) because God is wont ordinarily to convert nations and peoples by some of their own countrymen who are nearest to them, and can best speak, and most of all pity their brethren and countrymen, but yet if the least beginnings be made by the conversion of two or three, it's worth all our time and travail, and cause of much thankfulness for such seeds, although no great harvests should immediately appear; surely this is evident, first that they never heard heartbreaking prayer and preaching before now in their own tongue, that we know of, secondly, that there were never such hopes of a dawning of mercy toward them as now, certainly those abundant tears which we saw shed from their eyes, argue a mighty and blessed presence of the spirit of heaven in their hearts, which when once it comes into such kind of spirits will not easily [come] out again.

33. "In a Searching Condition"

As Indians were being taught to pray to God and talked to their families and fellow tribesmen about Him and Jesus Christ, they wrestled with such questions as: "If but one parent believe, what state are our children in?" [1] *"How is the spirit of God in us? And where is it principally present?"* *"How shall I know when God accepts my prayers?"* [2] Another question went this way:

> ... What is the reason, that when a strange Indian comes among us whom we never saw before, *yet if he pray unto God, we do exceedingly love him: but if my own brother, dwelling a great way off, come unto us, he not praying to God, though we love him, yet nothing so as we love that other stranger who doth pray unto God.* [3]

And, of course, there also were queries like "Whether English men were ever at any time so ignorant of God and Jesus Christ as themselves?" and, after listening to Eliot relate the story of Noah, "How all the world is become so full of people, if they were all once drowned in the Flood?" [4]

Eliot publicized the questions raised by the Indians as evidence of Indian intelligence and faith and as an aid to his fund-raising efforts in Old England. The following is a collection of questions Eliot put together: [5]

The *Indians* about us which I constantly teach, do still diligently and desirously attend, and in a good measure practice (for the outward part of religion, both in their families and Sabbaths) according to their knowledge; and by degrees come on to labor. I should be over-tedious and troublesome to you to run into particulars, only let me give you a taste of their knowledge by their questions, a few whereof I did sometimes set down, though I have skipped many, and very material ones; these questions being asked at sundry times, and at sundry meetings of the *Indians.*

Quest. *How many good people were in Sodom when it was burned?*
I know not how to pray to Christ and the Spirit, I know a little how to pray to God?
Doth the Devil dwell in us as we dwell in an house?
When God saith, honor thy father, doth he mean three fathers? our father, and our sachem, and God?
When the soul goes to heaven, what doth it say when it comes there? And what doth a wicked soul say when it commeth into hell?

If one sleep on the Sabbath at meeting, and another awaketh him, and he be angry at it, and say, it's because he is angry with him that he so doth, is not this a sin?

If any talk of another man's faults, and tell others of it when he is [not] present to answer, is not that a sin?

Why did Christ die in our stead?

Seeing Eve was first in sin, whether did she die first?

Why must we love our enemies, and how shall we do it?

How doth Christ redeem and deliver us from sin?

When every day my heart thinks I must die, and go to hell for my sins, what shall I do in this case?

May a good man sin sometimes? Or may he be a good man, and yet sin sometimes?

If a man think a prayer, doth God know it, and will He bless him?

Who killed Christ?

If a man be almost a good man, and dieth; whither goeth his soul?

How long was Adam good before he sinned?

Shall we see God in heaven?

If a wicked man pray, whether doth he make a good prayer? or when doth a wicked man pray a good prayer?

If a man repent, doth God take away his sins, and forgive him?

Whether did God make hell before Adam sinned?

If two families dwell in one house, and one prayeth and the other not, what shall they that pray do to them that do not?

Did Abimeleck *know* Sarah *was Abraham's wife?*

Did not Abraham *sin in saying she is my sister?*

Seeing God promised Abraham *so many children, like the stars for multitude, why did He give him so few? and was it true?*

If God made hell in one of the six days, why did God make hell before Adam *sinned?*

Now the Indians desire to go to heaven, what shall we do that we may go thither when we die?

How shall I bring mine heart to love prayer?

· *If one man repent, and pray once in a day, another man often in a day; whether doth one of them go to heaven, the other not? or what difference is there?*

I find I want wisdom, what shall I do to be wise?

Why did Abraham *buy a place to bury in?*

Why doth God make men sick?

How shall the resurrection be, and when?

Do not Englishmen spoil their souls, to say a thing cost them more than it did? and is it not all one as to steal?

You say our body is made of clay, what is the sun or moon made of?

If one be loved of all Indians good and bad, another is hated of all saving a few that be good, doth God love both these?

I see why I must fear hell, and do so every day. But why must I fear God?

How is the tongue like fire, and like poison?

What if false witnesses accuse me of murder or some foul sin?

What punishment is due to liars?

If I reprove a man for sin, and he answer, why do you speak thus angrily to me: Mr. Eliot teacheth us to love one another, is this well?

Why is God angry with murderers?

If a wife will put away her husband because he will pray to God, and she will not, what must be done in this case?

If there be a young woman pray to God, may such as pray to God marry one that will not pray to God? or what is to be done in this case?

Whether doth God make bad men dream good dreams?

What is salvation?

What is the Kingdom of Heaven?

If my wife do some work in the house on the night before Sabbath, and some work on the Sabbath night, whether is this a sin?

If I do that which is a sin, and do not know it is a sin, what will God say to that?

Whether is faith set in my heart, or in my mind?

Why did Christ die for us, and who did kill him?

By these questions you may see they somewhat favor the things of God and Christ, and that their souls be in a searching condition after the great points of religion and salvation. And I will say this solemnly, not suddenly, not lightly, but before the Lord, as I apprehend in my conscience, were they but in a settled way of civility and government cohabiting together, and I called (according to God) to live among them, I durst freely join into church fellowship amongst them, and could find out at least twenty men and women in some measure fitted of the Lord for it, and soon would be capable thereof: and we do admit in charity some into our churches of our own, of whose spiritual estate I have more cause of fear, than of some of them: but that day of grace is not yet come unto them. When God's time is come, He will make way for it & enable us to accomplish it. In the meantime, I desire to wait, pray, and believe....

34. "Root Out Their *Powwows*"

The Indian had an understandable concern for his health. If he acceded to the Puritan injunction to forsake the medicine of his powwow, would he not place himself in jeopardy? Furthermore, since the tribal healers opposed the Puritan missionary efforts, they might well refuse to minister to the needs of "praying Indians." Eliot had some thoughts on the subject and a proposal to help remedy the situation.[1]

There is another great question that hath been several times propounded, and much sticks with such as begins to pray, namely, *If they leave off powwowing, and pray to God, what shall they do when they are sick?* for they have no skill in physic, though some of them understand the virtues of sundry things, yet the state of man's body, and skill to apply them they have not: but all the refuge they have and rely upon in time of sickness is their *powwows,* who by antic, foolish and irrational conceits delude the poor people; so that it is a very needful thing to inform them in the use of physic, and a most effectual means to take them off from their *powwowing.* Some of the wiser sort I have stirred up to get this skill; I have showed them the anatomy of man's body, and some general principles of physic, which is very acceptable to them, but they are so extremely ignorant, that these things must rather be taught by sight, sense, and experience than by precepts, and rules of art; and therefore I have had many thoughts in my heart, that it were a singular good work, if the Lord would stir up the hearts of some or other of His people in England to give some maintenance toward some school or college exercise this way, wherein there should be anatomies and other instructions that way, and where there might be some recompense given to any that should bring in any vegetable or other thing that is virtuous in the way of physic; by this means we should soon have all these things which they know, and others of our countrymen that are skillful that way, and now their skill lies buried for want of encouragement, would be a searching and trying to find out the virtues of things in this country, which doubtless are many, and would not a little conduce to the benefit of the people of this country, and it may be of our native country also; by this means we should train up these poor *Indians* in that skill which would confound and root out their *powwows,* and then would they be far more easily inclined to leave those ways, and pray unto God, whose gift physic is, and whose blessing must make it effectual.

35. "Near Unto Good Examples"

The problem was that few Indians were flocking to Christianity just because John Eliot was gospelizing them. And it was difficult for those who were attracted to Christianity to break with the past, to break with the tribes and the sachems who saw Puritan missionary activity as a direct threat to their political and economic power. The knowledge that the "praying Indians" were establishing "praying towns" sent sachems into a fury. In the following two documents from the missionaries' accounts of their efforts, the controversy with sachems comes into sharp relief and reveals the tactics the missionaries used to influence Indians to convert to Christianity.[1]

A.

This business of praying to God (for that is their general name of religion) hath hitherto found opposition only from the powwows and profane spirits; but now the Lord hath exercised us with another and a greater opposition; for the *sachems* of the country are generally set against us, and counter-work the Lord by keeping off their men from praying to God as much as they can; and the reason of it is this, they plainly see that religion will make a great change among them, and cut them off from their former tyranny; for they used to hold their people in an absolute servitude, insomuch as whatever they had, and themselves too were at his command; his language was, as one said, *(omne meum;)* now they see that religion teaches otherwise, and puts a bridle upon such usurpation; besides their former manner was, that if they wanted money, or if they desire anything from a man, they would take occasion to rage and be in a great anger; which when they did perceive, they would give him all they had to pacify him; for else their way was to suborn some villain (of which they have no lack) to find some opportunity to kill him; *this keeps them in great awe of their sachems,* and is one reason why none of them desire any wealth, only from hand to mouth, because they are but servants, and they get it not for themselves; but now if their *sachem* so rage, and give sharp and cruel language, instead of seeking his favor with gifts (as formerly) they will admonish him of his sin; tell him that is not the right way to get money; but he must labor, and then he may have money, that is God's command, &c. And as for tribute, some they are willing to pay, but not as formerly. Now these are great temptations to the *sachems,* and they had need of a good measure both of wisdom and grace to swallow this pill, and it hath set them quite off; and I suppose that hence it is, that (I having requested the Court of Commissioners for a general way to be thought of to instruct all the Indians in all parts, and I told the Indians that I did so, which they would soon spread; and still in my prayers, I pray for the *Mohegans, Narragansetts, &c.)* the *Mohegan* Indians were much troubled lest the Court of Commissioners should take some course to teach them to pray to God; and *Uncas* their *sachem* went to *Hartford* this Court (for there they sat) and expressed to Elder [Thomas] *Goodwin* his fear of such a thing, and manifested a great unwillingness thereunto; this one of our Commissioners told me at his coming home.

This temptation hath much troubled *Cutshamoquin* our *sachem,* and he was raised in his spirit to such an height, that at a meeting after lecture, he openly contested with me against our proceeding to make a town; and plainly told me that all the *sachems* in the

country were against it, &c. When he did so carry himself, all the
Indians were filled with fear, their countenances grew pale, and
most of them slunk away, a few stayed, and I was alone, not any
Englishman with me; but it pleased God (for it was His guidance of
me, and assistance) to raise up my spirit, not to passion, but to a
bold resolution, telling him it was God's work I was about, and He
was with me, and I feared not him, nor all the *sachems* in the
country, and I was resolved to go on, do what they can, and they
nor he should hinder that which I had begun, &c. And it pleased
God that his spirit shrunk and fell before me, which when those
Indians that tarried saw, they smiled as they durst, out of his sight,
and have been much strengthened ever since; and since I understand that in such conflicts their manner is, that they account him
that shrinks to be conquered, and the other to conquer; which, alas,
I knew not, nor did I aim at such a matter, but the Lord carried me
beyond my thoughts and wont; after this brunt was over, I took my
leave to go home, and *Cutshamoquin* went a little way with me, and
told me that the reason of this trouble was, because the Indians that
pray to God, since they have so done, do not pay him tribute as
formerly they have done; I answered him that once before when I
heard of his complaint that way, I preached on that text, *Give unto
Caesar what is Caesar's and unto God what is God's;* and also on
Rom. 13, naming him the matter of the texts (not the places of
which he is ignorant.) But he said it's true, I taught them well, but
they would not in that point do as I taught them [to pay tribute];
and further he said, this thing are all the *sachems* sensible of, and
therefore set themselves against praying to God; and then I was
troubled, lest (if they should be sinfully unjust) they should hinder
and blemish the Gospel and religion; I did therefore consult with
the magistrates and Mr. [John] *Cotton* and other elders; Mr.
Cotton's text by God's providence, the next lecture gave him
occasion to speak to it, which I foreknowing, advised some that
understood English best, to be there; and partly by what they
heard, and by what I had preached to the like purpose, and told
them what Mr. *Cotton* said, &c. They were troubled, and fell to
reckon up what they had done in two years past, a few of them that
lived at one of the places I preached unto; I took down the
particulars in writing, as followeth. At one time they gave him
twenty bushels of corn, at another time more than six bushels; two

hunting days they killed him fifteen deer; they brake up for him two acres of land, they made for him a great house or wigwam, they made twenty rod of fence for him, with a ditch and two rails about it, they paid a debt for him of 3 pounds 10 shillings only some others were contributors in this money; one of them gave him a skin of beaver of two pound, at his return from building, besides many days' works in planting corn altogether, and some severally; yea they said they would willingly do more if they would govern well by justice, and as the Word of God taught them; when I heard all this, I wondered, for this cometh to near 30 pounds and was done by a few, and they thought it not much if he had carried matters better; and yet his complaint was, they do nothing; but the bottom of it lieth here, he formerly had all or what he would; now he hath but what they will; and admonitions also to rule better, and he is provoked by other *sachems,* and ill counsel, not to suffer this, and yet doth not know how to help it; hence arise his temptations, in which I do very much pity him. Having all this information what they had done, and how careless his complaint and discontent was, I thought it a difficult thing to ease his spirit, and yet clear and justify his people, which I was to endeavor the next day of our meeting after the former contestations, therefore I was willing to get somebody with me; and by God's providence, Elder [Isaac] *Heath* went with me, and when we came there, we found him very full of discontent, sighing, sour looks, &c. but we took no notice of it.

I preached that day out of *Matthew,* the temptations of Christ; and when I came at that temptation, of the Devil's showing Christ the kingdoms and glories of the world, thereby to tempt Him from the service of God, to the service of the Devil; I did apply it wholly to his case, showing him the Devil was now tempting him, as he tempted Christ; and Satan showeth him all the delights and dignities, and gifts and greatness that he was wont to have in their sinful way; Satan also tells him he shall lose them all if he pray to God, but if he will give over praying to God he shall have them all again; then I showed him how Christ rejected that temptation, and exhorted him to reject it also, for either he must reject the temptation, or else he will reject praying to God; if he should reject praying to God, God would reject him.

After our exercise was ended, we had conference of the matter, and we gave him the best counsel we could (as the Lord was pleased to assist) and when we had done, Elder *Heath* his observation of him was, that there was a great change in him, his spirit was very much lightened, and it much appeared both in his countenance and carriage, and he hath carried all things fairly ever since.

B.

Soon after your departure hence, the awakening of these *Indians* in our town raised a great noise among all the rest round about us, especially about *Concord* side, where the *sachem* (as I remember) and one or two more of his men, hearing of these things and of the preaching of the Word, and how it wrought among them here, came therefore hither to *(Nonantum),* to the *Indian* lecture, and what the Lord spoke to his heart we know not, only it seems he was so far affected, as that he desired to become more like to the English, and to cast off those *Indian* wild and sinful courses they formerly lived in; but when divers of his men perceived their *(sachem's)* mind, they secretly opposed him herein; which opposition being known, he therefore called together his chief men about him, & made a speech to this effect unto them, *"viz.* That they had no reason at all to oppose those courses the English were now taking for their good, for (saith he) all the time you have lived after the *Indian* fashion under the power and protection of higher *Indian* sachems, what did they care for you? They only sought their own ends out of you, and therefore would exact upon you, and take away your skins and your *kettles* & your *wampum* from you at their own pleasure, & this was all that they regarded: but you may evidently see that the English mind no such things, care for none of your goods, but only seek your good and welfare, and instead of taking away, are ready to give to you;["] with many other things I now forget, which were related by an eminent man of that town to me. What the effect of this speech was, we can tell no otherwise than as the effects showed it; the first thing was, the making of certain laws, for their more religious and civil government and behavior, to the making of which, they craved the assistance of one of the chief *Indians* in *Nonantum,* a very active *Indian* to bring in others to the knowledge of God; desiring withal an able faithful man in *Concord* to record and keep in writing what they had generally agreed upon. Another effect was, their desire of Mr. *Eliot's* coming up to them, to preach, as he could find time among them; and the last effect was, their desire of having a town given them within the bounds of *Concord* near unto the English. This latter when it was propounded by the *sachem* of the place, he was demanded why he desired a town so near, when as there was more room for them up in the country. To which the *sachem* replied, that he therefore desired it because he knew that if the *Indians* dwelt far from the English, that they would not so much care to pray, nor would they be so ready to hear the Word of God, but they would be all one *Indians* still; but dwelling near the English he hoped it might be otherwise with them then. The town therefore was granted them; but it seems that the opposition made by some of themselves more malignantly set against these courses, hath kept them from any present settling down; and surely this opposition is a special finger of *Satan* resisting these budding beginnings; for what more hopeful way of doing them good than by cohabitation in such towns, near unto good examples, and such as may be continually whetting upon them, and dropping into them of the things of God? What greater means at least to civilize them? as is evident in the *Cusco* and *Mexico Indians,* more civil than any else in this vast continent that we know of, who were reduced by the politic[al] principles of the two great conquering princes of those countries after their long and tedious wars, from their wild and wandering course of life, unto a settling into particular towns and cities; but I forbear, only to confirm the truth of these things, I have sent you the orders agreed on at *Concord* by the *Indians,* under the hand of two faithful witnesses, who could testify more, if need were, of these matters; I have sent you their own copy and their own hands to it, which I have here inserted.

Conclusions and Orders made and agreed upon by divers Sachems and other principal men amongst the Indians at Concord, in the end of the eleventh month, An. 1646.

1. That every one that shall abuse themselves with wine or strong liquors, shall pay for every time so abusing themselves, 20 *s.*

2. That there shall be no more *powwowing* amongst the *Indians.* And if any shall hereafter *powwow,* both he that shall *powwow,* & he that shall procure him to *powwow,* shall pay 20 *s.* apiece.

3. They do desire that they may be stirred up to seek after God

4. They desire they may understand the wiles of Satan, and grow out of love with his suggestions, and temptations.

5. That they may fall upon some better course to improve their time, than formerly.

6. That they may be brought to the sight of the sin of lying, and whosoever shall be found faulty herein shall pay for the first offense 5*s.* the second 10 *s.* the third 20 *s.*

7. Whosoever shall steal anything from another, shall restore fourfold.

8. They desire that no *Indian* hereafter shall have any more but one wife.

9. They desire to prevent falling out of *Indians* one with another, and that they may live quietly one by another.

10. That they may labor after humility, and not be proud.

11. That when *Indians* do wrong one to another, they may be liable to censure by *fine* or the like, as the *English* are.

12. That they pay their debts to the *English.*

13. That they do observe the Lord's Day, and whosoever shall profane it shall pay 20 *s.*

14. That there shall not be allowance to *pick lice,* as formerly, and eat them, and whosoever shall offend in this case shall pay for every louse a penny.

15. They will wear their *hair* comely, as the *English* do, and whosoever shall offend herein shall pay 5 *s.*

16. They intend to reform themselves, in their former greasing themselves, under the penalty of 5 *s.* for every default.

17. They do all resolve to set up prayer in their *wigwams,* and to seek to God both before and after meat.

18. If any commit the sin of fornication, being single persons, the man shall pay 20 *s.* and the woman 10 *s.*

19. If any man lie with a beast he shall die.

20. Whosoever shall play at their former games shall pay 10 *s.*

21. Whosoever shall commit adultery shall be put to death.

22. Willful murder shall be punished with death.

23. They shall not disguise themselves in their mournings, as formerly, nor shall they keep a great noise by howling.

24. The old ceremony of the maid walking alone and living apart so many days 20 *s.*

25. No *Indian* shall take an *English* man's canoe without leave under penalty of 5 *s.*

26. No *Indian* shall come into any *English* man's house except he first knock: and this they expect from the *English.*

27. Whosoever beats his wife shall pay 20 *s.*

28. If any *Indian* shall fall out with, and beat another *Indian,* he shall pay 20 *s.*

29. They desire ... [there] may be a town, and either to dwell on this side the *Bear Swamp,* or at the east side of Mr. *Flint's Pond.*

Immediately after these things were agreed upon, most of the Indians of these parts, set up prayer morning and evening in their families, and before and after meat. They also generally cut their hair, and were more civil in their carriage to the *English* than formerly. And they do manifest a great willingness to conform themselves to the civil fashions of the *English.* The Lord's Day they keep a day of rest, and minister what edification they can to one another. These former orders were put into this form by Captain *Simon Willard* of *Concord,* whom the *Indians* with unanimous consent entreated to be their recorder, being very solicitous that what they did agree upon might be faithfully preserved without alteration.

THOMAS FLINT.   SIMON WILLARD.

These things thus wrought in a short time about *Concord* side, I look upon as fruits of the ministry of the Word. . . .

36. "Stubborn and Rebellious Children"

Praying Indians had to endure mockery and other tribulations at the hands of their tribes. As though this were not enough, Eliot and other Puritan missionaries rarely took the feelings of the natives into account when discussing God and Christ. Failing to understand Indian cultural attitudes and practices, the missionary didn't hesitate to address even willing Indians with condescension. The following documents illustrate these points: [1]

A.

... the next they propounded ... was this, viz. How come the English to differ so much from the Indians in the knowledge of God and Jesus Christ, seeing they had all at first but one father?

We confessed that it was true that at first we had all but one father, but after that our first father fell, he had divers children, some were bad and some good, those that were bad would not take his counsel but departed from him and from God, and those God left alone in sin and ignorance, but others did regard him and the counsel of God by him, and those knew God, and so the difference arose at first, that some together with their posterity knew God, and others did not; and so we told them it was at this day, for like as if an old man, an aged father amongst them, have many children, if some of them be rebellious against the counsel of the father, he shuts them out of doors, and lets them go, and regards them not, unless they return and repent, but others that will be ruled by him, they learn by him and come to know his mind; so we said English men seek God, dwell in His house, hear His word, pray to God, instruct their children out of God's book, hence they come to know God; but Indians' forefathers were stubborn and rebellious children, and would not hear the Word, did not care to pray, not to teach their children, and hence Indians that now are, do not know God at all: and so must continue unless they repent, and return to God and pray, and teach their children what they now may learn: but withal we told them that many Englishmen did not know God but were like to Cutshamoquin's drunken Indians; nor were we willing to tell them the story of the scattering of *Noah's* children since the flood, and thereby to show them how the Indians come to be so ignorant, because it was too difficult, and the history of the Bible is reserved for them (if God will) to be opened at a more convenient season in their own tongue.

B.

One of them ... replied to us, that he was a little while since praying in his *wigwam,* unto God and Jesus Christ, that God would give him a good heart, and that while he was praying, one of his fellow *Indians* interrupted him, and told him, that he prayed in vain, because Jesus Christ understood not what *Indians* speak in prayer, He had been used to hear *English* men pray and so could well enough understand them, but *Indian* language in prayer he thought He was not acquainted with it, but was a stranger to it, and therefore could not understand them. His question therefore was, whether Jesus Christ did understand or God did understand Indian prayers.

This question sounding just like themselves, we studied to give as familiar an answer as we could, and therefore in this as in all other of our answers, we endeavored to speak nothing without clearing of it up by some familiar similitude; our answer summarily was therefore this, that Jesus Christ and God by Him made all things, and makes all men, not only *English* but *Indian* men, and if He made them both (which we know the light of nature would readily teach as they had been also instructed by us) then He knew all that was within man and came from man, all his desires, and all his thoughts, and all his speeches, and so all his prayer; and if He made *Indian* men; then He knows all *Indian* prayers also: and therefore we bid them look upon that *Indian* basket that was before them, there was black and white straws, and many other things they made it of, now though others did not know what those things were who made not the basket, yet he that made it must needs tell all the things in it, so (we said) it was here.

Another propounded this question after this answer, Whether English men were ever at any time so ignorant of God and Jesus Christ as themselves?

When we perceived the root and reach of this question, we gave them this answer, that there were two sorts of English men, some are bad and naught, and live wickedly and loosely, (describing them) and these kinds of English men we told them were in a manner as ignorant of Jesus Christ as the *Indians* now are; but there are a second sort of English men, who though for a time they lived wickedly also like other profane and ignorant English, yet repenting of their sins, and seeking after God and Jesus Christ, they are good men now, and now know Christ, and love Christ, and pray to Christ, and are thankful for all they have to Christ, and shall at last when they die, go up to heaven to Christ; and we told them all these also were once as ignorant of God and Jesus Christ as the *Indians* are, but by seeking to know Him by reading His book, and hearing His word, and praying to Him, &c. they now know Jesus Christ, and just so shall the *Indians* know Him if they so seek Him also, although at the present they be extremely ignorant of Him.

How can there be an image of God, because it's forbidden in the Second Commandment?

We told them that image was all one picture, as the picture of an *Indian,* bow and arrows on a tree, with such little eyes and such fair hands, is not an *Indian* but the picture or image of an *Indian,* and that picture man makes, and it can do no hurt nor good. So the image or picture of God is not God, but wicked men make it, and this image can do no good nor hurt to any man as God can.

37. "Conformed Is a Great Word"

In 1673, in the twilight of his life, John Eliot wrote responses to a series of questions that had been put to him. The whole was entitled "An Account of Indian Churches in New England" and reported on the status of missionary work at that time. While Eliot chose to take the position that the "praying towns" all operated successfully in accordance with the pattern outlined in the Bible, he could not claim his efforts—covering twenty-seven years among the Indians—had been crowned with the kind of success he had hoped for. Here is his account: [1]

REV. AND BELOVED BROTHER,

You told me that a friend of yours desired to be informed in the present state of the gospel work among the Indians, and desired me to furnish you with matter of information. I find you propose an hard work, especially considering how much variety of employments lieth on me, but if you would propose any questions to me, I would endeavor to give you a short answer thereunto, which you accepted and do propose.

Q. How many churches are gathered, and where?

A. There be (through the grace of Christ) six churches gathered, according to the order of gathering churches among the English, one at Natick, one at Hassanamesit, 28 miles to the west, one at Mashpee, 20 miles east of Plymouth, two at Martha's Vineyard, and one at Nantucket.

Q. What is the manner usually of their inchurching?

A. The same (so near as we can) that is practiced in gathering churches among the English. ...

Q. What number of members in each church are in full communion?

A. I have not numbered them, nor can I, though all baptized, both adult and infants, are registered in the church at Natick; as also burials of such as are baptized yet I know not if any of the other churches do so.

Q. Whether brotherly watch is observed among them according to Mat. 18, &c.

A. Yes, it is so, and one is under admonition at this day, yea they are so severe that I am put to bridle them to moderation and forbearance.

Q. Whether are all furnished with church officers; if not, which or how many are destitute?

A. All are furnished with officers, saving the church at Natick, and in modesty they stand off, because so long as I live, they say, there is no need; but we propose (God willing) not always to rest in this answer.

Q. Whether are they able and willing to provide for the outward subsistence of their Elders, that they may live of the Gospel?

A. They are willing according to what they have, and not according to what they have not; they willingly pay their tithes and the Commissioners allow them a man [pastor] per annum which renders their subsistence above their brethren, though low at the best.

Q. Whether their pastors do administer the sacrament among them?

A. They do so.

Q. Whether praying to God, reading of the Scriptures, and catechising, &c. be attended in their families duly?

A. According to their ability it is so, but sundry cannot read; all Christians learn and rehearse catechism.

Q. What is their discipline in their churches, and whether they have consented to any model of church ordinances?

A. They both consent unto and practice the same discipline and ordinances as we practice in the English Congregational churches, they studiously endeavor to write after the English copy in all church order.

Q. Whether the Indian churches are settled in a way of communion of churches one with another by synods, or how?

A. Our churches have communion in the sacraments and send messengers to gatherings of churches, but have yet had no occasion of synods.

Q. Whether they are conscientious of the Sabbath day?

A. Through the grace of Christ they are so.

Q. Whether powwowing be practiced among them?

A. It is abandon'd, exploded, and abolish'd, as also games by lottery and for wager, &c.

Q. Whether they observe any days of fasting and thanksgiving?

A. All days of public fasting and thanksgiving which are exercised among us, they do religiously observe, even as they do the Sabbaths, and sometimes we have fasting days among ourselves.

Q. Whether there are daily added to the church new converts, and that upon the Lord's blessing upon the Word preached by the pastors?

A. This is too strict, daily added is a private word in a numerous church of religious and enlightened people; we are a blind, thin and scattered wild people; 20 or 30 years time have made a visible appearance of a divine work, and I observe a great blessing to follow the labors of their own countrymen who labor among them.

Q. What is the manner of their admission of any new converts into the churches?

A. They are diligently instructed and examined both publicly and privately in the catechism; their blameless and pious conversation is publicly testified, their names are publicly exposed as desiring to make confession and join into the church. The teachers and chief brethren do first hear their preparatory confessions, and when they judge them meet they are called publicly to confess, confederate and be baptized, both themselves and their children, if not up grown; the up grown are called upon to make their own confession, and so to be baptized as their parents were.

Q. Whether they are acknowledged by any of the churches of English, and accepted to communion occasionally in the churches?

A. Once when I was at the Vineyard, I administered the sacraments in the English church, and they accepted the Indian church to join with them, I told them that Christ did please first to beautify this His little spouse with this jewel of love to embrace into their communion the Indian converts in church ordinances; another time I administered the sacraments in the Indian church, and such of the English church as saw meet joined with us. Brother, if you know not, you may know how I have moved and argued among the Elders, that it will be an act of honor to Christ, to the churches, and to yourselves, and but a fit yea necessary encouragement unto the work to accept them into your communion which the Lord hath so manifestly, undeniably accepted. I am quiet in the plea of the diversity of language.

Q. What is their church care for their children, and whether nothing of anabaptism hath leavened them?

A. They see with the eyes of their own children, who have been trained up religiously and at schools, are now become teachers in the assembly of praying Indians, and in the exercise of their gifts at Natick, do approve themselves good proficients in religion which maketh both them and me desirous a few schools to be erected at Natick. Two praying Indians of the Vineyard were seduced by the English anabaptists of Nantucket, but all the rest are steadfast, I praise God for it, and whether they are recovered I cannot say.

Q. Whether any spirit or way of heterodoxy hath sprung up among them?

A. Not any; they have a deep sense of their own darkness and ignorance, and a reverent esteem of the light and goodness of the English, and an evident observation that such English as warp into errors do also decline from goodness, by which means Satan hath yet found no door of entrance into them. They have often discourses and sometimes variety of apprehensions which is speedily brought to me, and all rest in such Scripture determinations as I express.

Q. Whether they have any schools, and the order thereof, and the proficiency that hath done therein?

A. We have schools; many can read, some write, sundry able to exercise in public, are sent by the church to teach in new praying places and who live remote from the churches and some or other of them do every lecture day, at Natick, exercise their gifts two or three on a day, and I moderate. I desire to carry on school work strongly, but alas we want means, it would be a means to further the work greatly to found a free school amongst them.

Q. How do those Indians that are not in church order carry it towards their neighbors that are in church state?

A. With reverence and good esteem. Such as are approved and received by the church, are advanc'd to a good degree in the eyes of all the people, and the rather it is so, because they know it is free for them to have the same privilege, and they are exhorted to it, pains taken with them, to bring them to it, and they are sensible that only their ignorance and other sins keep them from it.

Q. What encouragement is there (as to outward matters) for any of the nations of England or Scotland to undertake the work of the ministry among them, by devoting himself wholly or mainly thereunto?

A. Nothing but poverty and hardships, unsupportable in a constant way by our cloathed and housed nations. He that doth undertake the work must be a giver and not a receiver, in outward matters, and the fuller his hand is, to be a giver, the more room he will find in the acceptation of the worst of men; who knoweth not this to be the frame of all mankind? Their national customs are connatural to them. Their own nation trained up and schooled unto ability for the work, are the most likely instruments to carry on this work, and therefore a few schools among themselves, with true hearted governors and teachers, is the most probable way of advancing this work.

Q. How do the converted Indians stand affected towards the English, by means of whom they have received the Gospel?

A. They have a great reverence and esteem of them, and ordinarily in their prayers they thank God for them, and pray for them as the instrument of God for their good; but the business about land giveth them no small matter of stumbling, but than for the ruling part of the English to be right carried.

Q. Whether as to their civil government, they are wholly conformed to the English, or have any peculiar ordering of their own whereby they are ruled?

A. Conformed is a great word; we are expressly conformed to the Scriptures, and to that form of government which we find Israel was under at the first, and never quite lost, to have rulers of ten, of fifty, of an hundred, we have yet gone no higher. Capt. Gookin and I did lately visit the now praying towns, some of them in Nipmuck, and he appointed a ruler (who is their ancient sachem, a godly man) over 5 or 6 or 7 towns, and a general constable. All the praying Indians have submitted themselves to the English government. The General Court hath (after the decease of others, as Mr. Noel, Mr. Atherton,) authorized Capt. Gookin with the power of a county court to rule, make officers, laws with the consent of the people, and keep courts together with such as he hath invested with civil authority among them, and he hath ordained rulers of 10, of 50, &c. but Captain, who hath acted more effectually (as having more matured opportunity) than any of his predecessors, can give you more ample satisfaction about their civil government than I can. Thus have I briefly gone through all your questions, the Lord add His blessing, so prayeth

> Your loving brother
> in the Lord Jesus,
> JOHN ELIOT.

Roxbury, this 22 of the 6th, '73

Chapter V

"To Dispossess Us of the Land"

King Philip's War

For centuries, historians have been debating the question of moral responsibility for King Philip's War (1675–76), the cataclysm that broke the back of Indian resistance in New England and symbolized, as well, the decline of Puritan vitality. Who started the war? The first killer (a white man) or the first destroyer of private property (an Indian)? Was the instigator Metacom, known as King Philip, who clearly felt that his authority as Wampanoag leader was being eroded by English aggression? Or was the instigator the Plymouth Court, which repeatedly accused Metacom of conspiring with other tribes against the English and peremptorily executed three Wampanoags for the alleged murder of an Indian who had been acting as an English spy? Was there, for that matter, any Indian conspiracy at all prior to the first shot?

The trouble with speculation like this is that it forces the student of Puritan-Indian relations into a maze of detail in an attempt to assign guilt. Perhaps, therefore, one should stand back and consider, instead, the much larger issue of overall responsibility. Only then can one avoid the mistake of assigning blame on the basis of a simple act arising out of decades of interaction between opposing cultures.

First of all, it is crucial for the student of King Philip's War to understand that the leaders of Massachusetts Bay and Plymouth, given their theological view of the universe, not only felt that they had not "provoked" Metacom into war, but that they, as Puritans and Pilgrims, were fundamentally incapable of provoking Indians to do anything. Cotton Mather's argument that "the Devil decoyed those miserable savages [to New England], in hopes that the Gospel of the Lord Jesus Christ would never come here to destroy or disturb His *absolute empire* over them" finds its corollary in William Hubbard's insistence that Satan "instigated" the Indians in King Philip's War out of "envy" or "fear" that the "power of the Lord Jesus" was "filling the whole earth" in the New World. Consequently, the violent reaction to God's presence had transpired, Hubbard concluded, with "no cause of provocation being given by the English." [1]

Yet, even as they insisted on Satan's manipulation of his native children, Puritan writers occasionally conceded a kind of secondary provocation in themselves. John Eliot hoped, in a letter to the Governor of Connecticut, that the war would "humble the English, to do the Indians justice, and no wrong about their lands," a plea seconded by Increase Mather (Cotton Mother's father) and Hubbard.[2] Moreover, Mather and Hubbard excoriated the private Puritan traders who sold rum (and guns) to Indians in violation of the law, thus heightening their "barbarous" passions.[3] Mather even suggested, in his history of the war, that the meager effort to convert Indians to Christianity might have been a contributing cause.[4] These "provocations" are similar to the ones expressed by Metacom himself on the eve of the war: that the English made Indians drunk and then cheated them in land transactions; that English cattle and horses repeatedly destroyed Indian corn, prompting drunken natives to kill the livestock; that, like the Narragansetts, the Wampanoags "had a great fear lest any of their Indians should be called or forced to be Christian Indians" (to which objection Mather undoubtedly would have suggested a redoubling of missionary efforts in order to save Indians from their own pride and savagery).[5] There is a fundamental difference, however, between the nature of Eliot's, Mather's, and Hubbard's admissions and the Wampanoags' complaints. When examined closely, what seem to be confessed provocations of Indians become, instead, provocations of God, who then permits Satan to use his "instruments"—the natives—to punish Puritans for their sins against Him. Eliot's worry about Indian lands was primarily a fear of inciting God's wrath, not the pride of the offended natives (though the first might become the second). Likewise, Mather and Hubbard, in criticizing land hunger, trading houses, and feeble missionary efforts, were declaiming against the spiritual pride and materialism of Puritans, not their injustice toward Indians.

Nowhere is this view more apparent than in the Massachusetts General Court's explanation for the onset of the war. Its catalog of causes concentrates on the failure of Puritans to follow the daily precepts of their faith: stern child-rearing, modest clothing, intolerance toward Quakers, moderate drinking, obedience to authority, and refusal to sell liquor to Indians, among others.[6] Using the same reasoning, Increase Mather concluded that the war was won by the Puritans because "God hath let us see that He could easily have destroyed us, *by such a contemptible enemy as the Indians have been in our eyes,* yea, He hath convinced us that we ourselves could not subdue them. ... So that we have no cause for glory, for it is God which hath thus saved us, and not we ourselves." [7] Thus God began the war to rebuke the Puritans, and He ended it because He chose, in His wisdom, to be merciful toward His sinful chosen people at the expense of their "contemptible enemy." In this involved spiritual drama, the Puritans played only bit parts, but the Indians never even appeared on stage.

Mather saved the most important statement in his history of the war for last:

We may truly say of Philip, and the Indians, who have fought to dispossess us, of the land, which the Lord our God hath given to us, as sometimes Jepthah, and the Children of Israel said to the King of Ammon, I have not sinned against thee, but thou dost me wrong to war against me; the Lord the Judge, be Judge this day between the Children of Israel, and the Children of Ammon. And as Jehoshaphat said, when the heathen in those days, combined to destroy the Lord's People; And now behold the Children of Ammon, and Moab and Mount Seir, whom Thou [God] would not let Israel invade when they came out of the land of Egypt, but they [the Children of Israel] turned from them, and destroyed them not, behold how they reward us, to come to cast us out of Thy possession, which Thou hast given us to inherit, O God wilt Thou not judge them? [8]

Mather is saying here that anything short of a brutal invasion of Indian lands by the Puritans was a kindness on God's part, since He had already ordained the lands for the inheritance of the Puritans as latter-day "Children of Israel." Thus Wampanoag resistance to English presence in New England was a Satanic effort "to dispossess us." This is the crux of the conflict known as King Philip's War: both sides sincerely claimed the disputed territory of eastern Massachusetts for themselves and accused each other of dispossession.

The military phase of the conflict began on June 24, 1675, when eleven English settlers were killed in retaliation for the murder of an Indian the previous day. Thereafter, homes, villages, and noncombatants were repeatedly decimated in an intense guerrilla warfare that lasted through the following summer. By war's end, fifty-two Puritan towns had been attacked, twelve destroyed, and countless Indian villages had been leveled. Perhaps as many as nine thousand people died, two-thirds of them Indians, who lost half of their population in casualties. In all, 30 percent of the entire population of the territories of Massachusetts, Plymouth, and Rhode Island did not survive the war. The severity of such casualties, following thirty-eight years of coexistence between cultures in New England, begs for some kind of explanation and focuses the student's attention, in his search for a cause of the war, on the intervening years between 1637 (the Pequot War) and 1675.

Perhaps a clue to the distant and underlying reasons for the conduct of the war, as well as its origin, lies in the fact that the first major English military action in 1675 did not involve Metacom's own tribe. The Commissioners of the United Colonies, meeting in Boston in November, authorized on flimsy grounds a December strike against the Narragansetts in Rhode Island, the only major tribe not yet at war with the English. Rhode Island refused to provide soldiers for the attack but was helpless to prevent the invasion from Massachusetts. On December 19, the Puritan army surprised a huge Narragansett gathering in a swamp and burned the village to the ground, killing one hundred able-bodied men and, by a conservative estimate, three hundred women and children. The English lost about twenty dead and two hundred wounded. There is a striking similarity between this attack—the single most violent encounter of the war—and the massacre of Pequot Indians in Mystic Fort in 1637. And the similarity is not accidental. The communal Puritan spirit, always on guard against being cast out of its New World home, seems to have required both peacetime coexistence with native neighbors and wartime holocaust. There was no Indian, in peace or war, who was not an enemy in Puritan eyes: the Wampanoags were indeed enemies, and fought against the Puritans in 1675; but the Narragansetts, neutrals who kept their distance for decades in territory shared with heretic Rhode Islanders and coveted by Puritans, were condemned as proud and insolent; and the Mohegans, allies of the Puritans, were treated with suspicion to the last. Even the Christianized Massachuset Indians were forbidden participation in King Philip's War until the Puritans desperately needed their knowledge of the wilderness. That assistance turned the tide of battle in the English favor, but years later the Commissioners of the United Colonies still refused to pay these Indians for their services.[9] Following the war, all Indians, those who had remained peaceful as well as a few combatants who had not been executed or sold into a slavery were required to live on four (later three) reservations in Massachusetts Bay, with the "House of Correction or Prison" awaiting those who refused to comply.[10]

The hallmark of Puritan society, and the faith that undergirded it, was a volatile mixture of self-assurance in their status as God's saviors of Christianity and fear of enemies at their doorstep: Indians, Quakers, Catholics, and the backsliders in their own midst. Calm self-assurance, in contrast to the hot-headed aggressiveness of colonists in Virginia, could for a time keep them from succumbing to the temptations of war; but their fears sooner or later would have to break forth. When the faith of the Puritan community seemed to wane in the 1660s and 1670s, the time was ripe for what Richard Slotkin has called a "regeneration through violence." [11]

King Philip's War was a Pyrrhic victory. Convinced that God, not they, wielded the sword, the Puritans rejoiced in victory and then denied responsibility for what had transpired. In their own eyes, they were still humble. But in the eyes of their countrymen in England, they appeared either demented or shameless.[12] The war invited the King of England to assert his jurisdiction over his subjects in New England, who seemed to have forfeited some of their humanity in the name of a distorted version of Christianity. The spoils of war, too, did the Puritans no good. The new lands wrested from the Indians became a contributing factor to the internal and external weakening of Puritan society. Acquiring these tracts and capitalizing on their sale was too enticing for the growing numbers of less than scrupulous entrepreneurs in Puritan society, and the king himself, to resist.

In the aftermath of a hard-won victory, the New Jerusalem was further from reality than it had been on that day in 1630 when the *Arbella* first came to the land inhabited by New England natives. Increase Mather's confidence at the close of the war proved drastically mistaken:

> This Jerusalem ... shall be unto [God] a name of joy, a praise and an honor before all the nations of the earth, which shall hear all the good that He will do unto us, and they shall fear and tremble for all the goodness, and for all the prosperity He will procure.[13]

What once was Indian land became, in 1691, the King of England's royal province, and the days of Puritan rule in Massachusetts and Connecticut were finished.

38. "The Peccant and Offending Party"

The official Plymouth account of the causes of King Philip's War, which appears below, should be compared to the excerpt from the "Easton Narrative" that follows it.[1] Even together, the two accounts—as different as they are—give an incomplete picture of the political conflict between the English and the Indians on the eve of the war. Some additional facts, not provided by either narrative, need to be considered:

1. The Pilgrims repeatedly ordered Metacom's appearance before their courts in the 1660s and 1670s on the first rumor of a native conspiracy. Once there, Metacom was subjected to severe penalties in money, arms (used for hunting), and sovereignty. The Plymouth account fails to indicate, for example, the humiliation that must have accompanied Metacom's making "himself and his people absolute subjects to our Sovereign Lord King Charles the Second; and to that his Colony of New Plymouth," a submission that exceeded the earlier friendly desires of Massasoit, Metacom's father.

2. Sassamon, the dead Indian, may have been "faithful to the interest of God and of the English," but he was also, in common language, an English spy.

3. The "Indian appearing to testify" was actually in debt to the Indians whom he accused of Sassamon's murder.

4. The first person killed in the war was an Indian (on June 23), not Thomas Layton of Fall River on June 24.

5. John Easton, the author of the second account, was the Lieutenant Governor of Rhode Island and a Quaker. Some historians, therefore, have discerned an anti-Puritan bias in his narrative. Yet Easton was not above reminding Metacom that the English in Rhode Island, including himself, would fight with the Puritans

against the Wampanoags if it came to war. Essentially Easton was opposed to fighting itself, not to the Indians or the Puritans.

6. Metacom's charge in Easton's account that the English habitually allowed their livestock to ruin the cornfields of the Indians seems to be his most valid complaint, since Plymouth's own colonial records refer continually to this problem. One solution proposed by Plymouth's leaders was to require Englishmen to help Indians put up fences.[2] There is an irony in this situation: the English, who defended their right to land in the New World on the basis of private property, fences, and agriculture, were damaging the property of agrarian Indians with their own unfenced animals.

The reader of these and the following documents should be reminded that both sides in the dispute over who provoked whom in King Philip's War could defend their own behavior with conviction. One example is the Plymouth statement that since 1671 "we know not that the English ... have been injurious to him or his, that might justly provoke them to take up arms against us." Read carefully, this is not a hypocritical denial of injuries to the Wampanoags, only an assertion that those injuries did not "justly" provoke the Indians into fighting (assuming, of course, that they started the war).

A

A BRIEF NARRATIVE of the beginning and progress of the present trouble between us and the Indians; taking its Rise in the Colony of New Plymouth.

Anno Domini 1675

Not to look back further than the troubles that were between the Colony of New Plymouth and Philip, sachem of Mount Hope, in the year 1671, it may be remembered that the settlement and issue of that controversy obtained and made principally by the mediation and interposed advice and counsel of the other two confederate colonies, who upon a careful inquiry and search into the grounds of that trouble found that the sachem's pretense of wrongs and injuries, from that colony were groundless and false; and that he (although first in arms) was the peccant and offending party; and that Plymouth had just cause to take up arms against him; and it was then agreed that he should pay that colony a certain sum of money, in part of their damage and charge by him occasioned; and he then not only renewed his ancient covenant of friendship with them; but made himself and his people absolute subjects to our Sovereign Lord King Charles the Second; and to that his Colony of New Plymouth since which time we know not that the English of that or any other of the [United] Colonies have been injurious to him or his, that might justly provoke them to take up arms against us; but sometime last winter the Governor of Plymouth was informed by Sassamon, a faithful Indian, that the said Philip was undoubtedly endeavoring to raise new troubles, and was endeavoring to engage all the sachems round about in a war against us; some of the English also that lived near the said sachem, communicated their fears and jealousies concurrent with what the Indian had informed; about a week after John Sassamon had given his information, he was barbarously murdered by some Indians for his faithfulness (as we have cause to believe) to the interest of God and of the English; some time after Sassamon's death Philip, having heard that the Governor of Plymouth had received some information against him and purposed to send for or to him to appear at their next Court that they might inquire into those reports, came down of his own accord to Plymouth a little before their Court, in the beginning of March last; at which time the Council of that colony upon a large debate with him, had great reason to believe, that the information against him might be in substance true, but not having full proof thereof and hoping that the discovery of it so far would cause him to desist they dismissed him friendly; giving him only to understand that if they hear further concerning that matter they might see reason to demand his arms to be delivered up for their security; which was according to former agreement between him and them; and he engaged [pledged] on their demand they should be surrendered unto them or their order; at that Court we had many Indians in examination concerning the murder of John Sassamon but had not then testimony in the case but not long after, an Indian appearing to testify; we apprehended three by him charged to be the murderers of Sassamon; and secured them to a trial at our next Court (held in June) at which time, a little before the Court, Philip began to keep his men in arms about him and to gather strangers unto him and to march about in arms towards the upper end of the neck on which he lived and near to the English houses; who began thereby to be somewhat disquieted, but took as yet no further notice but only set a military watch in the next towns; as Swansea and Rehoboth some hints we had that Indians were in arms while our Court was sitting but we hoped it might arise from a guilty fear in Philip; that we would send for him and bring him to trial with the other murderers; and that if he saw the Court broken up and he not sent for, the cloud might blow over; and indeed our innocency made us very secure and confident it would not have broken out into a war. But no sooner was our Court dissolved but we had intelligence from Lieut. John Brown of Swansea that Phillip and his men continued constantly in arms, many strange Indians from several places flocked in to him & that they sent away their wives to Narragansett; and were giving our people frequent alarms by drums and guns in the night and invaded their passage towards Plymouth; and that their young Indians were earnest for a war; on the 7th of June Mr. Benjamin Church being on Rhode Island, Weetamoo and some of her chief men told him that Philip intended a war speedily with the English, some of them saying that they would help him; and that he had already given them leave to kill Englishmen's cattle and rob their houses; about the 14th and 15th of June Mr. James Brown went twice to Philip to persuade him to be quiet but at both times found his men in arms and Philip very high and not persuadable to peace; on the 14th June our Council wrote an amicable friendly letter to Philip therein showing our dislike of his practices; and advising him to dismiss his strange Indians and command his own men to fall quietly to their business that our people might also be quiet; and not to suffer himself to be abused by reports concerning us, who intended no wrong, nor hurt towards him; but Mr. Brown could not obtain an answer from him; on the 17th June Mr. Paine of Rehoboth and several others of the English going unarmed to Mount Hope to seek their horses at Philip's request, the Indians came and presented their guns at them and carried it very insolently though no way provoked by them; on the 18th or 19th Job Winslow his house was broken up and rifled by Philip's men; June the 20th being our Sabbath, the people at Swansea were alarmed by the Indians, two of our inhabitants burned out of their houses and their houses rifled; and the Indians were marching up as they judged to assault the town; and therefore entreated speedy help from us; we hereupon the 21 of June sent up some forces to relieve that town and dispatched more with speed; on Wednesday the 23 of June a dozen more of their houses at Swansea were rifled; on the 24th Thomas Layton was slain at the Fall River; on the 25th of June divers of the people at Swansea slain; and many houses burned until which time, and for several days, though we had a considerable force there both of our own and of the Massachusetts (to our grief and shame), they took no revenge on the enemy; thus slow were we and unwilling to engage ourselves and neighbors in a war; having many insolencies almost intolerable from them, of whose hands we had deserved better;

JOSIAH WINSLOW
THOMAS HINCKLEY
[Plymouth Commissioners to the United Colonies]

B.

... We said we knew the English said the Indians wronged them and the Indians said the English wronged them, but our desire was [that] the quarrel might rightly be decided in the best way, and not as dogs decide their quarrels. The Indians owned that fighting was the worst way, then they propounded how right might take place, we said by arbitration. They said all English agreed against them, and so by arbitration they had had much wrong, many miles square of land so taken from them, for English would have English arbitrators, and once they were persuaded to give in their arms, that thereby jealousy might be removed, [then] the English having their arms would not deliver them as they had promised, until they consented to pay 100 pounds, and now they had not so much land or money, that they were as good be killed as leave all their livelihood. We said they might choose an Indian king, and the English might choose the Governor of New York, that neither had cause to say either were parties in the difference. They said they had not heard of that way and said we honestly spoke, so we were persuaded if that way had been tendered they would have accepted. We did endeavor not to hear their complaints, said it was not convenient for us now to consider of, but to endeavor to prevent war, said to them when in war against English, blood was spilt that engaged all Englishmen, for we were to be all under one kind. We knew what their complaints would be, and in our colony [Rhode Island] had removed some of them in sending for [Narragansett] Indian rulers in so far as the crime concerned Indians' lives, which they very lovingly accepted and agreed with us to their execution and said so they were able to satisfy their subjects when they knew an Indian suffered duly, but said what was only between their Indians and not in townships that we had purchased, they would not have us prosecute and that they had a great fear lest any of their Indians should be called or forced to be Christian Indians. They said that such were in everything more mischievous, only dissemblers, and then the English made them not subject to their kings, and by their lying to wrong their kings. We knew it to be true, and we promising them that however in government to Indians all should be alike and that we knew it was our King's will it should be so, that although we were weaker than other colonies, they having submitted to our King to protect them, others dared not otherwise to molest them, so they expressed they took that to be well, that we had little cause to doubt but that to us, under the King, they would have yielded to our determinations in what any should have complained to us against them, but Philip charged it to be dishonesty in us to put off the hearing [of] the complaints. Therefore we consented to hear them. They said they had been the first in doing good to the English, and the English the first in doing wrong, said when the English first came their king's father [Massasoit] was as a great man and the English as a little child, he constrained other Indians from wronging the English and gave them corn and showed them how to plant and was free to do them any good and had let them have a 100 times more land than now the king had for his own people, but their king's brother when he was king came miserably to die by being forced to court, as they judged poisoned, and another grievance was if 20 of their own Indians testified that an Englishman had done them wrong, it was as nothing, and if but one of their worst Indians testified against any Indian or their king, when it pleased the English that was sufficient. Another grievance was when their kings sold land, the English would say it was more than they agreed to and a writing must be proof against all them, and some of their kings had done wrong to sell so much. He left his people none, and some being given to drunkenness the English made them drunk and then cheated them in bargains, but now their kings were forewarned not to part with land for nothing in comparison to the value thereof. Now whom the English had owned for king or queen they [the English] would disinherit, and make another king that would give or sell them their land, that now they had no hopes left to keep any land. Another grievance the English cattle and horses still increased, that when they removed 30 miles from where English had anything to do, they could not keep their corn [there] from being spoiled, they never being used to fence, and thought when the English bought land of them that they [the English] would have kept their cattle upon their own land. Another grievance, the English were so eager to sell the Indians liquor that most of the Indians spent all in drunkenness and then ravened upon the sober Indians and, they did believe, often did hurt the English cattle, and their kings could not prevent it. We knew before [that] these were their grand complaints, but then we only endeavored to persuade that all complaints might be righted without war, but could have no other answer but that they had not heard of that way for the Governor of York and an Indian king to have the hearing of it. We had cause to think if that had been tendered it would have been accepted. We endeavored that, however, they should lay down their arms, for the English were too strong for them. They said then the English should do to them as they did when they were too strong for the English. . . .

39. "He Sent Our Enemies to Be Our Lords"

John Kingsley's letter to a minister in Hartford, Connecticut, gives an especially graphic picture of the devastation created in Puritan villages once Metacom's soldiers began to coordinate their attacks.[1] Rehoboth, Kingsley's village, was right on the edge of Wampanoag territory, and its citizens were often guilty of the trespass and damage cited by Metacom in John Easton's narrative. Pleading from a

traditional theological position, however, Kingsley is sure that Rehoboth's destruction reflects the anger of "the blessed and loving
God" (not the anger of the Indians) and prays for a "prophet" to
identify "New England's sin" for him.

Sir, I salute you with all that call on the Lord Jesus, their Lord &
ours. I did dispatch a few lines to New Norwich & so to you & the
rest on your river, but fearing it should not come to your hand &
those which it concerns, I now, in my sickness that the Lord hath
laid on us as He did on Job—I am now in a fever or ague, yet I do
judge I follow [St.] Paul, I can say truly that since our wars begun
my flesh is so gone with fear, care & grief & now this sickness, my
skin is ready to cleave to my bones. Now being unknown to you
below on the river, I say I am the 1 man & only left of those that
gathered the church that is now in Dorchester, yet of late have lived
at Rehoboth or Seconk & hath suffered deep, with my neighbors.
Now to tell you what we have & how we are like to suffer, my
heart will not hold to write & sheets would [not] contain. I am not
able to bear the sad stories of our woeful day [March 28, 1676],
when the Lord made our wolfish heathen to be our lords, to fire our
town, shout & holler, to call to us to come out of our garrisons.
Some did go out alive, with success; but had not our God
restrained them, they were now to have swallowed us all up. They
burnt our mills, brake the stones, yea, our grinding stones; & what
was hid in the earth they found, corn & fowls, killed cattle & took
the hindquarters & left the rest, yea, all that day that the Lord gave
license they burnt cart wheels, drive away our cattle, sheep, horses,
in a word had not the Lord restrained they had not left one to have
told of our woeful day. We lost but one silly man that day. We are
shut up in our garrison & dare not go abroad far to our outlands,
without some strength. Some of our soldiers are removed. Nobody
comes to say, how do ye. Counsel from Bost. & Plymouth was to
stay, unless all had gone that could & left the rest to perish, yet
now every rod of ground near garrison is broken up & where house
& barn stood now put in beans & squashes; but alas, what will do
against famine!
    Now to leave all our danger, fear of sword, famine stares us in
the face. Now to my comfort I hear you have store of corn, yea,
though you do not sow in some years. Now misery calls for mercy

but I consave [?] is distress. The truth is my heart will not bear to write. Ah, the burden that I bear night & day, to see the blessed & loving God thus angry, & we have not a prophet to tell how long, & to say this or these are New England's sin. For general sin calls usually for general plague; which is now. Dear brethren, if there be power in your hands, do not say, go away & come again. It is better to die by sword than famine. Therefore I beg in my Lord's name, to send us some meal; for if we send it Rhode Island there is one wolf in the way, & he will have money, which one of 40 hath not it to pay, though they starve; yea, 1sh for 1 bushel, caring & bringing. There is another, that is the miller, & he takes an 8 part. O New England, when wilt thou leave oppressing. It may be in some of your minds to say, why do not the head men write, but only this old poor man. I say only, I will lay a mantel on my shoulder & go backwards. There is but two that knows of my writing, & the one discouraged me; but I know how earnest Paul begged prayers that which he calls grace might be expected.

I pray if this come into the hand of any that fear God, do not stifle it, but impart it to others, that those who have a willing mind may have a hand to save us from famine. I do not beg for money to build houses. Ah no, no. If any will send meal, pray let Deacon Walker distribute it. I know no man like minded.

It would be a dishonor to such a people as you, to use arguments to stir you up to such a work. I leave this & you all to the good hand of God, through Jesus Christ, who is the divine head of that blessed Covenant of Grace & fountain of all good. Bear with my writing, who came of my sickbed to make an end of these lines.

JOHN KINGSLEY

4 or 5 of 3 Mon. 1676

If any that hear or read will trust me one barrel of Indian meal & one of wheat, I do promise to pay, I or mine, when the Lord shall turn to His people with peace.

If any know or hear that Enos Kingsley be alive, at Northampton, let know that I his father am alive though no shelter for my gray hair, only with one swine God left when He sent our enemies to be our lords, & blessed be His holy name; He gave & He took. I prayed seven years to be fitted to suffer common calamity; so the thing I feared is come on me; but alas I am ready to faint in the day of adversity & show my strength is small.

40. "Awful Tokens of Divine Displeasure"

The view of the war from the relative safety of Boston is best expressed by Increase Mather's *Diary*. In it, the desperation of the Puritan faithful is evident. While the war itself has bypassed the city, a smallpox epidemic has not; and both occurrences seem to be judgments of God. Indeed, Mather attributes to God everything besides his own sins and the particularly heinous murders of Indians by whites, which, he confesses, "may occasion the Indians to seek to revenge their blood.... And if justice be not done upon the murderers, God will take vengeance." The single most tragic image of the war appears at the end of this excerpt from the *Diary*: Indians and whites being executed side by side on Boston Common while the plague and the war rage in and out of the city.[1]

[13 *January* 1675]. As to public concerns. 1. The sword is not yet put into the scabbard. 2. The army hath read a rebuke in that 6 captains have been lately slain at once. 3. There are sad diseases and terrible in the country. e.g. At Plymouth there is a malignant fever that is very mortal. At Gloucester the smallpox is in several families. Diverse already dead there. 4. Boston is under awful tokens of divine displeasure. Several dead (and many sick still) of that fever. Yea and the smallpox is now come into the town. One died yesterday nearby. (As to private concerns. 1. My old sins. 2. Plagues of heart. 3. Unthankfulness for special favors. God has continued health to me and mine. God hath provided for me in these difficult times but alas I have not been thankful as I should have been.) 5. There fears of an approaching famine. 6. Reformation doth not go forward. Magistrates too slow in that matter. Humble requests to God in court. As to public. 1. That the arms may be preserved. The Lord keep them from this terrible disease of the smallpox. And rebuke the heathen. 2. Heal His people. 3. In special, let the Lord have compassion upon Boston; & suffer not this disease to spread here. Enemies are risen up against us; & therefore let not the compassionate God, rise up against us too at the same time. 4. Sanctify these judgments, so as to cause a reformation of evils. . . .

August 7, [1676]. Some of those Indians (women & children) who lately submitted themselves to the English as they were gathering huckleberries in Concord were murdered by 4 Englishmen. A sad thing. It may be it will occasion the Indians to seek to revenge their blood which has been shed & new troubles to arise. And if justice be not done upon the murderers, God will take vengeance. . . .

In the latter end of August many sick with fever & fluxes (especially in Boston) which proved mortal. Above 50 died in August in this town. In the last week in August I hear of 11 that died in 2 days. . . .

Sep 13 [1676]. There were 8 Indians shot to death in Boston of those that were brought in from the eastward.

21. There were 3 Indians hanged & an Englishman hanged also, for murdering the Indians not far from Concord. Also another Englishman that was condemned should this day have been hanged but he died in prison. The like not known that a man should die or be sick on the day appointed for his execution. A sad thing also that English & Indians should be executed together.

We hear that 40 Indians have submitted themselves to the English at the eastward, because afraid of the Mohawks, who have killed several.

22. This day Sagamore Sam was hanged at Boston. And the sick Englishman that should have been executed last week (whose name was Goble) was hanged with him. It seems a madwoman got away the rope which should have hanged the Englishman, wherefore he was hanged with the very same rope which had hanged the Indian just before.

The same day 3 other Indians hanged, viz the Sagamore of Quaboag, one-eyed John, & Jethro. They were betrayed into the hands of the English by Indians.

Nov. 4 [1676]. Mugg, the Indian captain, came to Boston to treat about peace with the eastern Indians.

11. Discoursing with Mugg, he told me that this winter many Indians at the eastward had starved to death & particularly that there were 3 sachems starved to death. . . .

41. "They Will Not This Next Twenty Years Recover"

Kingsley's letter and Mather's diary leave a dramatic impression of the war's impact on Boston and its outskirts; Mather even mentions the starvation which, more than any other factor, eventually defeated the Indians. For an insight into the economic impact of the war on the Puritan colonies as a whole, the best source is a letter dated April, 1676, from William Berkeley, Governor of Virginia, to Thomas Ludwell.[1] Since at this time Virginia was also enduring an English-Indian war, Berkeley assumes a widespread native conspiracy (as did the Puritans when they learned of Virginia's troubles). Berkeley clearly pities the suffering Puritans; but he also felt that the Puritans had provoked God and, therefore, begun the war by their rejection of Anglicanism—an ironic twist of the Puritan conviction that they had provoked God by their failure to be Puritan enough.[2]

A new tax is laid upon us for the Indians are generally combined against us in all the northern parts of America. They have destroyed divers towns in New England, killed more than a thousand fighting men, seldom were worsted in any encounter and have made the New England men desert above a hundred miles of ground of that land which they had divers years seated and built towns on. I have not heard from thence this fortnight but expect to hear no very good news when I do for they either have not or pretend not to have money to pay their soldiers. But whatever the success be, they will not this next twenty years recover what they have lost and expended in this war. They had taken in their last harvest before the Indians invaded them and declared the war against them, yet now they are in such want of provisions that they have sent to us abundance of vessels to buy of us great quantities of all sort as pork beef and corn in so much that I and the Council

first and since the General Assembly have been forced to promul-
gate a severe law that no more provisions shall be exported from
hence and I think all considering men conclude that one year's
want of provision does impoverish kingdoms and states (of all
natures) more than seven years of luxury, but this is not half the
New England men's misery, for they have lost all their beaver
trade, half at least of their fishing and have nothing to carry to the
Barbados with whose commodities they were wont to carry away
our tobacco and other provisions. Add to this the new tax of one
penny per pound on tobacco which my officers rigorously exact of
them: to conclude this, if this war lasts one year longer they in New
England will be the poorest, miserablest people of all the plantations of the English in America. Indeed ... I should pity them had
they deserved it of the King or his blessed father.

42. "The Indians Come In Daily"

Accounts of the effect of the war on Indians are much harder to
come by than Kingsley's and Berkeley's letters or Mather's diary.
One, however, is found in the William Harris Papers, published by
the Rhode Island Historical Society.[1] Harris was a rival of Roger
Williams and, in his high-handed land transactions, hardly a friend
of the Narragansetts. But his description of the defeated, destitute,
and traitorous Indians straggling into Providence in the summer of
1676 is one of the lasting images of the war.

... Ever since the taking of the great man of Narragansett
[Canonicus] the war hath gone most against the Indians, and within
two or three days after a great army of Indians, supposed a
thousand, boasted of their victories at Providence over the English,
in a parley there the aforesaid great man was taken by Connecticut
forces, from which time March to this 12th of August 1676, two
thousand Indians have been killed taken & come in and supposed
fifteen hundred before, and some say a thousand English from the
first slain, but I doubt nearer fifteen hundred.

The Indians come in daily, and fight presently against the Indians they came from and betray one another into the hands of the English.

And because Connecticut forces are most constantly active & kill all save boys & girls, the Indians haste into the Massachusetts & Plymouth to scape them that are most like (by the help of Indians that are with them) to kill them.

Another occasion of their coming in is want of powder, which is hard to be got now, having but little to buy it and go to buy it in great danger of their lives by reason of the Indians called Mohawks, their enemies, that meet with them that used to kill & eat their enemies but formerly they have said they had powder of the Dutch about Fort Albany.

There have more Indians died since the war began by sickness & hunger than by the sword, so that dead come in & transported since the war each way about seven thousand. It hath been God's heavy hand on them as well as on the English, for they now are not only in danger of the English & divers sorts of Indians but of their own supposed friends having been so much trepanned [entrapped] by them that they are afraid of all they see but least of those of Rhode Island, for there they come in & are as well accommodated as ever they were in their lives only they are called servants, but soon after peace is concluded they will run all away again as the captives formerly did after the Pequot War forty years since. . . .

Just now news is brought that this 12th of August early in the morning Philip was slain in a swamp within a mile of Mount Hope [his home] & about a mile & half from Rhode Island. He was with a few men there & set upon by one Captain Benjamin Church of Plymouth & Captain Pealeg Sanford of Rhode Island, each of them with forty men, & the said Philip shot through the heart by an Indian that lives on Rhode Island and his head & hands are now on the said Island. . . .

43. "To Kill and Destroy Them"

The Indians Harris describes found relative safety in Rhode Island as long as Connecticut soldiers could be avoided. The fate that awaited surrendering Indians in Massachusetts was somewhat different. There no marauding army intervened, but an order from the Governor's Council in August of 1675 permitted any white to shoot on sight any Indian outside the boundaries of five of John Eliot's "praying towns." Such a law is understandable in wartime, though the order severely inconvenienced Indians loyal to the Puritan cause in their hunting and farming. What is more alarming is that the same Massachusetts authorities also invited all Indians not already confined in the five towns to submit themselves to Puritan examination and mercy by walking into Boston from its rural outskirts. Thus Edward Rawson's response to James Quanhpohkit and four other Indians loyal to the Puritans is little more than an invitation to any Indian—enemy, neutral, or friend—to be shot by some trigger-happy white.[1]

A.

At a Council held in Boston, August 30th, 1675.

The Council judging it of absolute necessity for security of the English and Indians in amity with us, that they be restrained their usual commerce with the English and hunting in the woods, during the time of hostility with those that are our enemies; do order, that all those Indians, that are desirous to approve themselves faithful to the English, be confined to the several places underwritten, until the Council shall take further order, and that they so order the setting of their wigwams that they may stand compact in one place of their plantations respectively, where it may be best for their own provision and defense, and that none of them do presume to travel above one mile from the center of such of their dwellings unless in company of some English, or in their service, excepting for gathering in their corn with one Englishman in company, on peril of being taken as our enemies, or their abettors. And in case any of them be taken without the limits aforesaid except as above said, and do lose their lives, or be otherwise damnified by English or Indians; the Council do hereby declare that they shall account themselves wholly innocent, and their blood, or other damage by them sustained, will be upon their own heads. Also it shall not be lawful for any Indians that are now in amity with us, to entertain or receive any strange Indians, or to receive any of our enemies' plunder, but shall from time to time make discovery thereof to some English that shall be appointed for that end to sojourn with them, on penalty of being accounted our enemies, and to be proceeded against, as such.

Also, whereas it is the manner of the heathen that are now in hostility with us, contrary to the practice of civil nations, to execute their bloody insolences by stealth, and skulking in small parties, declining all open decision of the controversy, either by treaty or by the sword; the Council do therefore order, that after the publication of the provision aforesaid, it shall be lawful for any person, whether English or Indian, that shall find any Indian travelling in any of our towns or woods, contrary to the limits abovenamed, to command them under their guard and examination, or to kill and destroy them as they best may or can. The Council hereby declaring, that it will be most acceptable to them, that none be killed or wounded, that are willing to surrender themselves into custody.

The places of the Indians' residence are, Natick, Punquapog, Nashobah, Wamesit, and Hassanamesit. And if there be any that belong to other places, they are to repair to some one of these.

By the Council.

 EDWARD RAWSON, SECRETARY.

B.

In answer to the petition of James Quanhpohkit, James Speen, Job, Andrew Pittimee, and John Magus. [June, 1676]

Capt. Tom being a lawful prisoner at war, there needs no further evidence for his conviction; yet he having had liberty to present his plea before the Council why he should not be proceeded against accordingly, instead of presenting anything that might alleviate his withdrawing [as a Christianized Indian] from the government of the English and joining with the enemy, it doth appear by sufficient evidence that he was not only (as is credibly related by some Indians present with him) an instigator to others over whom he was by this government made a captain, but also was actually present and an actor in the devastation of some of our plantations; and therefore it cannot consist with the honor and justice of authority to grant him a pardon.

Whereas the Council do, with reference to the faithful service of the petitioners, grant them the lives of the women and children by them mentioned. And, further, the Council do hereby declare, that, as they shall be ready to show favor in sparing the lives and liberty of those that have been our enemies, on their coming in and submission of themselves to the English government and your disposal, the reality and complacency of the government towards the Indians sufficiently appearing in the provisions they have made, and tranquility that the Pequots have enjoyed under them for over forty years; so also it will not be available for any to plead in favor for them that they have been our friends while found and taken among our enemies.

Further the Council do hereby declare that none may expect privilege by his declaration, that come not in and submit themselves in 14 days next coming.

By the Council,

EDW. RAWSON, CLERK.

44. "The Terror of Selling Away Such Indians"

The next two documents deal with the aftermath of the war for the Indians who fought against the Puritans. The first is John Eliot's plea against selling native survivors into slavery, a practice begun after the Pequot War (see Document 28).[1] Though Puritans themselves had occasional black and Indian slaves (the latter, for the most part, spoils of war), their chief involvement in slavery was the provision of Indian slaves for Caribbean colonies. Eliot was horrified by this practice, though he himself had a Pequot servant for years.[2]

The second document—a series of extracts from letters to the General Court at Plymouth—concerns the issue of whether to sell Metacom's nine-year-old son into slavery or to execute him.[3] The final decision—slavery—was undoubtedly viewed by Plymouth leaders as a humane gesture and can be taken as an implicit reply to Eliot's arguments.

A.

To the Honorable the Governor & council,
sitting at Boston this 13th of the 6th [August] [16]75
the humble petition of John Eliot
Showeth

That the terror of selling away such Indians, unto the Islands for perpetual slaves, who shall yield up themselves to your mercy, is like to be an effectual prolongation of the war & such an exasperation of them, as may produce, we know not what evil consequence, upon all the land. Christ hath said, blessed are the merciful, for they shall obtain mercy. This usage of them is worse than death. To put to death men that have deserved to die, is an ordinance of God, & a blessing is promised to it. It may be done in faith. The design of Christ in these last days, is not to extirpate nations, but to gospelize them. He will spread the Gospel round the world about. Re [velations]. 11. 15. The Kingdoms of the Lord & of His Christ, His sovereign hand, & grace hath brought the Gospel into these dark places of the earth. When we came, we declared to the world, & it is recorded, yea we are engaged by our letters patent to the King's Majesty, that the endeavor of the Indians' conversion, not their extirpation, was one great end of our enterprise, in coming to these ends of the earth. The Lord hath so succeeded that work, as that (by His grace) they have the Holy Scriptures as sundry of themselves able to teach their countrymen, the good knowledge of God. The light of the Gospel is risen among those that sat in darkness, & in the region of the shadow of death. And however some of them have refused to receive the Gospel, & now are incensed in their spirits unto a war against the English: yet by that good promise Ps [alms] 2. 1. 2. 3. 4. 5. 6. etc. I doubt not but the meaning of Christ is, to open a door for the free passage of the Gospel among them, & that the Lord will fulfill that Word v. 6 yet have I set my King, my annointed, on my holy hill of Sion, though some rage at it. My humble request is, that you would follow Christ His design, in this matter, to promote the free passage of religion among them, & not to destroy them. To send them away from the light of the Gospel, which Christ hath graciously given them, unto a place, a state, a way of perpetual darkness, to the eternal ruin of their souls, is (as I apprehend) to act contrary to the mind of Christ. God's command is, that we should enlarge the Kingdom of Jesus Christ, Isaiah 54. 1. enlarge the place of thy tent. It seemeth to me, that to sell them away for slaves, is to hinder the enlargement of His Kingdom. How can a Christian soul yield to act, in casting away their souls, for whom Christ hath, with an eminent hand provided an offer of the Gospel? To sell souls for money seemeth to me a dangerous merchandise. If they deserve to die, it is far better to be put to death, under godly governors, who will take religious care, that means may be used, that they may die penitently. To sell them away from all means of grace, when Christ hath provided means of grace for them, is the way for us to be active in the destroying their souls, when we are highly obliged to seek their conversion, & salvation, & have opportunity in our hands so to do. Deut [eronomy] 23. 15-16. A fugitive servant from a pagan master, might not be delivered to his master, but be kept in Israel for the good of his soul. How much less lawful is it to sell away souls from under the light of the Gospel, into a condition, where their souls will be utterly lost, so far as appeareth unto men. All men (of reading) condemn the Spaniard for cruelty, upon this point, in destroying men, & depopulating the land. The country is large enough, here is land enough for them & us too. P[roverbs] 14. 28. In the multitude of people is the King's honor. It will be much to the glory of Christ, to have many brought in to worship His great name.

I beseech the honored Council to pardon my boldness, & let the case of conscience be discussed orderly, before the thing be acted.

Cover my weakness, & weigh the reason & religion that laboreth in this great case of conscience.

B.

At a General Court specially called in Boston, 6 September 1676.

There being many of our Indian enemies seized & now in our possession, the Court judgeth it meet to refer the disposal of them to the honored Council, declaring it to be their sense that such of them as shall appear to have imbrued their hands in English blood should suffer death here, & not be transported into foreign parts.

No. 2.

The question being propounded to us by our honored rulers, whether Philip's son be a child of death—our answer hereunto is, That we do acknowledge that the rule in Deut. 24. 16. ["The fathers shall not be put to death for the children, neither shall the children be put to death for the fathers; every man shall be put to death for his own sin"] is moral, & therefore perpetually binding, *viz.*, that in a particular act of wickedness, though capital, the crime of the parent doth not render his child a subject of punishment, by the civil magistrate; yet, upon serious consideration, we humbly conceive that the children of notorious traitors, rebels & murderers, especially of such as have been principal leaders & actors in such horrid villainies, & that against a whole country, yea, the whole interest of God therein, may be involved in the guilt of their parents, & may, *salva republica*, be adjudged to death, as to us seems evident by the Scripture instances of Saul, Achan, Haman, the children of whom were cut off by the sword of justice for the transgressions of their parents, although concerning some of those children it be manifest that they were not capable of being co-actors therein.

SAMUEL ARNOLD.
JOHN COTTON.

Plymouth, September 7, 1676.

No. 3.

I hope you have seen my letter to the Governor, if it had not been out of mind when I was writing I should have said something about Philip's son. It is necessary that some effectual course be taken with him. This makes me think of Hadad, who was a little child when his father, chief sachem of the Edomites, was killed by Joab, & had not others fled away with him, I am apt to think that David would have taken a course that Hadad should never have proved a scourge to the next generation. [Kings 11, 17]

Your affectionate Brother,   INCREASE MATHER.
Boston, October 20, 1676.
To John Cotton, Plymouth

No. 4.

I long to know what becomes of Philip's wife & son. I know there is some difficulty in Psalm 137. 8, 9, though I think it may be considered whether there be not some specialty & somewhat extraordinary in it. The law, Deut. 24. 16, compared with the commended example of Amasias, 2 Chron. 25, 4, doth sway much with me in the case under consideration. I hope God will direct those whom it doth concern to a good issue. Let us join our prayers at the Throne of Grace with all our might, that the Lord would so dispose of all public motions & affairs, that His Jerusalem in this wilderness may be the habitation of justice & mountain of holiness; that it may be a quiet habitation, a Tabernacle that shall not be taken down.

JAMES KEITH
Bridgewater, Oct. 30, 1676.
To John Cotton, Plymouth

45. "They Strip, They Bind, They Ravish"

It is always difficult to determine the extent to which the senti-
ments of religious and governmental leaders are shared by the
general population. Increase Mather's conviction that God was
punishing the Puritans for their sins by permitting successful Indian
attacks might not have been a strongly held belief on the Puritan
frontier itself. There, one could argue, settlers feared Indians more
than Mather feared them, but were also more aware than he of white
injustices. One frontier minister in Connecticut, for example, wrote to
Mather in the summer of 1676, long after the war had begun, asking
him for help in persuading his parishioners that the Plymouth
colonists were "wholly innocent" in the outbreak of war, despite the
"uncomfortable and dishonorable reports concerning them, which I
was grieved to hear." [1]

There are some documents, however, not written by politicians or
ministers, that seem to give a clearer picture of popular attitudes to
the war. The excerpt printed here from Benjamin Thompson's
widely-read poem *New England's Crisis* pictures the Wampanoags
and Metacom as motivated solely by sadism, lust, greed, and love of
liquor. [2] One should compare the words Thompson puts into Metacom's mouth with Metacom's own statements in John Easton's
narrative. Thomas Wheeler, in his "True Narrative of the Lord's
Providences . . . ," repeats the claim that the Indians "hate us without
a cause," but goes beyond Thompson in praying, with Increase
Mather, that God's anger "may cease towards us and He may be
pleased either to make our enemies at peace with us, or more,
destroy them before us". [3] Finally, Mary Rowlandson's famous narrative of her captivity among the Wampanoags adds her own "provok-

ing sins" to Wheeler's assumption that Puritan "hearts" in general have temporarily turned from God and invited His punishment.[4] The most notable characteristic of Rowlandson's narrative, however, is her determination to credit the Indians' vices to their savage nature and their virtues to God. Published in 1682, the narrative is one of the best examples of a Puritan observer who recorded truths about native life in New England but could not interpret those truths as evidence of normal human conduct: desperation, sorrow, kindness, shrewdness, and, in the most general terms, simple self-interest. By the end of King Philip's War, the Puritan capacity to understand native culture had, if anything, declined in the forty-six years since the landing of the *Arbella.*

A.

In seventy-five the critic of our years
Commenced our war with Philip and his peers.
Whether the sun in Leo had inspired
A fev'rish heat, and pagan spirits fired?
Whether some Romish agent hatcht the plot?
Or whether they themselves? appeareth not.
Whether our infant thrivings did invite?
Or whether to our lands pretended right?
Is hard to say; but Indian spirits need
No grounds but lust to make a Christian bleed.
    And here methinks I see this greasy lout
With all his pagan slaves coiled round about,
Assuming all the majesty his throne
Of rotten stump, or of the rugged stone
Could yield; casting some bacon-rind-like looks,
Enough to fright a student from his books,
Thus treat his peers, and next to them his commons,
Kenneled together all without a summons.
"My friends, our fathers were not half so wise
As we ourselves who see with younger eyes.
They sell our land to Englishmen who teach
Our nation all so fast to pray and preach:
Of all our country they enjoy the best,

And quickly they intend to have the rest.
This no wunnegin, no big matchit law,
Which our old fathers' fathers never saw.
These English make and we must keep them too,
Which is too hard for them or us to do,
We drink we so big whipt, but English they
Go sneep, no more, or else a little pay.
Me meddle squaw me hanged, our fathers kept
What squaws they would whether they waked or slept.
Now if you'll fight I'll get you English coats.
And wine to drink out of their captains' throats.
The richest merchants' houses shall be ours.
We'll lie no more on mats or dwell in bowers;
We'll have their silken wives, take they our squaws,
They shall be whipt by virtue of our laws.
If ere we strike 'tis now before they swell
To greater swarms than we know how to quell.
This my resolve, let neighboring sachems know,
And everyone that hath club, gun, or bow."
This was assented to, and for a close
He stroked his smutty beard and cursed his foes.
This counsel lightning like their tribes invade,
And something like a muster's quickly made,
A ragged regiment, a naked swarm,
Whom hopes of booty doth with courage arm,
Set forth with bloody hearts, the first they meet
Of men or beasts they butcher at their feet.
They round our skirts, they pare, they fleece, they kill,
And to our bordering towns do what they will.
Poor hovels (better far then Caesar's court
In the experience of the meaner sort)
Receive from them their doom next execution,
By flames reduced to horror and confusion:
Here might be seen the smoking funeral piles
Of wildered towns pitcht distant many miles.
Here might be seen the infant from the breast
Snatcht by a pagan hand to lasting rest:
The mother Rachel-like shrieks out, "My child!"
She wrings her hands and raves as she were wild.

The brutish wolves suppress her anxious moan
By cruelties more deadly of her own.
Will she or nill the chastest turtle must
Taste of the pangs of their unbridled lust.
From farms to farms, from towns to towns they post,
They strip, they bind, they ravish, flea and roast....

B.

Thus I have endeavored to set down and declare both what the Lord did against us in the loss of several persons' lives, and the wounding of others, some of which wounds were very painful in dressing, and long ere they were healed, besides many dangers that we were in, and fears that we were excercised with; and also what great things He was pleased to do for us in frustrating their [the Indians'] many attempts, and vouchsafing such a deliverance to us. The Lord avenge the blood that hath been shed by these heathen, who hate us without a cause, though He be most righteous in all that hath befallen there, and in all other parts of the country; He help us to humble ourselves before Him, and with our whole hearts, to return to Him, and also to improve all His mercies, which we still enjoy, that so His anger may cease towards us and He may be pleased either to make our enemies at peace with us, or more, destroy them before us. I tarried at Marlborough with Captain Hutchinson until his death, and came home to Concord, August the 21, (though not thoroughly recovered of my wound) and so did others that went with me. But since I am reasonable well, though I have not the use of my hand and arm as before: my son Thomas, though in great hazard of life for some time after his return to Concord, yet is now very well cured, and his strength well restored! Oh that we could praise the Lord for His great goodness towards us. Praised be His name, that though He took away some of us, yet was pleased to spare so many of us, and add unto our days; He help us whose souls He hath delivered from death, and eyes from tears, and feet from falling, to walk before Him in the land of the living, till our great change come, and to sanctify His name in all His ways about us, that both our afflictions, and our mercies may quicken us to live more to His glory all our days.

C.

But before I go any further, I would take leave to mention a few remarkable passages of providence, which I took special notice of in my afflicted time.

1. Of the fair opportunity lost in the long march, a little after the fort fight, when our English army was so numerous, and in pursuit of the enemy, and so near as to take several and destroy them: and the enemy in such distress for food, that our men might track them by their rooting in the earth for ground-nuts, whilst they were flying for their lives. I say, that then our army should want provision, and be forced to leave their pursuit and return homeward: and the very next week the enemy came upon our town, like bears bereft of their whelps, or so many ravenous wolves, rending us and our lambs to death. But what shall I say? God seemed to leave His people to themselves, and order all things for His own holy ends. *Shall there be evil in the city and the Lord hath not done it? They are not grieved for the affliction of Joseph, therefore shall they go captive, with the first that go captive.* It is the Lord's doing, and it should be marvelous in our eyes.

2. I cannot but remember how the Indians derided the slowness, and dullness of the English army, in its setting out. For after the desolations at Lancaster and Medfield, as I went along with them, they asked me when I thought the English army would come after them? I told them I could not tell: it may be they will come in May, said they. Thus did they scoff at us, as if the English would be a quarter of a year getting ready.

3. Which also I have hinted before, when the English army with new supplies were sent forth to pursue after the enemy, and they understanding it, fled before them till they came to Baquaug River, where they forthwith went over safely: that that river should be impassable to the English. I can but admire to see the wonderful providence of God in preserving the heathen for farther affliction to our poor country. They could go in great numbers over, but the English must stop: God had an over-ruling hand in all those things.

4. It was thought, if their corn were cut down, they would starve and die with hunger: and all their corn that could be found, was destroyed, and they driven from that little they had in store, into

the woods in the midst of winter; and yet how to admiration did the Lord preserve them for His holy ends, and the destruction of many still amongst the English! strangely did the Lord provide for them; that I did not see (all the time I was among them) one man, woman, or child, die with hunger.

Though many times they would eat that, that a hog or a dog would hardly touch; yet by that God strengthened them to be a scourge to His people.

The chief and commonest food was ground-nuts: they eat also nuts and acorns, artichokes, lilly roots, ground-beans, and several other weeds and roots, that I know not.

They would pick up old bones, and cut them to pieces at the joints, and if they were full of worms and maggots, they would scald them over the fire to make the vermine come out, and then boil them, and drink up the liquor, and then beat the great ends of them in a mortar, and so eat them. They would eat horses guts, and ears, and all sorts of wild birds which they could catch: also bear, venison, beaver, tortoise, frogs, squirrels, dogs, skunks, rattle-snakes; yea, the very bark of trees; besides all sorts of creatures, and provision which they plundered from the English. I can but stand in admiration to see the wonderful power of God, in providing for such a vast number of our enemies in the wilderness, where there was nothing to be seen, but from hand to mouth. Many times in a morning, the generality of them would eat up all they had, and yet have some farther supply against they wanted. It is said, Psal. 81, 13, 14. *Oh, that my people had hearkened to me, and Israel had walked in my ways, I should soon have subdued their enemies, and turned my hand against their adversaries.* But now our perverse and evil carriages in the sight of the Lord, have so offended Him, that instead of turning His hand against them, the Lord feeds and nourishes them up to be a scourge to the whole land.

5. Another thing that I would observe is, the strange providence of God, in turning things about when the Indians was at the highest, and the English at the lowest. I was with the enemy eleven weeks and five days, and not one week passed without the fury of the enemy, and some desolation by fire and sword upon one place or other. They mourned (with their black faces) for their own losses, yet triumphed and rejoiced in their inhumane, and many times devilish cruelty to the English. They would boast much of their

victories; saying, that in two hours time they had destroyed such a
captain, and his company at such a place; and such a captain and
his company at such a place; and such a captain and his company
in such a place: and boast how many towns they had destroyed,
and scoff, and say, they had done them a good turn, to send them
to heaven so soon. Again, they would say, this summer that they
would knock all the rogues in the head, or drive them into the sea,
or make them fly the country: thinking surely, Agag-like, *The
Bitterness of Death is Past*. Now the heathen begins to think all is
their own, and the poor Christians' hopes to fail (as to man) and
now their eyes are more to God, and their hearts sigh heaven-ward:
and to say in good earnest, *Help Lord, or we perish*: when the Lord
has brought His people to this, that they saw no help in anything
but Himself: then He takes the quarrel into His own hand: and
though they made a pit, in their own imaginations, as deep as hell
for the Christians that summer, yet the Lord hurled themselves into
it. And the Lord had not so many ways before to preserve them,
but now He hath as many to destroy them.

But to return again to my going home, where we may see a
remarkable change of providence: At first they were all against it,
except my husband would come for me; but afterwards they
assented to it, and seemed much to rejoice in it; some asked me to
send them some bread, others some tobacco, others shaking me by
the hand, offering me a hood and scarf to ride in; not one moving
hand or tongue against it. Thus hath the Lord answered my poor
desire, and the many earnest requests of others put up unto God
for me. In my travels an Indian came to me, and told me, if I were
willing, he and his squaw would run away, and go home along with
me: I told him No: I was not willing to run away, but desired to
wait God's time, that I might go home quietly, and without fear.
And now God hath granted me my desire. O the wonderful power
of God that I have seen, and the experience that I have had: I have
been in the midst of those roaring lions, and savage bears, that
feared neither God, nor man, nor the Devil, by night and day,
alone and in company: sleeping all sorts together, and yet not one
of them offered me the least abuse of unchastity to me, in word or
action. Though some are ready to say, I speak it for my own credit;
but I speak it in the presence of God, and to His glory....

Conclusion

"They Thought Their Way Was Good"

I

History was not kind to the governments that clashed in King Philip's War. Autonomous Indian rule disappeared forever from New England when the last stronghold of native self-determination, the Mohegans, declared their official submission to Connecticut in 1682; two years later, James II revoked the Massachusetts Bay charter. Even as King Philip's War was drawing to a close with Puritan victory in sight, a special agent of the crown, Edward Randolph, arrived in Boston to find and expose the vices of Puritan rule. Among other charges that Randolph relayed to the mother country was the accusation that Puritans in general, not the Pilgrims of Plymouth Colony in particular, had provoked the war by harassing Metacom and selling liquor and arms to the Indians.[1] Technically, some of Randolph's charges were unfounded; but in their overall import they were true enough: persecution and paranoia had been on the rise in New England, especially in Massachusetts, since the end of Puritan rule in England in 1658. And the final, desperate outbreak of that paranoia—the Salem witchcraft trials—was still to come in 1692, one year after the conversion of Massachusetts into a dependent royal province. The new charter of the Bay Colony, replacing the one that Winthrop had carried with him to New England in 1630, spoke again of "winning" the natives to "the only true God" by the "good life and orderly conversation" of Englishmen.[2] But the zeal to save the

entire world, founded upon Puritan identification with the original
Israelites of the Bible, was eliminated once and for all from the
realm of politics. Henceforth, New England's governance would be
broadened and secularized to a degree that the immigrants on the
Arbella would have considered unimaginable.

There were still Indians to deal with, however; and royal rule was
no more benign than Puritan control had been. Randolph himself
had called the Indians "rude and licentious" when he criticized
Puritan treatment of them, and long-standing Indian complaints
about English arrogance and land encroachment continued una-
bated. In his grand defense of Puritan faith, *Magnalia Christi
Americana*, Cotton Mather quoted a Martha's Vineyard Indian
protesting in 1689 against Englishmen who "would have forcibly
taken sheep from thence; and we are much threatened therewith. . . . We hope we shall not see (as is too much practis'd in other
places) an Englishman pretending an Indian to be in his debt, to
come to our houses and pay himself; or, in other cases, beat our
people."³ Years later, the London coordinator of the missionary
effort to the remaining Indians in New England, after congratulat-
ing the Province of Massachusetts on the purchase of part of the
same Martha's Vineyard, noted the legitimate complaints of the
"unjust encroachments made upon the poor Indians at the places
[in Massachusetts] appropriated for their settlements" and regretted
that no provision had yet (in 1712) been "made law" in the colony
"to prevent these instrusions."⁴ Thus, although Indians had been
restricted to scattered sites in Massachusetts (which by then included the former Plymouth Colony as well as Martha's Vineyard
and Nantucket), they had no legal protection for the few acres they
retained.

The complex fate of New England natives under post-Puritan
provincial rule is apparent in the contrast between a Cotton Mather
sermon from 1700 and a Cotton Mather letter from 1718. In the
sermon, "A Monitory, and Hortatory Letter, To those English, who
debauch the Indians, By Selling Strong Drink unto them," Mather
declaims against the inveterate "impiety" of colonists who "feed the
lust of drunkenness among the Indians . . . to obtain a little bit of
money."⁵ "Sometimes," Mather says, these men will "screw them
into bargains full of cruel oppression and extortion [of furs, corn,
and money], which afterwards throw them into the extremest

inconveniences."6 Though Mather insists that New England is "to better purpose possessed and occupied by the English" than by the formerly temperate natives, he adds that it is the Devil's work to cause "those forlorn creatures [to] stumble into such horrible pits of sin. ... The Indians were the children of hell before; but by their drunkenness, they are twofold more so."7 Not only do drunken Indians resist work and become violent, their health and life itself are repeatedly threatened (by drowning and accidental fires). Above all, according to Mather, "the evangelical work" among Christianized Indians, "which already too much comes to little," is jeopardized by alcohol: some "old men among the Indians" say that "when they were heathens, many of them were not such great villains, as they are since they were Christians."8 Mather concludes that God may therefore decide once again to "commission" these same Indians to be the "executioners of His wrath" upon the English in another Indian war.9

This partially sympathetic picture of native degradation and resistance to Christianity is complemented by a different kind of complaint in Mather's letter to the General Assembly of Connecticut on October 8, 1718. There he regrets that "in the very heart of a colony renowned for the profession of Christianity, there should for fourscore [80] years together be a body of the aboriginals [Mohegans] persisting in the darkest and most horrid paganism." "We do importunately beseech you," Mather continues, "to quiet the minds of your Indians, with all possible security for their peaceable enjoyment of that small portion of lands which has been reserved for them" through "a clear, firm, lasting settlement of claims," so that the conversion of the Mohegans to the true faith can proceed.10 (A generation later, following a drawn-out settlement of those very land claims, a Puritan minister found the Indians in the backcountry of Connecticut still celebrating their traditional paganism.11)

The overall picture of native life one draws from these two Mather documents suggests not that Indians were mired in sin, but that New England natives, despite extreme economic and jurisdictional pressures, continued to maintain a measure of indigenous culture. This conclusion is supported by the most detailed record of early eighteenth-century native attitudes in New England: Experience Mayhew's journal of his futile missionary efforts among three different tribes in 1713 and 1714. A Narragansett sachem, still asserting his authority over his people, confidently asked Mayhew "why I did not make the English good in the first place" and pointed out to him that English masters in Rhode Island forcibly removed their indentured Indian servants from tribal meetings. The Pequot Indians rebuffed Mayhew because they had more pressing concerns: Connecticut whites were squatting on their remaining lands. And the Mohegans, whom Mayhew finally reached in Connecticut, responded to his sermon with the following arguments:

> Some of them said they did acknowledge that there was a God and did worship Him, but as several nations had their distinct way of worship, so they had theirs; and they thought their way was good, and that they had no reason to alter it.... Others said some Indians that had seemed most forward to profess religion had soon after forsaken the English and joined with their enemies, which they would not have done if they had found such excellency in religion as we pretended there was. Others said they could not see that men were ever the better for being Christians, for the English that were Christians would cheat the Indians of their land and otherwise wrong them, and that their knowledge of books made them the more cunning to cheat others and so did more hurt than good.[12]

II

Among tribes to the north of Massachusetts, native pride led to further bloodshed on a large scale: King William's War, 1690–97; Queen Anne's War, 1702–14; and "Lovewell's War," 1722–25. Once these "ravenous howling wolves," in Cotton Mather's words, went to war, the royal English government—like the Puritan magistrates before them—conducted a no-holds-barred campaign, but with a new wrinkle: the scalp bounty.[13] Rewards were posted for the scalps of male or female Indians, children as well as adults. And the traditional practice (dating from the Pequot War) was continued of awarding confiscated Indian lands as payment for English military service. The additional fact that the French government, operating out of Canada, did its part to incite the natives of northern New England against the English only heightened anti-Indian feelings to the south. As a result, instead of imagining a spiritual Satan manipulating his native children, Protestants of all varieties had visible satans—Catholic priests—to point to.

French Catholic manipulation, however, helped to eradicate a crucial theological aspect of earlier Puritan war narratives. No longer were English Protestants in Massachusetts inclined to look inward for the sins against God that made Him use Indians as agents of punishment. Now the Indians were agents of French priests, who clearly must be acting against God's wishes in the battle between Protestantism and Catholic heresy. In eighteenth-century war narratives the image of natives was still satanic, but the image of Protestantism in the New World as deserving chastisement had vanished. To eighteenth-century Protestants—except for a few traditional Puritan soul-searchers—God might prevent the destruction of his Protestant children, but He would not authorize Indian attacks in the first place.

A similar theological shift is evident in the captivity narratives that became ghoulishly popular following the decline of Puritan rule in Massachusetts. In 1682, Mary Rowlandson had seriously considered her own "provoking sins" as a contributing factor in her "heathenish" treatment among the Wampanoags. But the later, more secular successors to her captivity narrative, notably Hannah Duston's account of her efficient execution of her Indian captors, celebrate white retaliatory violence against Indians far more than they remind their readers of their own sinful state.[14] Intercultural violence in the eighteenth century, in short, was increasingly justified by the supposedly savage character of the Indians themselves, rather than by God's authorization of Indian wars as an opportunity for Englishmen to overcome their own spiritual failings.

From an Indian's point of view, the difference is hardly crucial: it is a distinction between the earlier Puritan violence of conscience and the later colonial violence of hate. As a case in point, Samuel Penhallow, in his *History of the Wars of New England with the Eastern Indians* (1726), clearly enjoys telling his bloody story in a way that Increase Mather, fifty years earlier, would have found complacent and shocking.[15] As the eighteenth century wound on toward the French and Indian Wars of the 1750s and the American Revolution itself, the increasing secularization of New England society deprived the remaining natives within its borders of even a symbolic theological role in its history. Even Jonathan Edwards, the last great Calvinist preacher in New England, devoted his only account of his missionary service at the isolated Indian outpost in Stockbridge, Massachusetts, to the political advantage of converting natives to Protestantism in the face of Jesuit overtures from French Canada.[16]

III

If Puritan control over New England politics was gone by 1692 and Puritan self-castigation was lost in the eighteenth-century accounts of Indian fiendishness, did later American policy toward hundreds of other Indian tribes owe no debt to Puritan attitudes and behavior? Indeed it did—though not in theological form. What even twentieth-century Americans have clearly inherited from New England Puritans, far more than from the other English colonists, is a need to see themselves as divinely appointed users of the earth for the good of all mankind. In essence, this conviction is no more than a simplified form of the Puritan belief in *vacuum domicilium*: the biblical investiture of untilled ground—"virgin land"—in the hands of Christian farmers. Nineteenth-century politicians seldom referred to Genesis 1:28 when they argued that Indians had to forfeit their territory because they did not do anything with it besides hunting, gathering, and fishing; but the essence of their claim was no different from John Winthrop's to the "vacant" lands of New England.[17] Even when individual tribes like the Cherokees in Georgia demonstrated their long-standing commitment to an agricultural economy, their continued interest in hunting and rejection of land as private property disqualified them as farmers in the proper, Christian sense of the term. Yet Cherokee society, by that time, bore a closer resemblance than white American society to the tribal life of the Israelites in the Bible that inspired the Puritans.[18] America took from the Puritans what it needed—a sense of territorial destiny—and rejected most of the rest. But that sense of territorial destiny was the cornerstone of the Bible Commonwealth in New England, and its survival—with or without scriptural citations—was critical to the formation of American society.[19]

This is most apparent in the effect that the Louisiana Purchase of 1803 had on American Indian policy. Thomas Jefferson, as President, negotiated that acquisition, yet it precipitated a policy of Indian removal that contravened his own philosophical attitudes toward Native Americans. As America's most influential Enlightenment thinker, Jefferson believed firmly in the importance of assimilating Indians into white society by persuading them that it was in their own best interest to trade their hunting grounds for white expertise in farming. With the Louisiana Purchase, however, it occurred to Jefferson that Indians who were beset by white encroachment on their tribal lands might want to move to another area in the territory of the United States, which stretched beyond the Mississippi River to the Rocky Mountains. But if the Indians chose not to become farmers or move across the Mississippi, Jefferson was not in favor of coercing them.

Eventually, however, during the presidential administration of Andrew Jackson (1828–36), coercion became official policy. Prior to 1830, American Indian policy offered natives the same basic alternatives as Puritans had offered before the Pequot War: total conversion to a Puritan way of life or relinquishment of land by purchase or treaty. Later, Puritans had moved toward a belief that Indians were constitutionally unable to convert themselves into good Christian citizens. The year 1830 signaled a similar turning point in the nineteenth century. It marked the passage of the Indian Removal Bill in Congress, which gave eastern Indians the impossible choice (from their point of view) of submitting to state laws and tribal extinction or moving into other Indian lands west of the Mississippi. It also marked the first articulate expression of a growing sentiment among Americans that Indians were racially incapable of changing their way of life and assimilating into white American society. A key article by Lewis Cass (shortly to become Jackson's Secretary of War) in the liberal *North American Review* argued at great length that an "inherent difficulty" arising from Indian "character" (not simply Indian culture) prevented fulfillment of Jefferson's original hope that Indians could be dealt with rationally.[20]

Following the administrative example of Jackson and the intellectual example of Cass, a range of American theoreticians popularized the idea that Indians were doomed by their own biological character to be left out of American history. At one end of the spectrum, the influential "American School" of ethnology asserted during the 1830s, '40s, and '50s the concept of "polygenesis" (separate and unequal creation of individual races). At the other end was Henry Wadsworth Longfellow's "Song of Hiawatha" (1855), long taken by Americans as a paradigm of noble savagery. Longfellow's Christlike Indian emissary from God to American Indians has a vision at the end of the poem of a "wild and woeful" future for his people among white Americans, thanks, apparently, to some inherent native tendency to vice and disloyalty, which Longfellow leaves unexplained. When "Hiawatha" was published, the discovery of gold in California was bringing an endless succession of wagon trains west of the Mississippi, and Indians there were beginning to assert their right to their homelands. Longfellow tacitly suggested in his otherwise benign poem that American Indians were not proud enough to play a cooperative or uncooperative part in the westward marches of hardy pioneers, who, unlike hopelessly disloyal Indians, had "but one heart-beat in their bosoms."[21]

Just as Puritan opinion of Indians hardened as the seventeenth century wore on, so, too, did nineteenth-century opinion. White society was unable to conceive of Indians as defending, for good reason, a human culture of their own. There is certainly a difference between viewing Indians as pawns of God and viewing them as genetically inferior: but both views deny natives a capacity for rational self-determination and make possible George Armstrong Custer's conclusion in the 1870s that Indians were "a race incapable of being judged by the rules or laws applicable to any other known race of men." It was only a short step from that belief to Custer's justification for killing noncombatants in attacks on Indian villages.[22]

Time and again in the nineteenth century, liberal and conservative politicians in Washington passed laws designed to make natives abandon what remained of their multifaceted economies and become independent farmers. Every attempt failed, even with the assistance of isolated but devoted missionaries, not because (as some politicians concluded) Indians were inherently unable to work or change, but because the consequences of such a change would have been catastrophic for Indians: total relinquishment of their cultures.[23] Using the earth for private gain had always been unconscionable for the majority of Native Americans; even though they sold some land to whites for reasons of expedience, in general they believed that land was not a salable possession and not ordained for anyone by any god. From the native point of view, a particular culture might have been given a particular territory by the Creator, but this hardly justified encroachment or exploitation of resources. If anything, it mandated the opposite: respect for sovereign boundaries and reverence for all the resources, animate and inanimate, that their own national territory provided. Nineteenth-century Americans, like their Puritan forebears, felt that Indian tribes had no sense of territoriality. They saw no difference between shared and overlapping occupation and absence of boundaries, whereas in fact cultures that do not value private property often share the wealth of a territory without sharing the sovereignty.[24] In this century our judicial system has continued the mistake: even some sympathetic courts, hearing Indian claims for compensation for lost lands, have required tribes to demonstrate exclusive use (rather than perpetual use) before they will confirm the original Indian title to the lands.[25]

We in this century are not the agrarian society we were when Jefferson spoke of the moral superiority of the yeoman farmer. Yet that agrarian concept is still with us, secularized and drained even further of its biblical associations. In our own day, the idea of using the land has been broadened and refocused on natural resources in every form. Jefferson's defense of the farmer's private investment of labor can be applied, with no wrenching of terms, to a corporation's private investment of capital in the oil fields of Alaska. Even though America's moral superiority is now defined as technological rather than manual, nature is still yielding its treasures to our hands, and our hands are converting those treasures, at a remarkable rate, into goods for the pleasure of the world.

The Indians, however, remain—in Arizona, in Alaska, wherever a decision is made, in Puritan fashion, that new resources are designed to augment our nation's destiny as a world leader. And they are resisting the loss of their remaining lands as surely as Metacom resisted the loss of Wampanoag power and territory. Only their weapons have changed. Now they are lawsuits, sit-ins, and boycotts.[26] Seneca, Tuscorora, and Onondaga Indians have taken legal steps to oppose eminent domain proceedings against parts of their treaty-protected reservations. Four years ago Northern Cheyenne in Montana refused a deal offered by Consolidation Coal

Company, by which Consolidation would build a hospital on the reservation and increase the lease rate in return for a mining monopoly. The Cheyenne knew that a mining monopoly on the reservation would considerably increase the white working population surrounding their territory and so increase pressure to sell or lease more land. The Northern Cheyenne later brought suit to terminate some coal leases altogether.

Perhaps more significantly, some Indian tribes like the Passamaquodies and Penobscots in Maine, the Narragansetts in Rhode Island, and the Menominees in Wisconsin have been fighting in the courts to regain lands that they claim were fraudulently taken from them in the past. At the heart of many of these disputes are Native American demands that the federal government, not individual states or localities, has the primary constitutional responsibility for dealing with Indian tribes, and that the tribes must be dealt with as defeated but autonomous nations. The federal government, according to this argument, must concern itself with the destiny of all political and racial entities within its borders, not only Anglo-Saxon culture. It must "comprehend the nature and meaning of culture."[27]

IV

In the last analysis, seventeenth-century Puritans did not bequeath to later Americans the materialism that is constantly attributed to our society; nor did Puritans give us our republican form of government. Compared to other European colonists, Puritans had no distinctive commitment to an agrarian way of life or to the concept of private property. They cannot be singled out from their countrymen along the Atlantic coast for particularly harsh treatment of Indians. Their distinguishing mark is their overriding belief in themselves as a community saved by God for a special purpose in the world. Under the umbrella of that sense of destiny, materialism, agrarianism, private property, republican government, industrialism, and belief in native inferiority could each, in time, find its safe and proper niche.

Racism derives group moral differences from group genetic differences; cultural status follows automatically from biological classification. So in recent years there has been a tendency to deny cultural distinctions between racial groups as a means of eradicating racism. This had led to Native Americans legally resisting the application of the 1964 Civil Rights Act to Indian life because it imposes a younger, alien form of government on the indigenous cultures of America. And U.S. courts have, at times, supported this resistance:

> No provision in the Constitution makes the First Amendment applicable to Indian nations nor is there any law of Congress doing so. It follows that neither, under the Constitution or the laws of Congress, do the Federal courts have jurisdiction of tribal laws or regulations, even though they [the tribal laws] may have an impact to some extent on forms of worship.[28]

Though moral distinctions between races are invalid, it does not follow that cultural distinctions between races are also invalid, particularly if the issue is political or religious sovereignty.

The most remarkable aspect of American Indian history is that Indians have survived at all as quasi-independent nations. Perhaps the resurgence of hundreds of Native American cultures in the 1960s and 1970s is an indication that Indians can teach white American society—as they could not teach the Puritans—a great deal about destiny, vitality, and endurance.

Suggested Readings for Future Study

The two recent books about Puritan-Indian relations—Alden T. Vaughan's *New England Frontier: Puritans and Indians, 1620–1675* (Boston, 1965) and Francis Jennings's *The Invasion of America: Indians, Colonialism, and the Cant of Conquest* (Chapel Hill, N.C., 1975)—are rarely in agreement on any points of interpretation. Vaughan trusts Puritan accounts of Indians; Jennings distrusts them. Vaughan emphasizes the missionary effort to the Indians; Jennings deemphasizes it. Vaughan is interested in Puritan culture, not native cultures; Jennings has it the other way around. In the end, Vaughan's book is appealing because of its trust, but Jennings's book is built on better research techniques and a broader sense of culture. Neither scholar, however, is sufficiently interested in the nature of Puritan theology and how it determined racial policy. The best accounts of Pilgrim-Indian relations at Plymouth reflect a similar conflict of interpretation: George F. Willison's *Saints and Strangers* (New York, 1945) is distinctly distrustful and unsympathetic toward the Pilgrims; David Bushnell's "The Treatment of the Indians in Plymouth Colony," *New England Quarterly*, 26 (1953), 193-218, and George D. Langdon, Jr.'s *Pilgrim Colony: A History of New Plymouth* (New Haven, Conn., 1966) are distinctly trusting and sympathetic.

There are several essays that provide a basic introduction to the European attitudes and myths that lay behind the exportation of Puritanism to North America: David Hall, "Understanding the Puritans," in Herbert J. Bass, ed., *The State of American History* (Chicago, 1970), 330-349; Fred M. Kimmey, "Christianity and Indian Lands," *Ethnohistory*, 7 (1960), 44-60; George H. Williams, "The Wilderness and Paradise in the History of the Church," *Church History* 28 (1959), 3-24; and Nicholas P. Canny, "The Ideology of English Colonization: From Ireland to America," *William and Mary Quarterly*, 3rd series, 30 (1973), 575-598. For an understanding of the native cultures that awaited the invading Europeans, the most important sources are Regina Flannery, *An Analysis of Coastal Algonquian Culture*, Catholic University of America Anthropological Series, 7 (Washington, 1939); Anthony F. C. Wallace, "Political Organization and Land Tenure among the Northeastern Indians, 1600-1830," *Southwestern Journal of Anthropology*, 13 (1957), 301-321; and Frank Shuffelton, "Indian Devils and Pilgrim Fathers: Squanto, Hobomok, and the English Conception of Indian Religion," *New England Quarterly*, 49 (1976), 108-116. Professor Neil Salisbury of Smith College is now at work on a book that should synthesize and surpass the Flannery, Wallace, and Shuffelton studies.

On specific aspects of Puritan-Indian relations, many articles and books are virtually indispensable. The relationship between Puritan theology and Puritan behavior toward Indians is discussed most effectively in Roy Harvey Pearce's ground-breaking article, "The 'Ruines of Mankind': The Indian and the Puritan Mind," *Journal of the History of Ideas*, 13 (1952), 200-217, while the economic aspects of Indian-Puritan contact are analyzed in Bernard Bailyn, *The New England Merchant in the Seventeenth Century* (Cambridge, Mass., 1955). For the political complexity of Puritan and Indian alliances and conflicts, the best single essay is John Sainsbury's "Miantonomo's Death and New England Politics," *Rhode Island History*, 30 (1971), 111-123; and the most thorough, most perceptive analysis of the Puritan missionary effort to the Indians is Salisbury's "Red Puritans: The 'Praying Indians' of Massachusetts Bay and John Eliot," *William and Mary Quarterly*, 3rd Series, 31 (1974), 27-54. See Douglas Leach, *Flintlock and Tomahawk: New England in King Philip's War* (New York, 1958) for a balanced treatment, following a misleading opening chapter, of that conflict, and Pearce's article, "The Significance of the Captivity Narrative," *American Literature*, 19 (1947), 1-20, for an understanding of the popular literature stimulated by Indian wars in New England. The ever-present fear of Indians among Puritans is described most clearly in Peter N. Carroll, *Puritanism and the Wilderness: The Intellectual Significance of the New England Frontier, 1629-1700* (New York, 1969), and the extent to which that fear drove Puritans to treat all Indians harshly after King Philip's War is documented in Yasu Kawashima, "Legal Origins of the Indian Reservation in Colonial Massachusetts," *American Journal of Legal History*, 13 (1969), 42-56. To understand the contrast between Puritan-Indian relations in New England and French-Indian relations in Canada, see Bruce G. Trigger, "The Jesuits and the Fur Trade," *Ethnohistory*, 12 (1965), 30-52, and A. G. Bailey, *The Conflict of European and Eastern Algonkian Cultures, 1504-1700* (Toronto, 1969).

For students who want to do their own research into the primary materials of Puritan-Indian contact, the following works are good places to begin: *The Colonial Laws of Massachusetts*, William H. Whitmore, ed. (Boston, 1889) is, in part, a compilation of statutes passed in the key Puritan colony to control Indian behavior; the five volumes of *Winthrop Papers*, Allyn B. Forbes, ed. (Boston, 1929-47) give the quickest insight into the characteristic thinking of Puritan leaders; William Bradford's *Of Plymouth Plantation, 1620-1647*, S. E. Morison, ed. (New York, 1963) does the same for Pilgrim leaders; and Daniel Gookin, "History of the Christian Indians," American Antiquarian Society, *Transactions and Collections*, 2 (1836), 423-534, and Charles H. Lincoln, ed., *Narratives of the Indian Wars, 1675-1699* (New York, 1913) provide a graphic starting point for understanding the popular attitudes of Puritans and Indians toward each other.

Lastly, several general works that put the Puritan-Indian experience in a larger historical context deserve mention. Gary B. Nash's *Red, White, and Black: The Peoples of Early America* (Englewood Cliffs, N. J., 1974) is an excellent summary of the best scholarship on all forms of race relations in colonial America; and William Christie MacLeod's *The American Indian Frontier* (New York, 1928) is still the most thoughtful narrative of the events and forces that led to the radical dispossession of American Indians by the twentieth century, though MacLeod's pessimism about the rapid disappearance of Indians and their cultures has proven, fortunately, to be unfounded. For a thorough documentary approach to the sweep of Indian-white relations in America, Wilcomb Washburn's *The Indian and the White Man* (New York, 1964) is unsurpassed. It is fitting to end this bibliographical essay by mentioning one of Washburn's many works, since he, more than any other modern scholar, has given the field of Indian-white studies a long-overdue status and dignity.

Notes

Introduction
"For the Sake of Our Religion"

1. Gary B. Nash, *Red, White, and Black: The Peoples of Early America* (Englewood Cliffs, N.J.: Prentice-Hall, 1974). See pp. 26-27, 106-107, 119-120.

2. Spain's very mixed record of genocide and wholesale conversion of natives to nominal Christianity is explained, largely, by the presence in the Americas of two rival Spanish groups: wealth-seeking military men and religious orders, like the Franciscans, charged specifically with a missionary purpose. The Puritans had no such religious orders.

3. Nash, *Red, White, and Black*, p. 120.

4. John Demos, ed., *Remarkable Providences, 1600-1760* (New York: George Braziller, 1972), pp. 13-14.

5. For Powhatan's conduct, see Nash, pp. 56-57; for Custer's attitude, see his autobiography, *My Life on the Plains* (Lincoln: University of Nebraska Press, 1966), p. 362.

6. See Clifford K. Shipton, "The New England Frontier," *New England Quarterly*, 10 (1937), 25-36; and Alan Heimert, "Puritanism, The Wilderness, and The Frontier," *New England Quarterly*, 26 (1953), 361-382.

7. Cotton Mather, *Magnalia Christi Americana* (Hartford, 1853), 2:659-664.

8. The essential difference between the "Separatist" Pilgrims and the "nonseparating" Puritans lay in their conceptions of themselves as religious communities, not in their theological beliefs. Pilgrims sought independence from the "popish" Church of England—the Anglican Church—and based their church organization on their geographical isolation. As a result, the eventual splitting of their community at Plymouth had a profound effect on

their original group identity. The Puritans, on the other hand, chose to reform the Church of England through the purity of their own example and did not technically separate from it. In doing so, they retained a degree of bureaucracy that united various Puritan communities and were able, therefore, to tolerate and even encourage the expansion of individual churches into remoter areas of New England. From the native point of view, the two groups were virtually identical, particularly after the political organization of the United Colonies of New England in 1643, which included Plymouth.

9. Francis Jennings, *The Invasion of America: Indians, Colonialism, and the Cant of Conquest* (Chapel Hill: University of North Carolina Press, 1975), pp. 28-29.

10. William Bradford, *Of Plymouth Plantation, 1620-1647,* Samuel Eliot Morison, ed. (New York: Alfred A. Knopf, 1963), p. 271.

11. John Cotton, "God's Promise to His Plantations" (1630), *Old South Leaflets,* No. 53 (Boston, 1896), p. 6.

12. Ibid., pp. 5-6

13. Edward Winslow, "Good News from New England ..." (1624), in Alexander Young, ed., *Chronicles of the Pilgrim Fathers* (Boston: Little, 1841), pp. 361-362; Roger Williams, *A Key into the Language of America: Or, An help to the Language of the Natives in that part of America, called New England ...* (1643), James Hammond Trumbull, ed., in *The Complete Writings of Roger Williams* (New York: Russell & Russell, 1963), 1:180, hereinafter cited as *RW.* See also, Anthony F. C. Wallace, "Political Organization and Land Tenure Among the Northeastern Indians, 1600-1830," *Southwestern Journal of Anthropology,* 13 (1957), pp. 301-321.

14. See, in particular, the accounts of voyages by Martin Pring (1603) and George Waymouth (1605) in Charles Herbert Levermore, ed., *Forerunners and Competitors of the Pilgrims and Puritans* (Brooklyn, N.Y.: New England Society of Brooklyn, 1912), 1. These episodes parallel the experience of Jacques Cartier in 1534, described in Henry Burrage, ed., *Early English and French Voyages, Chiefly from Hakluyt, 1534-1608* (New York: Charles Scribner's Sons, 1906), pp. 24-26.

15. Bradford, p. 62. Once settled at Plymouth, Bradford wrote about Indian torture of whites in extremely graphic terms (p. 26); there is no reliable evidence, however, that southern New England tribes practiced torture, scalping, or cannibalism. See Regina Flannery, *An Analysis of Coastal Algonquian Culture,* Catholic University of American Anthropological Series, 7 (Washington, D.C., 1939).

16. Cotton Mather, *Magnalia Christi Americana*, 2: 566; John Eliot, "Dedications to Eliot's Indian Bible, 1663," Massachusetts Historical Society, *Collections* (hereinafter cited as *MCH*), 1st Series, 7: 226.

17. *RW*, 1: Chapters 16 and 21.

18. William Hubbard, *The History of the Indian Wars in New England* ... (1677), S. G. Drake, ed. (Roxbury, Mass. 1865), 2: 277.

19. Ibid., p. 249.

20. See, for example, Document 12.

21. The best example of such legislation is the General Allotment Act of 1887 (also known as the Dawes Act), which mandated that the tribal landholdings of peaceful Indians be broken up and allotted to individual natives and whites. Supporters of the act assumed (1) that it did not matter if Indians did not want to become private landowners, and (2) that the individual possession of land (as opposed to communally owned land) would transform Indians into loyal, hard-working farmers within a white American economic system.

22. The Narragansetts, Pequots, Mohegans, and Wampanoags have functioning tribal organizations in 1977 and land claims cases in U.S. courts. The recent decision of a federal judge that Maine Indians are entitled to federal status and protection as tribes will also have a bearing on southern New England tribes. The government may now have to argue the Indians' land cases in court if there is evidence that the land was acquired after 1790 by individuals or states without the explicit approval of the United States as a nation. The most influential organization of New England tribes is the Coalition of Eastern Native Americans, Inc. (CENA), with offices at 733 15th St. NW, Suite 637, Washington, D.C. 20005.

Chapter I
"If Thy Belly Be Thy God": Land and Trade

1. Richard Baxter, *Christian Directory*, in *The Practical Works of Richard Baxter* (London, 1847), 1: 514.

2. Ibid., p. 94

3. Ibid., p. 219.

4. Quoted in Edmund S. Morgan, *Roger Williams: The Church and the State* (New York: Harcourt, Brace & World, 1967), p. 113.

5. Ibid., pp. 112-114. See also Winthrop S. Hudson, "Puritanism and the Spirit of Capitalism." *Church History*, 18 (1949), pp. 10-13.

6. Baxter, *Christian Directory*, p. 181.

7. Bernard Bailyn, *The New England Merchants in the Seventeenth Century* (Cambridge: Harvard University Press, 1955), p. 22.

8. John Winthrop, *The History of New England from 1630 to 1649*, James Savage, ed. (Boston, 1853), 1: 317, hereinafter cited as *Winthrop History*; John Cotton, *An Abstract of the Laws of New England* [*Moses His Judicials*] (London, 1655), reprinted in Thomas Hutchinson, ed., *The Hutchinson Papers*, The Prince Society, *Publications* (Albany, 1865), 1: 193-194.

9. *Winthrop History*, p. 315.

10. William Wood, *Wood's New England's Prospect*, The Prince Society, *Publications* (Boston, 1865), p. 87.

11. William B. Weeden, *Economic and Social History of New England, 1620-1789* (New York: Hillary House Publishers, 1963), 1: 37-38.

12. *Wood's New England's Prospect*, pp. 69-70.

13. Nathaniel B. Shurtleff, ed., *Records of the Governor and Company of the Massachusetts Bay in New England* (Boston, 1853), 1: 83, 323, hereinafter cited as *Massachusetts Colonial Records*.

14. David Pulsifer, ed., *Records of the Colony of New Plymouth* (Boston, 1859), 11: 65-66, hereinafter cited as *Plymouth Colonial Records; Massachusetts Colonial Records*, 3: 398. See also James R. Ronda, "Red and White at the Bench: Indians and the Law in Plymouth Colony, 1620-1691," Essex Institute, *Historical Collections*, 101 (1974), pp. 207-208.

15. *Massachusetts Colonial Records*, 1: 99-100.

16. Bailyn, *The New England Merchants in the Seventeenth Century*, pp. 30-32.

17. *Wood's New England's Prospect*, p. 100.

18. Jennings, *The Invasion of America*, p. 94; Weeden, *Economic and Social History of New England*, 1: 39-41.

19. Allyn B. Forbes, ed., *Winthrop Papers*, (Boston: Massachusetts Historical Society, 1929-47), 2: 141; Jennings, *The Invasion of America*, p. 138.

20. See Jennings, Chapter 8. See also Note 11 in Introduction above.

21. Jennings, 128-130. See also Charles E. Eisinger, "The Puritans' Justification for Taking the Land," Essex Institute, *Historical Collections*, 84 (1948), pp. 131-143.

22. *RW*, 2: 40. See also Wilcomb E. Washburn, "The Moral and Legal Justification for Dispossessing the Indians," in *Seventeenth-Century Amer-*

ica: Essays in Colonial History, James Morton Smith, ed. (Chapel Hill: University of North Carolina Press, 1959), p. 25.

23. *RW*, 2: 47.

24. See Jennings, *The Invasion of America*, pp. 144-145.

25. Baxter, *Christian Directory*, p. 151.

26. Cotton Mather, *Magnalia Christi Americana*, 2: 558; Roger Williams, *The Bloody Tenant Yet More Bloody* (1652), in *RW*, 4: 85.

27. Cotton Mather, *The Wonders of the Invisible World* (Boston, 1693), p. 63.

28. Increase Mather, *A Relation of the Troubles* (Boston, 1677), pp. 12-16.

29. See Sacvan Bercovitch, *Horologicals to Chronometricals: The Rhetoric of the Jeremiad*, in *Literary Monographs*, 3, Eric Rothstein, ed. (Madison: University of Wisconsin Press, 1970), 113-114.

1. "Abraham ... Among the Sodomites"

1. *Winthrop Papers*, 2: 91.

2. Ibid., p. 120.

2. "The Son of Adam or Noah"

1. John Cotton, "God's Promise to His Plantations," pp. 5-7.

3. "No Time to Pamper the Flesh"

1. Allen Johnson and Dumas Malone, eds., *Dictionary of American Biography* (New York, 1930), 5: 5. See also *Chronicles of the Pilgrim Fathers*, pp. 255-256 ff.

2. Ibid., pp. 258-265.

4. "The Governor Hath Sent Him a Coat"

1. "Bradford's and Winslow's Journal," in *Chronicles of the Pilgrim Fathers*, p. 202.

2. Ibid., pp. 203-206, 208-209.

5. "Some of You Steal Our Corn"

1. *MCH*, 4th Series, 4: 474.

2. Phineas Pratt. "A Declaration of the Affairs of the English People that First Inhabited New England," in ibid., pp. 480-485.

6. "They Saw ... a Walking Island"

1. Wood's New England's Prospect, pp. 87-89.

7. "For a Little Profit"

1. John Josselyn, "An Account of Two Voyages to New-England," MCH, 3rd Series, 3: 304-307.

8. "That All Interlopers ... Be Restrained"

1. Weeden, Economic and Social History of New England, 1: 179.
2. David Pulsifer, ed., Acts of the Commissioners of the United Colonies of New England, in Plymouth Colonial Records, 9: 22-23. The project never materialized, and the fur trade continued to be exploited successfully by individual traders.

9. "Till the English Taught Them"

1. "Cartwright's Answer to the Massachusetts Narrative of Transactions with the Royal Commissioners," in The Clarendon Papers, New-York Historical Society, Collections, 1869, pp. 90-93, 102-104.

Chapter II
"God Wraps Us in His Ordinances":
Government Relations

1. Quoted in Edward Rawson, "The Revolution in New England Justified ..." (1691), The Andros Tracts (Boston, 1868), 1: 88-89.
2. Winslow, "Good News from New England," pp. 359, 362; Williams, A Key into the Language, pp. 152-153; Edward Johnson, Johnson's Wonder-Working Providence, 1628-1651 (1654), J. Franklin Jameson, ed. (New York: Charles Scribner's Sons, 1910), pp. 162-163; Daniel Gookin, "Historical Collections of the Indians in New England," (1674), in MCH, 1st Series, 1: 154.

3. Cotton, "God's Promise to His Plantations," p. 7.

4. For the best discussion of the entire Miantonomo incident, see John Sainsbury, "Miantonomo's Death and New England Politics," *Rhode Island History*, 30 (1971), 111-123.

10. *"To Return the Patent Back Again to the King"*

1. The most famous of the Williams-Cotton debates is Williams's *The Bloody Tenent of Persecution for the Cause of Conscience* (1644) and Cotton's reply, *The Bloody Tenent Washed, and Made White in the Blood of the Lamb* (1647).

2. John Cotton, *A Reply to Mr. Williams his Examination*, in *RW*, 2: 45-47.

11. *"Thanks to the People"*

1. Jennings, *The Invasion of America*, pp. 187, 244-247.
2. Edward Winslow, "Good News from New England," pp. 360-362.

12. *"How Solidly and Wisely These Savage People Did Consider"*

1. *Johnson's Wonder-Working Providence*, pp. 161-163.

13. *"However His Death May Be Grievous"*

1. *Acts of the Commissioners of the United Colonies of New England*, 9: 14-15.

14. *"We Freely Give Over Ourselves"*

1. *Massachusetts Colonial Records*, 2: 55-56; John Russell Bartlett, ed., *Records of the Colony of Rhode Island and Providence Plantations, in New England* (Providence, R.I., 1856), 1: 134-136, hereinafter cited as *Rhode Island Colonial Records*.

15. *"There Is a Spirit of Desperation Fallen Upon Them"*

1. *RW*, 6: 144-45; *Acts of the Commissioners of the United Colonies*, 9: 55.

16. "Unnecessary Wars and Cruel Destructions"

1. *Rhode Island Colonial Records*, 1: 293, 294, 296, 298.

17. "It Was Reasonable to Succor One's Christian Brethren"

1. Reuben Gold Thwaites, ed., *The Jesuit Relations and Allied Documents: Travels and Explorations of the Jesuit Missionaries in New France, 1610-1791* (Cleveland, 1899), 36: 91-93, 95-97, 99-101.

18. "A Kind of Invocation Used Among Them"

1. Jennings, *The Invasion of America*, pp. 293-295.
2. *Rhode Island Colonial Records* (Providence, R.I., 1857), 2: 269, 270-271, 272-273.

19. "Minding Gain Than Godliness"

1. See Document 9 and Jennings, *The Invasion of America*, p. 325.
2. J. Hammond Trumbull, ed., *The Public Records of the Colony of Connecticut* (Hartford, 1852), 2: 473-474, hereinafter cited as *Connecticut Colonial Records*.

Chapter III
"If God Be with Us": The Pequot War

1. *Winthrop Papers*, 2: 303.
2. John Cotton, "God's Promise to His Plantations," pp. 5-7; Francis Higginson, "New England's Plantation," in Alexander Young, ed., *Chronicles of the First Planters of the Colony of Massachusetts Bay, From 1623 to 1636* (Boston, 1846), p. 259.
3. John Underhill, "News from America, or a late and experimental discovery of New England," in Charles Orr, ed., *History of the Pequot War* (Cleveland, 1897), pp. 82, 84. See also *RW*, 1: 204, for a report of a similar fighting posture among the Narragansetts.
4. Lion Gardiner, "Lt. Lion Gardiner his relation of the Pequot Wars," in *History of the Pequot War*, p. 130.

5. For a detailed pro-Indian discussion of the Pequot War, see Jennings, *The Invasion of America*, pp. 186-227. For a pro-Puritan approach to the Pequot War, see Alden T. Vaughan, *New England Frontier: Puritans and Indians, 1620-1675* (Boston: Little, Brown, 1965), pp. 122-154, and his "Pequots and Puritans: The Causes of the War of 1637," *William and Mary Quarterly*, 3rd Series, 21 (1964), 256-269.

6. The commercial losses resulted from the ill-fated House of Hope the Dutch had tried to establish in Pequot territory as a viable enterprise.

7. *Winthrop History*, 1: 176-177.

8. Jennings, *The Invasion of America*, p. 193.

9. *Winthrop History*, 1: 177.

10. Ibid., p. 176.

11. Ibid.

12. Ibid.

13. Ibid., p. 177.

14. *Winthrop Papers*, 3: 270-271.

15. Underhill, "News from America," p. 84.

16. Ibid., pp. 51-52, 63, 66.

17. Philip Vincent, "A True Relation of the Late Battle Fought in New England between the English and the Pequot Savages," in *History of the Pequot War*, p. 99.

18. Bradford, *Of Plymouth Plantation*, p. 26.

19. John Mason, "A Brief History of the Pequot War," in *History of the Pequot War*, p. 30.

20. Bradford, *Of Plymouth Plantation*, p. 296.

21. *Johnson's Wonder-Working Providence*, p. 148.

22. *Winthrop Papers*, 5: 155.

23. Ibid., 4: 409; William Hooke, *New England's Sense, of Old England and Ireland's Sorrows*, in Samuel Hopkins Emery, ed., *The Ministry of Taunton* (Boston, 1853), 1: 114.

20. *"By the Sword of the Lord"*

1. Jennings, *The Invasion of America*, pp. 206-208. Oldham probably did something to incur the wrath of the Narragansetts, but what this was is not known.

2. Ibid., 209.

3. *Winthrop History*, 1: 191.

4. Underhill, "News from America," pp. 49-55.

21. *"What Cheer, Englishmen.... What Do You Come For?"*

1. Underhill, "News from America," p. 55.
2. Ibid., pp. 55-60.

22. *"They Had Always Loved the English"*

1. On Miantonomo and Canonicus, see John A. Sainsbury, "Miantonomo's Death ... ," 111-123.
2. Jennings, *The Invasion of America*, p. 214.
3. *Winthrop History*, 1: 198-199.
4. On March 21, 1637, Winthrop recorded (Ibid., p. 259), Miantonomo
sent "forty fathom of wampum and a Pequot's hand," signifying agreement
on the peace treaty. See also Sainsbury, "Miantonomo's Death ... ," p.
113.

23. *"They Asked If We Did Use to Kill Women and Children?"*

1. Gardiner's Relation," p. 122.
2. Ibid., p. 130.
3. Ibid., pp. 130-133.

24. *"In the Name of the Lord"*

1. Dumas Malone, ed., *Dictionary of American Biography,* 9: 13-14.
2. *Winthrop Papers*, 3: 404-407.

25. *"To Do Execution ... on the Pequots"*

1. *Winthrop Papers*, 3: 412-414.
2. The smallpox epidemic of 1633-34 took seven thousand Narragansett
lives. It was the worst outbreak of native disease since the plague of 1616-
19. See *Johnson's Wonder-Working Providence*, p. 79; *Winthrop History*, 1:
115-116, 119-120; Jennings, *The Invasion of America,* pp. 207-208.

26. *"Every Faithful Soldier of Christ Jesus"*

1. *Johnson's Wonder-Working Providence*, p. 165.

2. Ibid., pp. 165-166.

27. *"Being Bereaved of Pity"*

1. *Connecticut Colonial Records*, 1: 9.
2. Jennings, *The Invasion of America*, pp. 217-218.
3. "Gardiner's Relation," p. 136.
4. Ibid.
5. Underhill, "News from America," pp. 77-81.

28. *"So Miraculously Did the Lord Preserve Them"*

1. Mason, "A Brief History of the Pequot War," p. 25.
2. *Winthrop Papers*, 3: 453-454.
3. Bradford, *Of Plymouth Plantation*, pp. 396-398.
4. In Puritan New England, March was the first month of the New Year.

Chapter IV
"Hiring Them to Hear Sermons"

1. *Winthrop Papers*, 2: 145.
2. Samuel Eliot Morison, *Builders of the Bay Colony* (Boston: Houghton Mifflin, 1930), p. 26.
3. Henry Whitfield, "Strength Out of Weakness; Or a Glorious Manifestation of the further Progress of the Gospel among the Indians in New England," in *MCH*, 3rd Series, 4: 156-157.
4. *Johnson's Wonder-Working Providence*, p. 59.
5. Gookin, "Historical Collections," pp. 144-145.
6. Quoted in J. F. Maclear, "New England and the Fifth Monarchy: The Quest for the Millennium in Early American Puritanism," *William and Mary Quarterly*, 3rd Series, 32 (1975), 229.
7. Edward Winslow, "The Glorious Progress of the Gospel, amongst the Indians in New England," in *MCH*, 3rd Series, 4: 91.
8. See Frank Shuffelton, "Indian Devils and Pilgrim Fathers: Squanto, Hobomok, and the English Conception of Indian Religion," in *New England Quarterly*, 49 (1976), 108-116.
9. Winslow, "Good News from New England," p. 357.

10. *Wood's New England's Prospect*, p. 92.

11. Winslow, "Good News from New England," pp. 355-356.

12. Williams, *A Key into the Language*, p. 154.

13. *Winthrop Papers*, 4: 17.

14. Henry Whitfield, ed., "The Light appearing more and more towards the perfect Day. Or, a farther Discovery of the present state of the Indians in New-England, Concerning the Progress of the Gospel amongst them," in *MCH*, 3rd Series, 4:111. Puritan divines consistently sought to demonstrate the superiority of the English God over the dieties worshipped by the red men and also claimed to exceed the curative powers of the powwows. (See Winslow, "The Glorious Progress," p. 77.) By downgrading the status and effectiveness of the native gods, Eliot and other Puritan missionaries held to a strategy that placed the red man in a position of psychological inferiority that made him, theoretically, more prone to accept the Puritan God.

15. Gookin, "Historical Collections," p. 182.

16. Francis Jennings, "Goals and Functions of Puritan Missions to the Indians," *Ethnohistory*, 18 (1971), p. 200.

17. Roger Williams, "Christenings Make Not Christians," Perry Miller, ed., in *RW*, 7: 36.

18. Williams, *A Key into the Language*, p. 163.

19. Winslow, "The Glorious Progress," p. 88. Why spend a considerable sum of money to help the "barbarous Indians, famous for nothing but cruelty"? To many Englishmen, Indians were no more than "a crafty people." (See *Johnson's Wonder-Working Providence*, p. 52; *Winthrop Papers*, 3: 17.)

20. [John Wilson?], "The Day-Breaking, If Not The Sun-Rising of the Gospel with the Indians in New-England," in *MCH*, 3rd Series, 4:18.

21. Whitfield, ed. "The Light appearing," pp. 112-113. Whatever success the Puritans had in converting Indians—and by 1674 there were only slightly more than 1,100 such converts—was due to the fact that these natives had been subjected to tremendous Puritan pressures and, unlike the overwhelming majority of their people, succumbed to the coercion. See also G. E. Thomas, "Puritanism, Indians, and the Concept of Race," in *New England Quarterly*, 48 (1975), p. 10.

22. For a different point of view, see Vaughan, *New England Frontier*, pp. 185-210.

23. Cartwright, "Cartwright's Answer to the Massachusetts Narrative," p. 86.

24. John Eliot to Commissioners of the United Colonies, Sept. 4, 1671, in Massachusetts Historical Society, *Proceedings,* 17 (1879–1880), pp. 248-249. See also Eliot, *A Brief Narrative of the Progress of the Gospel Among the Indians of New England, 1670* (Boston, 1868), p. 6.

25. Ibid., pp. 248-249, 250.

26. Ibid., p. 250

27. Jennings, *The Invasion of America,* pp. 249-250.

28. Vaughan, *New England Frontier,* p. 22.

29. *"Their Gods Made Them"*

1. Quoted in Richard S. Dunn, *Puritans and Yankees: The Winthrop Dynasty of New England, 1630–1717* (Princeton: Princeton University Press, 1962), p. 47.

2. Williams, *A Key into the Language,* pp. 147-161.

30. *"We Have Nothing to Do to Censure Indians"*

1. For a discussion of Separatists and non-Separatists, see Edmund S. Morgan, *Visible Saints: The History of a Puritan Idea* (New York: New York University Press, 1963), pp. 1-63.

2. Quoted in Jennings, *The Invasion of America,* pp. 235-236.

3. John Cotton, *The Way of Congregational Churches Cleared,* in Larzer Ziff, ed., *John Cotton on the Churches of New England* (Cambridge: The Belknap Press, 1968), pp. 268, 272-274, 278-279.

31. *"Preventing the Dishonor ... of the Most High God"*

1. Thomas Shepard, "The Clear Sunshine of the Gospel Breaking Forth upon the Indians in New England," in *MCH,* 3rd Series, 4:55.

2. Ibid.

3. Thomas Lechford, "Plain dealings: or news from New England," in *MCH,* 3rd Series, 3:80.

4. *Massachusetts Colonial Records,* 2: 176-179.

32. *"Such Dry and Rocky Ground"*

1. [Wilson?], "The Day-Breaking," pp. 14-16.

33. *"In a Searching Condition"*

1. Whitfield, ed., "The Light appearing," p. 132.
2. Winslow, "The Glorious Progress," p. 91.
3. Whitfield, ed., "The Light appearing," p. 125.
4. [Wilson?], "The Day-Breaking," pp. 6-7.
5. Winslow, "The Glorious Progress," pp. 84-86.

34. *"Root Out Their Powwows"*

1. Shepard, "The Clear Sunshine," pp. 56-67.

35. *"Near Unto Good Examples"*

1. Shepard, "The Clear Sunshine," pp. 38-41; Whitfield, ed., "The Light appearing," pp. 139-141.

36. *"Stubborn and Rebellious Children"*

1. [Wilson?], "The Day-Breaking," pp. 5-6, 10-11.

37. *"Conformed Is a Great Word"*

1. *MCH*, 1st Series, 10:124-129.

Chapter V
"To Dispossess Us of the Land": King Philip's War

1. Hubbard, *The History of the Indian Wars in New England,* 1:52-53.
2. *MCH*, 5th Series, 1:424-26; Increase Mather, *An Earnest Exhortation to the Inhabitants of New England* ... (Boston, 1676), pp. 6-7, 9; William Hubbard, *The Happiness of a People* ... (Boston, 1676), p. 59.
3. Mather, *An Earnest Exhortation*, p. 10; Hubbard, *The History of the Indian Wars*, 2:255-256, 258.
4. Increase Mather, *The History of King Philip's War* (1676), Samuel G. Drake, ed., (Albany, N.Y., 1862), pp. 42, 47, 216; Mather, *An Earnest Exhortation,* p. 17.

5. John Easton, "A Relation of the Indian War" (1675), in Charles H. Lincoln, ed., *Narratives of the Indian Wars, 1675–1699* (New York: Charles Scribner's Sons, 1913), p. 11.

6. *Massachusetts Colonial Records*, 5:59-63.

7. Mather, *The History of King Philip's War*, pp. 206-207.

8. Ibid., pp. 224-225.

9. John W. Ford, ed., *Some Correspondence between the Governors and Treasurers of the New England Company in London and the Commissioners of the United Colonies in America, the Missionaries of the Company and Others . . .* (London, 1896), p. 59.

10. William H. Whitmore, ed., *The Colonial Laws of Massachusetts. Reprinted from the Edition of 1672, with the Supplements through 1686* (Boston, 1890), pp. 251-252, 289.

11. Richard Slotkin, *Regeneration Through Violence: The Mythology of the American Frontier, 1600–1860* (Middletown, Conn.: Wesleyan University Press, 1972).

12. Robert N. Toppan, ed., *Edward Randolph Papers* (Boston, 1898), 2: 243-245; Wilcomb Washburn, "Governor Berkeley and King Philip's War," *New England Quarterly*, 30 (1957), 363-377.

13. Mather, *The History of King Philip's War*, p. 208.

38. *"The Peccant and Offending Party"*

1. *Acts of the Commissioners of the United Colonies*, 10:362-364; John Easton, "A Relation of the Indian War . . ." pp. 9-11.

2. David Bushnell, "The Treatment of the Indians in Plymouth Colony," *New England Quarterly*, 26 (1953), p. 206.

39. *"He Sent Our Enemies to Be Our Lords"*

1. *Connecticut Colonial Records*, 2:445-447.

40. *"Awful Tokens of Divine Displeasure"*

1. Increase Mather, *Diary, March 1675–December, 1676, Together with Extracts from Another Diary by Him, 1674–1687* (Cambridge, 1900), pp. 22-23, 46-47.

41. "They Will Not This Next Twenty Years Recover"

1. Public Record Office, London, Colonial Office, Series 1, Vol. 36, no. 37, quoted in Wilcomb Washburn, "Governor Berkeley and King Philip's War," p. 371.
2. Ibid., pp. 373, 377.

42. "The Indians Come In Daily"

1. Rhode Island Historical Society, *Collections* (Providence, 1902), 10: 177-178.

43. "To Kill and Destroy Them"

1. Daniel Gookin, "History of the Christian Indians," American Antiquarian Society, *Transactions* (Cambridge, Mass., 1836), 2:450-451, 528-529.

44. "The Terror of Selling Away Such Indians"

1. *Acts of the Commissioners of the United Colonies*, 10:451-453.
2. The key authority on New England colonial slavery practices is Almon Wheeler Lauber. *Indian Slavery in Colonial Times, Columbia University Studies in History, Economics, and Public Law*, 54 (1913).
3. *MCH*, 4th Series, 8:689-690.

45. "They Strip, They Bind, They Ravish"

1. *MCH*, 4th Series, 8:300.
2. Russel B. Nye and Norman S. Grabo, eds., *American Thought and Writing*, Vol. I (Boston: Houghton Mifflin, 1965), pp. 283-285.
3. Thomas Wheeler, "A True Narrative of the Lord's Providences ..." *Old South Leaflets*, No. 155 (Boston, n.d.), pp. 13-14.
4. "Narrative of the Captivity and Restoration of Mrs. Mary Rowlandson," in Lincoln, ed., *Narratives of the Indian Wars*, pp. 158-161.

Conclusion
"They Thought Their Way Was Good"

1. *Edward Randolph Papers*, 2:243-47.

2. *The Charter Granted by their Majesties* (Boston, 1692), pp. 5, 10. No. 616 in Charles Evans's *American Bibliography*.

3. Mather, *Magnalia Christi Americana*, 2:435.

4. Ford, ed., *Some Correspondence between the Governors and Treasurers of the New England Company* ... p. 94.

5. Cotton Mather, *A Monitory, and Hortatory Letter, To those English, who debauch the Indians, By Selling Strong Drink unto them* (Boston, 1700), pp. 1-2. No. 928 in Evans.

6. Ibid., pp. 2, 16.

7. Ibid., pp. 1, 5, 8.

8. Ibid., pp. 10-11.

9. Ibid., p. 15.

10. Kenneth Silverman, ed., *Selected Letters of Cotton Mather* (Baton Rouge: Louisiana State University Press, 1971), pp. 264-265.

11. "Treat Narrative," Connecticut Historical Society, *Collections*, 5:478-484.

12. Ford, ed., *Some Correspondence between the Governors and Treasurers of the New England Company* ... pp. 97-127. See especially pp. 110-11, 113-17, and 119-20.

13. Broadside, May 27, 1696. Province of Massachusetts Bay (Boston, 1696). No. 751 in Evans.

14. See Wilcomb Washburn, *The North American Indian Captivity* (New York: Garland, 1976).

15. Samuel Penhallow, *History of the Wars of New England with the Eastern Indians* [1726] (Cincinnati, 1859). For Mather—the last of the powerful Puritan ministers—a good Puritan, humble before the wrath of God toward Puritans and Indians alike, might enjoy God's victory over the satanic natives, but not consciously delight in the vicarious experience of telling the story of that victory.

16. *MCH*, lst Series, 10:142-153.

17. For an eloquent discussion of the white view since Puritan times that the Indian is an "impediment to the progress of civilization," see N. Scott Momaday, "The Morality of Indian Hating," *Ramparts*, 3 (1964), 33-40. Henry Nash Smith's important book, *Virgin Land: The American West as*

Symbol and Myth (New York: Random House, 1950), provides an excellent description of white attitudes toward the land in the nineteenth century but does not discuss the effect of those attitudes on Indian society or the contrast between those attitudes and native responses to nature.

18. See Dale Van Every, *Disinherited: The Lost Birthright of the American Indian* (New York: Morrow, 1966).

19. In Canada, Indians "have always suffered less pressure than in the United States because the whites were fewer, the land vaster, and the Indians in general less numerous than in the corresponding areas to the south," according to Palmer Patterson, "The Colonial Parallel: A View of Indian History," *Ethnohistory*, 18 (1971), p. 4. To these factors, however, should be added the following considerations: (1) Canadian Indian policy has always been somewhat influenced by the precedent of French colonial settlers, who were economically beholden to Indians and, therefore, more culturally accommodating than English Puritans to the south, and (2) Canadian territory, from the sixteenth to the nineteenth centuries, was not seized upon by whites as a haven from the corruptions of Europe; on the contrary, it was viewed as an extension of beneficent imperial control, during both French and English rule. Though an attitude of Manifest Destiny is apparent in Canadian history, it does not have the urgency that it has had in the United States of America.

20. [Lewis Cass], "Removal of the Indians," *North American Review*, 30 (1830), 62-121. See especially pp. 72-73.

21. Henry Wadsworth Longfellow, *The Song of Hiawatha* (Boston: Houghton Mifflin, 1908), p. 216.

22. George Armstrong Custer, *My Life on the Plains*, pp. 24, 320, 336.

23. See Loring Benson Priest, "The Congressional Decision to Use Force," in Richard N. Ellis, ed., *The Western American Indian* (Lincoln: University of Nebraska Press, 1972), pp. 119-132; and Wilcomb Washburn, *The Assault on Indian Tribalism: The General Allotment Act (Dawes Act) of 1887* (Philadelphia: Lippincott, 1975). The Indian Removal Bill of 1830 made the same demands of any natives who chose to retain their lands east of the Mississippi River; one Chickasaw leader described his tribe's options as (1) losing a homeland or (2) "losing our name and language" (*American State Papers, Indian Affairs*, 2:722).

24. Harold Driver, *Indians of North America*, 2nd ed. rev. (Chicago: University of Chicago Press, 1970), Chapters 14 and 17.

25. See Wilcomb Washburn, *Red Man's Land, White Man's Law* (New York: Charles Scribner's Sons, 1971), pp. 109-123.

26. The best source on current Indian political protests is *Akwesasne Notes*, a newspaper published via Rooseveltown, New York, 13683. For information on situations where militant protests have, fortunately, been unnecessary, another newspaper, *Wassaja* (American Indian Historical Society, San Francisco, Calif., 94117), is preferable. Both papers are published by Native Americans.

27. Vine Deloria, Jr., ed., *Of Utmost Good Faith* (New York: Bantam, 1972), pp. 141-142.

28. *Native American Church* v. *Navaho Tribal Council*, 272 F. 2d 131 (1959), quoted in Deloria, ed., *Of Utmost Good Faith*, p. 121. See also the final opinions in *Talton* v. *Mayes* (1896) and *Toledo* v. *Pueblo de Jemez* (1954), both included in Deloria's book.

Index

Index

Luther, Martin, 32

Magus, John, 202
Mahwissa, 29
Maine:
  colony, 29, 97, 99
  state, 224
Manecopungun, 101
Martha's Vineyard Island, 144–45, 147,
  175, 177, 216
Mascanomet, 89–90
Mascus, 87
Mason, John, 100, 111, 125, 134–38
Massachuset Indians, 31–32, 59–63, 81,
  89–91, 153–79, 185
Massachusetts:
  as English province, 186, 215–16, 219
  as Puritan colony, 27, 29, 31–32, 34,
    37–38, 42, 45–48, 50, 59, 63, 69–74,
    76–78, 80–82, 84, 87–93, 95, 97–99,
    103, 106–10, 113–14, 121–22, 127–29,
    131, 134, 137, 146–47, 149, 153, 155–
    58, 182–86, 191, 194, 200–1, 215
Massasoit, 55–59, 63, 82–84, 87–89, 187,
  192
Mather, Cotton, 29, 33, 49, 182, 216–18
Mather, Increase, 182–84, 186, 196–99,
  207–8, 219
Maverick, Samuel, 69
Mayhew, Experience, 217–18
Mayhew, Thomas, Sr., 145–47
Mayhew, Thomas, Jr., 36, 144–45, 147
Menasseh ben Israel, Rabbi, 143
Menominee Indians, 224
Metacom (King Philip), 66, 83, 100, 102,
  147–48, 181–84, 187–93, 200, 204,
  206–11, 215, 223
Miantonomo, 70–71, 78, 85–88, 92, 94,
  113, 121–22, 129–30, 152–53
Mixan, 93
Mohegan Indians, 78–79, 86–89, 93–94,
  97, 110, 127, 134, 165, 185, 215, 217–
  18
Mommenoteck, 120
Mononoto, 139–40
Mugg, 197–98
Mystic Fort, 84, 110, 131, 134–37, 185

Nantucket Island, 145, 147, 175, 177, 216
Narragansett Indians, 29, 31, 35, 71–72,
  74, 78–81, 84–89, 91–97, 100, 102–3,
  110, 113–17, 121–22, 129–31, 135,
144, 149–53, 165, 182, 184–85, 190,
  192, 199–200, 218, 224
Nash, Gary B., 25, 27
Nashowanon, 89–90
Natchez Indians, 27
Nattawhahore, 102
New England Company (for the
  propagation of the Gospel among
  Indians), 147
New Haven (Puritan colony), 34, 70, 78,
  87–88, 100, 110, 137
New York (Dutch and English colony),
  25–26, 69, 97, 100, 148, 191, 193
Nicolls, Richard, 69
Ninigret, 71, 100–2
Nipmuck Indians, 127, 139, 147, 179
Nonaconapoonog, 101
Northern Cheyenne Indians, 223–24
Norton, Walter, 117–18

Oldham, John, 110, 113–14, 125
Onondaga Indians, 223

Passamaquody Indians, 224
Patrick, Daniel, 138
Pecksuot, 60–63
Penhallow, Samuel, 219
Pennsylvania (English colony), 29
Penobscot Indians, 224
Pequot Indians, 29, 31, 71–72, 84–86, 97,
  101, 105–140, 185, 203–4, 218
Pequot War, 32, 75, 78, 84, 86, 97, 105–
  140, 184, 200, 203, 218, 221
Pessicus, 70–71, 92, 101
Pierce, William, 139
Pilgrims, 31–34, 46–47, 49, 54–63, 97,
  100, 110, 182, 215
Pittimee, Andrew, 202
Plymouth (Pilgrim colony), 27, 31–32, 45,
  47, 49, 54–63, 70, 73–74, 78, 87–89,
  97–99, 100, 109, 145, 150, 175, 181,
  184, 187–91, 193–95, 200, 204, 206–
  8, 215–16
Pocahontas, 29
Political organization:
  of Indians, 37–38, 47, 76–77, 82–
  84
  of Puritans, 37–38, 47, 76–77, 81
Population:
  of Indians, 31, 184
  of English in New England, 43
Potter, Robert, 93
Powhatan, 28–29, 31